BOYS
AND
TOYS

Cuba Gooding, Jr. in *Pearl Harbor*;
Will Smith and Tommy Lee Jones in *Men in Black*.

BOYS AND TOYS

ULTIMATE ACTION-ADVENTURE MOVIES

DOUGLAS BRODE

CITADEL PRESS
Kensington Publishing Corp.
www.kensingtonbooks.com

CITADEL PRESS BOOKS are published by

Kensington Publishing Corp.
850 Third Avenue
New York, NY 10022

All Kensington titles, imprints, and distributed lines
are available at special quantity discounts for bulk
purchases for sales promotions, premiums, fund-raising,
educational, or institutional use. Special book excerpts
or customized printings can also be created to fit
specific needs. For details, write or phone the office
of the Kensington special sales manager: Kensington
Publishing Corp., 850 Third Avenue, New York, NY
10022, attn: Special Sales Department,
phone 1-800-221-2647.

First printing: February 2003

10 9 8 7 6 5 4 3 2 1

Printed in the United States of America

Library of Congress Control Number: 2002104527

ISBN 0-8065-2381-6

For my son
Shane Johnson Brode
the original action-movie kid!

CONTENTS

ACKNOWLEDGMENTS

With special thanks to my son, Shane Johnson Brode, and the others who gave their time and help, including Harold "Rob" Thousand III, Erica Hayes, and Brian Miller.

   Also, to the film companies that generously allowed their publicity stills to be included: DreamWorks, Warner Bros., MGM, United Artists, Orion Pictures, Columbia, Paramount, 20th Century-Fox, Republic Pictures, American-International, Allied Artists, Buena Vista/Disney, Embassy Films, New Line Cinema, Roger Corman Productions, Mirisch, Seven Arts/ Hammer, Universal Pictures, Miramax Films, Fine Line Features, Samuel Goldwyn Films, and Playboy Productions.

1

INTRODUCTION: THE NAME OF ACTION

**In peace, there's nothing so becomes a man,
As modest stillness and humility:
But when the blast of war blows in our ears,
Then imitate the action of the tiger.**

—*Henry V* (by William Shakespeare)

In John McTiernan's *The Last Action Hero* (1993), a well-meaning high school teacher (Joan Plowright) suggests to her less-than-convinced class that "Hamlet was really the first action hero." Hoping to involve them with that 1599 masterwork, she tries to change their perception of the mournful prince from medieval wimp to mighty man of valor. Unfortunately, the lady undermines her own argument by screening the 1946 film directed by and starring Laurence Olivier. (An in-joke, for buffs: The teacher is portrayed by the widow of that late actor.) On-screen, Hamlet seems anything *but* an action hero, the first, the last, or in-between. Olivier actually embodies the antithesis of such a figure: soft and sensitive, truly Horatio's 'sweet prince.'

One boy, a devout Schwarzenegger fan, grows weary with this Hamlet's hesitations. "*Do something!*" he grimaces, closing his eyes, imagining how *Ah*-nold would handle such a situation. "Something's rotten in the state of Denmark," a narrator announces, as we see the lad's mental construction of a theatrical preview, "and Hamlet's here to set it right!" Schwarzenegger then enters the stylized set of Olivier's black-and-white film, replacing him as the central character. "Claudius, you killed my *fodda*!" Arnie shouts. "*Big* mistake!" Following a quick puff on his cigar, this pumped-up prince casually blows his arch enemy away.

More likely than not, this scene *does* approximate the Bard's desired reaction—Shakespeare wrote for an action-loving audience as enthralled with blood and guts as today's moviegoers. Still, that teacher's argument was wrong on one point. If Hamlet was indeed an action hero, he certainly wasn't the first. Consider the Hebrew warrior Joshua, winning the battle of Jericho for his philosophic mentor Moses, the predecessors of Obi-Wan Kenobi and

Luke Skywalker. Likewise, Jason of Greece organized his Argonauts much as Takashi Shimura and Yul Brynner assemble their magnificent groups in the landmark films *Seven Samurai* (1954) and *The Magnificent Seven* (1960). Theseus, a loner on a deadly mission, set the pace for the rugged individualists played, two and one half millennia later, by Bruce Lee and Bruce Willis. The action epic is the oldest story known to man. It is also the never-ending story, always in fashion. The central character in a ruggedly individualistic tale, beginning in Greek mythology with Perseus, or the group (Jason and his Argonauts with Hercules included) encounters much violent action before dragging home the prize: a Golden Fleece for the ancient world, the Holy Grail in the Christian era, a wad of money in the crass twentieth century, as in *Three Kings* (1999). The quest tradition of the round table neatly incorporates the two distinct possibilities for heroic action. On the one hand, they are members of a group, occasionally performing as such; on the other, each knight occasionally rides out alone, to rescue princesses from less chivalrous men of iron.

Over the ages, the substance of such stories remained much the same, even as the style changes. Sir Thomas Malory relates the round table myth in *L'Morte d'Arthur* (1485) as a bleak tale, inevitably leading to the hero's sacrificial end. Writing for a different audience and from another personal perspective, Alfred, Lord Tennyson emphasized the more glorious aspects of the epic in *Idylls of the King* (1842–1885). Sir Walter Scott's *Ivanhoe* (1819) became the model for such a saga as prose-narrative, the title character as gentle with women as he is merciless with those who endangered them. This figure was transported to America by Fenimore Cooper. "Hawkeye" (aka "Natty Bumppo") is Ivanhoe reimagined in the garb of Daniel Boone—a natural-born hero and gentleman, thanks to a romantic purity achieved by living in the as-yet-unspoiled woods.

As the frontier extended, the westerner replaced the woodsman as our abiding national hero. Coonskin caps gave way to stetsons, tall timber to vast prairies, though little else changed. As Kathryn C. Esselman noted, each successive dime novel or stage melodrama "helped strengthen the cowboy's identification with the knight" of old, if not in reality then certainly in our popular imagination. The American action tale became, as defined by scholar Peter Homans, "a story whose basic patterns of character, plot, and detail are repeated again and again" until it "embodies and sets forth certain meanings about what is good and bad, right and wrong—meanings regarded as important by those who view and participate in" each successive retelling.

How else can we explain the great appeal of ritualistically reading stories, seeing plays, or watching movies that tell the same essential story over and over again? As John G. Cawelti put it, this allows us to endlessly revisit an arena in which myth makers and their audiences unconsciously collaborate on "isolating and intensifying the encounter between social order and lawlessness." Since the outcome is always certain, no matter how terrible the odds, we take pleasure not only in the hero's courage and cleverness but also his "redemptive power." For always, he finds some way to slip out of the enemy's grasp and perform a simple, decisive act, saving any number of unwitting beneficiaries. There's something metaphysical about the heroic action, a contemporary equivalent to what ancients called *manna:* Some mysterious but palpable power, reaching far beyond the protagonist's physical abilities, however impressive they may be.

The presence of lawlessness (outlaws in westerns, terrorists in contemporary dramas) "required a strong sense of divine justice, untempered with mercy," according to Michael T. Marsden. The hero who arrives with a weapon—some "boy's toy," in our idiom—is the religious redeemer. Clint Eastwood hammered home this notion in *Pale Rider* (1985), in which a threatened child glances up from her Bible to spot the title character approaching on horseback. For Martin Nussbaum, such a hero's gun stands as "a symbol of divine intervention," carried by a good man who must bloody himself (spiritually as well as physically) in the process of eliminating evil. This notion is presented far more subtly in George Stevens's *Shane* (1952), a film Michael Marsden half-kiddingly referred to as "Savior in the Saddle." Robert Warshow writes that guns "constitute the moral center" of any action tale taking place during the past two hundreds years, "suggesting continually the possibility of violence" as the necessary means for closure, dramatic and moral.

The motion picture incarnation of such stories presents a key paradox. The action film as we know it today is the most recently created of all movie genres. In the earliest days of film, however, action was the essence of this new form of popular entertainment. The term "cinema" derives from a Greek word for action; in the first films, that's all there was. Consider a Lumiere brothers *actualite* (eight to ten seconds in length), shot in *fin-de-siecle* France. Workers exit a factory, a bicyclist is pummeled by snowball-wielding neighbors on an icy Paris street. In *Voyage to the Moon*, one of George Melies's fantasy films of that era, a professor informs his class that a rocket might reach the moon. The debate swiftly gives way to a fistfight that doesn't exist in the source, a Jules Verne novel. No sooner have the primitive astronauts

The essence of the action star was established early on, with Douglas Fairbanks playing any number of exotic swashbuckling heroes.

reached the moon's surface than they are engaged in an all-out battle with the horned creatures living there. Even the rocket's moon landing is violent, as the spaceship—an oversized bullet—smashes into the man in the moon's outraged face.

Consider this alongside today's films, in particular those we've come to call examples of the action genre. Little has changed except the level of technology, or, as industry insiders put it, the "state of the art." Whether movies take place in some modern city's mean streets or in outer space—whether we are dealing with Martin Scorsese or George Lucas—a champion always invokes what Hamlet called "the name of action," still the most basic appeal of moviegoing. This "gallant hero," as Richard W. Etulain once described him, "is always eager to combat any foe, regardless of the odds."

The very first screen action hero was not a man, but a dog named Rin-Tin-Tin. A veteran of The Great War, Rinty drew in late Victorian-era audiences, eager to see the wonder dog thwart bad guys. Déclassè as they might be, these screen vehicles were popular enough with the public to, as nostalgist Joe Franklin has noted, "pay off the losses on the costly prestige pictures with John Barrymore." More surprising still is that, however much action films may be perceived as masculine domain, the genre's first human superstar was a woman. Pearl White was pursued by countless villains in a chapter play, *The Perils of Pauline* (1914). At one episode's end, she dangled from a mountain precipice. It was at that moment the term "cliffhanger" was born.

The earliest male action heroes of the American screen were cowboys, beginning with Edwin S. Porter's *The Great Train Robbery* (1903). This simple story of robbers and the rangers who pursue them offers twelve minutes of non-stop action. One of the actors in that film, G. M. Anderson, sensed potential. Soon, he made a name for himself in a series of "Broncho Billy" features, such fare dismissed as superficial escapism. Tony Thomas noted of these movies that "the intellectual view is that they are vicarious pleasures for frustrated romantics, would-be heroes, armchair travelers, the dreamers and the discontents." Wisely, he added, that pretty much sums up *all of us* who constitute the moviegoing audience, whether we prefer something as serious as John Huston's *The Treasure of the Sierra Madre* (1948) or something as removed from everyday reality as *Goldfinger* (1964).

If all action films, realistic or romanticized, have one thing in common, it's the ability to thrust viewers, safely ensconced in their seats, into some deadly affair in which they can partake emotionally without risking life or limb. Such cheap thrills existed long before the advent of movies. As far back as Homer's adventures of world-traveler Odysseus, myth and legend provided a similar outlet. Yet nothing so effectively conveys action as a film, what Robert Warshow once referred to as "the *immediate* experience." The movies, even lesser ones, do not merely *suggest* but *actualize* grand-scale action.

Anderson's crude screen rendering of the American cowboy-hero swiftly gave way to more artistic approaches: the rugged realism of William S. Hart, the drugstore cowboy antics of Tom Mix, and—occupying a middleground between them—the sentimental yet historically accurate portraits by Harry Carey, particularly under the direction of young John Ford. In time, other action heroes emerged, including the period-piece swashbucklers of Douglas Fairbanks (Sr.), whose acrobatic vehicles had him scaling the sides of castles and swinging on chandeliers. A more contemporary vision appeared in movies starring Victor McLaglen, the big, burly Irish immigrant who owned every modern mean street he walked down. And there were the comics, beginning with Mack Sennett's pie-in-the-face antics for the Keystone Cops. While Charlie Chaplin was winning the world's collective heart with a cinematic combination of mime and ballet, Buster Keaton and Harold Lloyd dazzled the eyes with elaborate "gags" (to this day, the industry term for a stunt, owing to their work). Specifically, Buster stood tall on a speeding locomotive in *The General* (1925) while Harold hung from a clock high atop a skyscraper in *Safety Last* (1923).

Change, however, was in the air. D. W. Griffith, the first great director, was responsible for shifting the focus of movies away from short action quickies. In 1915, his masterwork, *The Birth of a Nation*, related the story of America before, during, and after the War Between the States. The epic, which runs (depending on projection speed employed today) as long as 192 minutes, contains some of the most startling action sequences ever filmed.

D. W. Griffith, the first great film director, understood full well that action could be choreographed into a visual poetry of violence, as the arrangements of figures in *The Birth of a Nation*'s Civil War battle makes clear.

His Civil War battle is on a scale that's impressive even today—the shootout between Ku Klux Klansmen and Black Militia still serves as a model for anyone planning to choreograph and orchestrate a fight sequence. However, such incidents were subordinated to the melodrama, involving romance, politics, plus comedy relief. With that film, the modern movie was born. Pure action films (though not action per se) slipped into hibernation as primitive nickelodeons gave way to the movie palaces of the twenties and thirties.

Then came *sound*. Following the success of a "partial talkie," *The Jazz Singer* (1927) with Al Jolson, studios began purchasing Broadway plays. For a time, movies became static; almost all action disappeared as dialogue came to dominate. Audiences quickly tired of sound for its own sake, though, so something altogether new emerged: the modern movie, combining the best elements of a play with the most visceral elements of silent films. The result was the adventure film. Such movies—pirate films, westerns, war stories, and crime sagas—invariably featured exciting scenes, with the biggest and best always saved for the conclusion. Even here, though, the action—however essential—would be abridged: The battle at Balaclava heights (*Charge of the Light Brigade*, 1936) or Custer's last stand at Little Big Horn (*They Died With*

Errol Flynn specialized in doomed romantic heroes, including the leader of the Balaclava Volunteers in *Charge of the Light Brigade.*

Their Boots On, 1941) comprises only the final 10 minutes of each movie's running time. This practice extended to the very cusp of what might be called modern moviemaking. John Wayne's enactment of the famed battle in San Antonio, Texas, consumed less than 20 minutes toward the end of his 161-minute epic, *The Alamo* (1960).

Not that the earlier action hero disappeared. He was alive and well and living in Saturday matinees, attended mostly by children. Be it the B-westerns of Buck Jones or the space operas featuring "Buck Rogers" (incarnated by Buster Crabbe), movies emphasizing action thrived in serials and program-

Olympic fame led to a long career for Johnny Weissmuller (with Maureen O'Sullivan) as Tarzan.

pictures churned out for kids. When Tarzan first reached the sound-era screen, in *Tarzan, the Ape Man* (1932) and *Tarzan and His Mate* (1934), the jungle king was marketed to grown-ups. However, MGM executives then decided the concept was juvenile, so star Johnny Weissmuller's movies were thereafter shot on ever smaller budgets. Kids continued to judge such films on how much action was crammed into any story, and that consideration remains the prime aesthetic of the action film to this day.

The filmmaking style that had developed during the late silent period and early sound era—roughly, the two decades between 1925 and 1945—might best be described as concerning, in the words of one keen observer, "a man who likes to roam and explore, to live by the skin of his teeth, to take risks, to gamble with his luck and tackle the unknown." He was Doug Fairbanks (Sr.) toned down enough to spend some time talking [i.e., Doug (Jr.) in *Gunga Din* (1939) and *Sinbad the Sailor* (1947)]. Such a character might be played, with a tough edge, by Errol Flynn, a tragic figure more often than not doomed to die at the end. Or he might appear in a gentler guise, played by Tyrone Power, whose easygoing ways allowed him to live and triumph in the final reel, as in *The Mark of Zorro* (1940) and *Captain From Castile* (1947). There were urban and western variations—the former most notably played by James Cagney and Humphrey Bogart, and the latter by Gary Cooper and John Wayne.

Invariably, the adventurer was something of an idealist. Such a man might seem the self-sufficient loner in the opening sequence, expressing an "I watch out for Number One!" attitude. In due time, though, he dedicates (and often sacrifices) himself to the common cause. In some (indeed, *many*) cases, such a figure initially becomes involved owing to the presence of a beautiful woman already grounded in the good side's apparently futile dream of rebellion against oppression. This dynamic holds as true for Harrison Ford's "Captain Solo," a futuristic space buccaneer in *Star Wars* (1977) as it did for Burt Lancaster's "Captain Vollo," a seventeenth-century Caribbean buccaneer in *The Crimson Pirate* (1952). In time, such a hero will do the right thing, if only at the last possible moment. This transformation constitutes his moral education. He is what the late mythologist Joseph Campbell tagged "the hero of a thousand faces," endless variations on a single basic and universal theme: Ancient patterns of heroism are defined by action, effectively revitalized via fresh treatments.

This tradition would be tested beginning in 1945. The full impact of World War II on Europe was at last evident; most horrifically undeniable of all was evidence of the Holocaust. At that moment, the face of evil at its most profound took on a terrifying new dimension. Shortly, the Cold War was upon us, whereby America and Russia would be able to decimate one another with nuclear weapons, by accident if not intent. Even at home, there were different demons, and no clear-cut knight in shining armor to slay them. McCarthyism all but destroyed America's sense of community, which had seemed tight-knit and permanent only a few years earlier. In the past, we'd always been able to shed our differences during extended periods of international combat. The Korean Conflict, referred to as a "police action" and an unwinnable prelude to Vietnam, failed to provide that. Americans were unable to fully support an undeclared war against a country that didn't seem particularly threatening to us. World War II suddenly felt like the good old days, before the world became too complex.

Obviously, movies had to change if they were to accurately reflect such an altered sensibility. They did so by slipping into a style the French would refer to as noir, films of the night, a cinema of shadows. In 1957, cult critic Manny Farber commented on the changes that had occurred during the past twelve years, noting that "the male action film" had been transformed, owing to a series of "melancholy masterpieces" rendered as "stiff, low-pulp material." These were mostly shot with a "low-budget ingenuity, which creates flashes of ferocious brassiness, an authentic practical-joke violence" and a sense of "brainless hell-raising." Obviously, the notion of what constituted a hero had to be rethought. Gone, at least from adult-oriented entertainment, was that perfect champion of the people. The idealist adventurer gave way to a glib, cynical realist, who more often than not expressed himself through violent action, and not always out of necessity. Detective Sam Spade, in Dashiell Hammet's *The Maltese Falcon*, turned his lover over to the police after discovering her to be a murderer. He does this reluctantly, with stony stoicism concealing his inner angst. Twenty years later, in Mickey Spillane's *I, the Jury*, Mike Hammer kills just such a woman himself while holding her tight for a final kiss. As the deliciously duplicitous dame crumples to the floor, she manages to ask with her dying breath how he could do it. The re-imagined gumshoe, making sure she hears his wise-guy retort, answers: "It was easy!" The modern man of action was crystallized then and there. "The heroic and the socially disillusioned," Jon Tuska noted, "serve as a convenient line of demarcation between the pre–World War II" protagonists and what followed. One of the first hit films of this era was titled *Brute Force* (1947), and for the lead, director Jules Dassin cast newcomer Burt Lancaster. The great adventure stars of the century's first half—Flynn, Power, Clark Gable, and others—would continue making movies, at least into the 1950s. But their golden hour was gone. Robert Mitchum, consigned to villainous roles before 1940 owing to bad-boy looks, appeared more appropriate for the emerging anti-heroic roles than conventionally handsome stars.

During WW II, a transformation from old-fashioned adventure films to the new modern action movie began, as rah!rah! propagandistic pictures gave way to a grimmer vision of combat and a darker view of life. Even after the magnificent seven have concluded their moral movement from self-serving loners to saviors of a small community, the final dialogue, spoken between two survivors, makes this clear. Chris (Yul Brynner) and Vin (Steve McQueen), about to ride away, glance down at the farmers below.

> CHRIS: They win. They *always* win.
> VIN: And . . . *us*?
> CHRIS: We *lose*. We *always* lose.

After the leader accomplishes the heroic task, he takes none of the pleasure from a difficult job well done that earlier incarnations of such men enjoyed. Chris and Vin are as penniless as they were at the beginning, and there is nowhere for them to go now that the last mission has been accomplished. Their cynicism, expressed in 1960, hardly rates as the be-all and end-all of the era's shifting mood. Six years later, in a similar film—*The Professionals*—like men pass beyond cynicism, growing pessimistic. Three years later, in *The Wild Bunch*, they openly embrace nihilism.

The rules (if there indeed are any) for today's action movies indicate a clear break from strict codes of the past. Writing in 1973, British film historian Ian Cameron noted that recent incidents involving great conflicts for survival, torn from newspaper headlines, intriguing owing to their ring of truth, "are liable to throw up heroes and heroines who can quickly be enshrined in film." The editor of *Movie* then claimed that, "even so, one can hardly see film-makers rushing to celebrate a remarkable feat of endurance by the survivors of (an) air crash, which kept alive on the snows of the Andes for an incredible length of time after the chocolate ran out by consuming the more nourishing parts of the conveniently deep-frozen corpses around them." A low-budget enactment of that incident, *Survive!*, appeared less than three years later. *Alive*, a far more elaborate version, debuted in 1993. Cameron may have been looking over his shoulder to the past, recalling a kind of bygone film in which such stuff would have been considered tasteless. In the new, more honest (if more vulgar) world of contemporary action, a tale involving cannibalism is made to order, such as the recent *Ravenous* (1999).

In the Old Hollywood, "adventure" existed as a blanket term for an element running through films as diverse as the big-budget western and the cheesy science-fiction flick. Today, the action movie constitutes a genre unto itself, if one that can incorporate such settings as the old west and outer space with equal aplomb. Again, of course, we can hear critics complaining that there's nothing serious to be found here. And, of course, they are wrong: No stories are *more* serious in import, if only by implication, than tales of action. "Standard plots, values, and character types" in such movies render them, in the words of Frederick Elkin, adult versions of the "fairy tale and folklore" of our childhood.

He continued:

> In most hero stories, the child can imagine himself in a world that is simple, clear-cut, and well-ordered. There are no unnecessary characters, no irrelevant intrusions, no complex personalities, and no problems left unresolved ... In identifying with the confident hero ... the child is reassured. No matter what the odds or dangers, the child in his imagination can, without the slightest fear or hesitation, overcome his adversaries and affirm his own strength and importance.

Those words were written in 1950, near the beginning of the postwar period, a time when most action films—for example, *The Seventh Voyage of Sinbad* (1958)—were designed with children in mind. Adult movies of the period— *A Streetcar Named Desire* (1949), *Marty* (1955), *Sweet Smell of Success* (1956), *The Three Faces of Eve* (1957)—were created under the assumption that adults could no longer believe in such stuff. As yet another cultural observer put it, traditional heroes with "the wooden absoluteness of their virtue represented little an adult could take seriously."

The modern action film features stunt work and special effects that the originators of the genre could only dream of, including dueling trucks in *License to Kill* (1989).

By decade's end, the tide was turning back. B-westerns for children all but disappeared. Adult westerns, beginning with *The Magnificent Seven* and continuing through Clint Eastwood's Man With No Name trilogy, returned with a vengeance, if in a meaner, leaner form. As action films, westerns or

otherwise, began to draw in an ever larger number of adults (often, accompanied by their kids), it became obvious this genre speaks to something essential not only in the child, but also the child that exists, however hidden, within every adult. To appear as grown-ups, we may wear suits and ties, attempting to pass ourselves off as mature. But, as our psychiatrists well know, this is life-as-theater; inside, insecurities with ourselves and feelings of inferiority in the world linger. We may have grown older, but we have not necessarily grown up. However loathe we may be to admit it, we need to be reassured, as only the action film can do.

When Tony Thomas penned *The Great Adventure Films* in 1976, he considered cutting the book off in 1965, insisting that the adventure film was dead by that point in time. "Tastes change," he bemoaned, "and the ever-increasing costs of production make the likelihood of costume epics slimmer." Period pictures *had* disappeared from the screen during the 1970s, when the moviegoing public grappled with modern issues in films as diverse as *Carnal Knowledge* (1971) and *Mean Streets* (1973). But what may momentarily appear to be a permanent change more often than not turns out to be a temporary pendulum swing. *Braveheart* (1995) and *Gladiator* (2000), huge commercial successes as well as Oscar-winning Best Pictures, make clear tastes can, and do, change back again.

As for those "ever-increasing costs," producers now solve that problem by having a handful of soldiers appear, through computer-generated F/X (special effects), as virtual armies, with no one harmed in the process except out-of-work extras. "Every era gets the beefed-up action-film demigod it deserves," Owen Gleiberman noted in *Entertainment Weekly*, and the shift in styles always reflects concurrent changes in society. His statement holds true for the movies themselves, for what they have to say and the manner in which they express it. What follows, then, is a guide to the action movie, beginning with its current identity, followed by an informal history, tracing the form back, era by era, to its roots in the films of World War II.

2

ESSENTIALS: INTO THE NEW MILLENNIUM

The opening years of the twenty-first century promise a golden age for action movies, both contemporary and historical. The action films of any one time reflect the mind-set of that age, and America is now at war, and with a new kind of enemy. A rah!rah! mind-set not seen since the 1940s' WWII films is with us once again, often in movies made now but about that long-ago era. Too bad John Wayne, whom we might dub the patron saint of the action movie, didn't live to see his old-fashioned brand of patriotism return!

Gladiator (2000)

CREDITS

Director, Ridley Scott; screenplay, John Logan, William Nicholson, and David H. Franzoni; producers, Franzoni, Douglas Wick, and Branko Lustig; original music, Klaus Badelt, Lisa Gerrard, and Hans Zimmer; cinematography, John Mathieson; running time, 154 min.; rating, R.

CAST

Russell Crowe (*Decimus Maximus*); Joaquin Phoenix (*Emperor Commodus*); Connie Nielsen (*Lucilla*); Oliver Reed (*Antonius Proximo*); Richard Harris (*Emperor Marcus Aurelius*); Derek Jacobi (*Senator Gracchus*); David Schofield (*Falco*); David Hemmings (*Cassius*); Billy Dowd (*Narrator*).

THE FILM

Gladiator won five Academy Awards, including Best Actor for Russell Crowe and Best Picture of the Year. Some believed that Crowe's award served as a compensation prize for the previous year, when he had not received the Oscar for his brilliant performance in *The Insider*, a far more psychologically complex portrait. The Best Picture statuette mainly acknowledged the vast canvas and epic sweep director Scott brought to this tale of the Roman

Empire in its final days, as greatness gave way to decadence. In truth, the script is certainly not in a class with the high-quality of writing that had provided *Spartacus* (1960)—the greatest gladiator movie ever made—with a level of literary sophistication. Mel Gibson's production of *Braveheart*, dealing with an entirely other historical era, more deserved its Best Picture award for effective blending of political intrigue and romantic drama. The dialogue in *Gladiator* is often perfunctory and seldom inspired.

The plot does not always progress logically as it follows the misadventures of General Decimus, cursed with the blessing of the dying emperor Marcus Aurelius, which angers that patrician's son, Commodus. This conflict leads to the murder of Decimus's wife and child, his banishment from Rome, enslavement, and eventual triumphant return as a gladiator-rebel. Crowe provides a simple, even cardboard, hero, and Phoenix portrays an over-the-top villain. The dramatic lines aren't very different from what we might expect from a Rambo film done in period costume. Still, Scott's directorial prowess allows him to neatly cover most of the script's weaknesses, creating such a strong visceral viewing experience, particularly in the large-scale battle sequences, that audiences fell in love with the film despite its deficiencies. *Gladiator* at least proves that the ancient world epic—believed by so many to be part of our moviemaking past—can be revived if done so in a way that makes such stories accessible to the contemporary audience.

X-Men (2000)

CREDITS

Director, Bryan Singer; screenplay, David Hayter, Tom DeSanto, and Bryan Singer; producers, Avi Arad, Stan Lee, Ralph Winter, and Lauren Shuler Donner; original music, Michael Kamen and Jeremy Sweet; cinematography, Newton Thomas Sigel; running time, 104 min.; rating, PG-13.

CAST

Patrick Stewart (*Prof. X/Prof. Xavier*); Ian McKellen (*Magneto/Erik Magnus Lehnsherr*); Hugh Jackman (*Wolverine/Logan*); Anna Paquin (*Rogue/Marie D'Ancanto*); Famke Janssen (*Dr. Jean Grey*); Halle Berry (*Storm/Ororo Munroe*); James Marsden (*Cyclops/Scott Summers*); Tyler Mane (*Sabretooth/Victor Creed*); Ray Park (*Toad/Mortimer Toynbee*); Rebecca Romijn-Stamos (*Mystique/Raven*).

THE FILM

Hugh Jackman as "Wolverine" in *X-Men*.

From Marvel Comics and Stan Lee comes the long-awaited screen version of this cult favorite. Two professors—one good (Xavier), one bad (Magneto)—compete for the minds, bodies, and souls of young people born with super powers, such mutants scorned by normal human beings. The forces of good and evil clash, particularly after a dangerous politician devises a bizarre final solution to "the mutant problem." The film, like the comic book, dares to touch on serious themes. Magneto was not born evil, but he has become so owing to his embitterment over the death of his parents during the Holocaust. His motivation is understandable, even if his means cannot be justified. For once, the villains become sympathetic as the "heroes" grow nihilistic. The great single figure from the comics—the rugged individualist, if you will, among the mutant community—is Wolverine.

Sensing how necessary it would be to make him totally authentic on-screen, Hugh Jackman took cold showers in hopes that this might stimulate the actor to project what Stan Lee refers to as Wolverine's "berserk rage." All ten of the Wolverine costumes, which had been fashioned out of leather, were decimated during the course of making the film.

Crouching Tiger, Hidden Dragon (2000)

CREDITS

Director, Ang Lee; screenplay, Hui-Ling Wang, Kuo Jung Tsai, and James Schamus, from the book by Du Lu Wang; producers, Lee, Phillip Lee, and Ping Dong and Li-Kong Hsu; original music, Jorge Calandrelli, Tan Dun, and Yong King; cinematography, Peter Pau; running time, 119 min.; rating, PG-13.

CAST

Chow Yun-Fat (*Master Li Mu Bai*); Michelle Yeoh (*Yu Shu Lien*); Ziyi Zhang (*Jen Yu*, aka *Xiou Long*); Chen Chang (*Lo Hu*, aka *Dark Cloud*); Sihung Lung (*Sir Te*); Pei-pei Cheng (*Jade Fox*); Fa Zeng Li (*Governor Yu*).

THE FILM

It's hard to believe, in retrospect, that Bruce Lee was *not* allowed to play the lead in *Kung Fu*. Though the TV series was developed specifically for him, the network expressed concern that the vast American audience might not accept an Asian as an action hero. If that was once true, then the country—and the movies—have certainly come a long way. *Crouching Tiger* was the top action film of its year, beloved by genre fans and mainstream moviegoers alike, with Asian actors in the leads. The movie introduced stateside audiences to a sub-genre of the martial arts movie, known as "wuxia" films—action epics with a fantasy orientation. In such stories, the characters are able to fly, with no explanation given or expected. Such films, shot in Asia, had been that continent's equivalent of our B-movies. They targeted a less-than-sophisticated audience, accounting for a great deal of unsubtle humor. Director Ang Lee set out to raise that genre to a high art, combining midair bouts of kung fu with an epic scope, a metaphysical theme, an assortment of well-wrought characters, a romantic plot, and a conclusion worthy of Greek tragedy.

Master Li Mu Bai and his female counterpart, Yu Shu Lien, have repressed their abiding love for more than a decade, each dedicated to idealistic purposes of honor and service. He hopes to enact vengeance for his slain master and recover the Green Destiny sword. Everything changes, however, when an irrepressible young woman, Jen Yu, slips away from her conventional lifestyle to enjoy forbidden adventures. She cannot guess her "innocent" double life will lead to an altered relationship between the older couple and the end of an entire way of existence. Director Lee employs this premise to mount an Asian epic that is steeped in genre but surpassing its usual limitations. Yuen Wo-ping staged the fight scenes much as a great choreographer of ballet would use dance patterns to express the individual personalities of each performer, allowing us to learn about a character by the way he or she fights. For a sense of literary beauty, Lee used Mandarin rather than Cantonese for the language, owing to its more poetic effect. Most notable were the time-altered sword fights in which characters soared through the night air, over rooftops and back again, adding a swooning sense of surrealism to the action.

Lord of the Rings (2000)

CREDITS

Director, Peter Jackson; screenplay, Fran Walsh, Philippa Boyens, and Peter Jackson, from the novel by J. R. R. Tolkien; producers, Peter Jackson, Tim Sanders, and Barrie M. Osborne; original music, Enya (songs) and Howard Shore; cinematography, Andrew Lesnie; running time, 178 min.; rating, PG-13.

CAST

Elijah Wood (*Frodo Baggins*); Ian McKellen (*Gandalf the Grey*); Viggo Mortensen (*Aragon/"Stryder"*); Sean Astin (*Samwise Gamgee*); Liv Tyler (*"Evenstar" Undómiel*); Sean Bean (*Boromir*); Cate Blanchett (*Lady Galadriel*); Ian Holm (*Bilbo Baggins*); Hugo Weaving (*Elrond*); Orlando Bloom (*Legolas*); Christopher Lee (*Saruman*).

Large-scale action sequences, within the context of mythic romance, and adventure, in *Lord of the Rings*.

THE FILM

In one of the more audacious gambles in movie history, all three installments of the famed fantasy-trilogy were shot back to back, to ensure that the entire cast would remain available. New Line budgeted $300 million for Peter Jackson to complete his dream project. The shoot went on for 274 days, a record. The fear was that if the first film flopped, New Line would be stuck with two expensive movies the public would not want. Fortunately, this was a gamble that paid off—the old-fashioned fantasy clicking with the New Age mentality that had, between the sixties and the nineties, gradually worked its way into mainstream thinking. Significant, too, is that the suitably subtitled "Fellowship of the Ring" worked as a self-sufficient work of entertainment while leaving the door wide open for the follow-ups, while offering a throwback to the grand adventure films of old Hollywood. Middle-earth, the mythological land that Tolkein, a revered professor, had been created out of ancient legend and his own imagination, was vividly realized. And there are the Rings of Power, engendering a hero quest. The 3½-foot hobbit Frodo (Elijah Wood) and his mentor, the 7¼-foot wizard Gandalf (Ian McKellan), journey through kingdoms of elves, dwarfs, wizards, and hobbits as they set out to destroy "The Ring" in the land of Mordor and hopefully overcome the powerful presence of evil. It's significant to note that the film, like so many classics, combines community and loyalty (The Fellowship of the Ring) and rugged individuality (Frodo's singular hero-quest, accompanied by his sidekick/squire).

Black Hawk Down (2001)

CREDITS

Director, Ridley Scott; screenplay, Ken Nolan and (uncredited) Steven Zaillian, from the book by Mark Bowden; producers, Scott and Jerry Bruckheimer; original music, James Michael Dooley and Hans Zimmer; cinematography, Slavomir Idziak; running time, 143 min.; rating, R.

CAST:

Josh Hartnett (*Sgt. Matt Eversmann*); Eric Bana (*Sgt. "Hoot" Hooten*); Ewan McGregor (*Ranger Danny Grimes*); Tom Sizemore (*Col. Danny McKnight*); Sam Shepard (*Gen. William F. Garrison*); Ewen Bremner (*Shawn Nelson*); William Fichtner (*Sgt. Sanderson*); Charlie Hofheimer

Josh Hartnett in
Black Hawk Down.

(*Jamie Smith*); Thomas Hardy (*Twombly*); Thomas Guiry (*Ed Yurek*);
Ron Eldard (*Mike Durant*); Orlando Bloom (*Todd*); Kim Coates
("*Wex*").

THE FILM

The war film was until recently considered even more "dead" a genre than the
western. During the late nineties, however, beginning with Steven Spielberg's
Saving Private Ryan, it was suddenly alive again, ranging from cinematic
reappraisals of World War II and Vietnam to considerably more esoteric areas
of combat. Ridley Scott, director of thinking-man's action films, drew from
just such a battle to fashion a modern masterpiece about loyalty, courage,
and ideology when tested by a nightmarish scenario. The movie recreates an
actual battle at Mogadishu in Somalia, on October 3, 1993. What was to have
been a relatively routine mission transforms, to the horror of U.S. Rangers
involved, into a long day's journey into self-discovery and salvation. The mil-

itary unit's objective is to capture key enemy officers for interrogation purposes, but that hope swiftly ends as a pair of helicopters employed for this purpose are brought down by rocket-propelled grenades. Some Americans find themselves in Mogadishu's hostile streets, surrounded by the enemy. With a "no one gets left behind" coda, the American forces involved make an effort to get them out and back to safety.

The film was produced by Jerry Bruckheimer who, with his late partner Don Simpson, had created a modern if notably superficial approach to action films (beginning with *Top Gun*, directed by Ridley Scott's brother Tony) in the mid-eighties. This film contained the kind of high-tech action of such earlier films but far more substance and complexity of character.

Spiderman (2002)

CREDITS

Director, Sam Raimi; screenplay, David Koepp, from the comic book by Stan Lee and Steve Ditko; producers, Ian Bryce and Laura Ziskin; original music, Danny Elfman; cinematography, Don Burgess; running time, 121 min.; rating, PG-13.

CAST

Tobey Maguire (*Peter Parker/Spider-Man*); Willem Dafoe (*Norman Osborn/The Green Goblin*); Kirsten Dunst (*Mary Jane Watson*); James Franco (*Harry Osborn*); Cliff Robertson (*Ben Parker*); Rosemary Harris (*Aunt May*); Randy Savage (aka, Poffo, *Boneshaw McGraw*); J. K. Simmons (*J. Jonah Jameson*); Joe Manganiello (*Flash Thompson*); Gerry Becker (*Maximillian Fargas*); Bill Nunn (*Joseph Robertson*); Bruce Campbell (*Ring Announcer*).

THE FILM

If never quite as mainstream a hit as *Superman* or *Batman*, the *Spiderman* comic book acquired a formidable cult following, particularly after a modestly successful TV series in the late 1970s. Later, even as those aforementioned superheroes were revived in the context of big-budget entertainments, the Spidey franchise remained relatively dormant, in large part owing to legal questions as to who owned the movie rights. Finally, *Spiderman* did get made and turned out to be a bigger hit even than devoted fans might have hoped.

In the early spring 2002 blockbuster sweepstakes, *Spiderman* all but

eclipsed the fifth *Star Wars* film (Episode 2). With a $114 million take on its opening weekend, *Spiderman* beat the $90 million record that had been set by *Harry Potter* the previous November. The movie's story line stuck close to the comic book conception. Peter Parker is a high school nerd bitten by a radioactive spider, causing his body chemistry to drastically alter. Shortly, he can scale the sides of buildings or walk on a ceiling. A breath of fresh air (and a modicum of reality) is featured; unlike other graphic-novel-type superheroes, he doesn't immediately decide to use these powers for altruistic purposes—i.e., fighting crime—but hopes to make as much money as possible. Then, his uncle is killed by the very crook Spiderman let go, altering Peter's vision of what Spidey can and should accomplish. Simultaneously, businessman/scientist Norman Osborn creates his own evil alter-ego, The Green Goblin, impossibly powerful and maniacally mean. Peter's task, as the unique Spidey, is to stop the Goblin while, as a normal kid, he wins the hand of the school's prettiest girl, Mary Jane Watson. The immense commercial (and, for the most part, critical) success ensured there would be sequels, though there was little doubt as to that. Tobey Maguire and Kirsten Dunst had already signed for the follow-up. So, early in the decade, the 2000+ plus generation had a super-hero as definitive for their generation as, in modern moviemaking terms, Superman had been for the eighties and Batman for the nineties. Sam Raimi's status as the film's director made clear that what had once been the fringe of moviemaking (this was the guy who, after all, gave us the *Evil Dead* movies) had become a part of the mainstream (see chapter 21 and "Bruce Campbell" in chapter 20).

Tobey Maguire in *Spiderman*.

3

YESTERDAY, TODAY, AND TOMORROW: ACTION STARS OF THE NINETIES AND BEYOND

Though the following performers all reached action-star status during the final years of the last millennium or the very beginning of the new one, many had been working in films for some time. Each achieved action stardom during the nineties and is likely to go on enjoying that status during the first decade of the new century.

(Jose) **Antonio** (Dominguez) **Banderas**

Antonio Banderas in *Desperado*.

Born August 10, 1960, in Malaga, Spain, to a policeman father and teacher mother. Antonio's initial dream was to be a soccer star, but such hopes ended when he broke his foot at age 14. Attracted by the mystique of theater, he became a street performer, later enrolling in Spain's premiere School of Dramatic Art. Antonio moved to Madrid, became a member of the National Theater of Spain's ensemble, and acquired a reputation as an intense, brooding, charismatic performer who dared to do avant-garde projects. In his first big break, Antonio was picked by Pedro Almodovar, an edgy erotic auteur of post-Franco Spain, to appear in *Women on the Verge of a Nervous Breakdown* (1988) and *Tie Me Up, Tie Me Down!* (1990). When American stardom beckoned, it was in the romantic *The Mambo Kings* (1992), as a throwback to an earlier generation of Latin lovers. He divorced first wife, Ana Leza, following an eight-year marriage, to wed Melanie Griffith. *Philadelphia* (1993), *Interview With the Vampire* (1994), and *Evita!* (1996) preceded his action stardom.

ACTION FILMOGRAPHY

Shoot! (1993); *Assassins* (1995); *Desperado* (1995); *Mask of Zorro* (1998); *The 13th Warrior* (1999); *The White River Kid* (1999); *Play It to the Bone* (1999); *The Body* (2000); *Spy Kids* (2001); *Spy Kids 2: Island of Lost Dreams* (2002); *Once Upon a Time in Mexico* (2002); *Femme Fatale* (2002).

MUST-SEE

Desperado (Robert Rodriguez, dir.). The director obtained a big Hollywood budget to remake his own earlier, cheaper, superior actioner, *El Mariachi* (see chapter 21). This time it's Antonio as the loner who, like Eastwood or Mifune, wanders into an isolated town (here, in Mexico) and becomes involved in violent gunplay. No shortage of action.

Spy Kids (Robert Rodriguez, dir.). Antonio and George Clooney unite, though in a film that plays action for the family viewer. Children, who realize they are the offspring of spies, decide to help when their parents are in jeopardy. Feel-good film with non-stop explosions, chases, etc.

Mask of Zorro (Martin Campbell, dir.). Providing a first-rate update of the legendary story, rightly played here as action flick, this movie is a tongue-in-cheek, rather than straightforward adventure. The tradition is handed down from old Zorro (Anthony Hopkins) to his heir (Antonio) who will fight for justice and romance spunky heroine (Catherine Zeta-Jones).

George (Timothy) Clooney

Born May 6, 1961, in Lexington, Kentucky. Father Nick (brother of jazz vocalist Rosemary) Clooney took a job as TV talk show host in Cincinnati. From age 5, George grew up in and around the broadcasting industry. Later attending Northern Kentucky U., George tried but failed to win a spot on the Cincinnati Reds baseball team. He was very aware of acting owing to Oscar-winner Uncle José Ferrer. Eventually, George drifted to L.A. and slept on the floor of a friend's apartment while trying to find jobs. Acting lessons at Beverly Hills Playhouse led to what was supposed to be George's big break: a role in 1984 on the TV medical show *E/R*. The show was a total flop, and quickly cancelled, leaving George to struggle for a long time thereafter. Ten years later, a similarly named dramatic series made his reputation.

George's marriage to actress Talia Balsam lasted from 1989 to 1992. He swears he will never marry again or have children.

The lead in *Three Kings* came his way only after Mel Gibson and Nicolas Cage passed on the project. George was the first guest ever to appear on *Rosie* TV talk fest. He is a diehard activist against media outlets that invade stars' privacy.

ACTION FILMOGRAPHY

Red Surf (1990); *From Dusk Till Dawn* (1996); *The Peacemaker* (1997); *Batman & Robin* (1997); *The Thin Red Line* (1998); *Out of Sight* (1998); *Three Kings* (1999); *The Perfect Storm* (2000).

MUST-SEE

From Dusk Till Dawn (Robert Rodriguez, dir.). Tarantino dreamed up this combo of violent road movie and vampire/stripper thriller, played at such a breakneck pace you don't have time to question its logic and/or morality. Clooney and Harvey Keitel make a great team. Salma Hayek's snake dance belongs in any self-respecting time capsule.

The Peacemaker (Mimi Leder, dir.). Wise-ass Clooney and ultra-serious Nicole Kidman are the odd couple trying to locate and eliminate terrorists who exploded an atomic bomb in Russia. Ignore the cheesy script and enjoy well-staged action/explosions.

Three Kings (see chapter 6).

The Perfect Storm (Wolfgang Petersen, dir.). Knock-your-socks-off F/X can't cover that the producers made a movie about the wrong characters; it should've been about the *real* heroes—the Coast Guard!—rather than drunken redneck sailors. Still, action fans will want to catch the remarkable storm scenes.

Benicio Del Toro

Born February 19, 1967, in San German, Puerto Rico. Benicio was the son of a sucessful lawyer team. After his mother died when he was 9, his father moved the family to a Pennsylvania farm. Finishing high school as a basketball star, Benicio headed for the University of California (San Diego) to study business, where he took an acting elective, sensing this was what he wanted to do. He dropped out of college and headed for L.A. to study with drama coach Stella Adler, then NYC's Circle in the Square Theatre. TV work followed, including *Miami Vice*. He was cast in his first action flick as "Dario," in *License to Kill*. At 21, Benicio was the youngest actor ever to portray the villain in a Bond film. Parts in numerous films of varying quality did little to bolster his career until an appearance in Oscar-winning thriller *The Usual Suspects*. Five years later, the Best Supporting Actor Oscar for *Traffic* propelled him into the Big Leagues. Benicio powerfully projects a combination of inner sensitivity and outward dangerousness, via Robert Mitchum–style sleepy eyes and a depth of personality reminiscent of Monty Clift.

Benicio Del Toro in *Traffic*.

ACTION FILMOGRAPHY

License to Kill (1989); *Christopher Columbus: The Discovery* (1992); *Fearless* (1993); *The Funeral* (1996); *Snatch* (2000); *Traffic* (2000); *The Hunted* (2002).

MUST-SEE

Snatch (Guy Ritchie, dir.). Yet another of the post-Tarantino violent action-thrillers, *Snatch* is about an assorted group of independently minded criminals setting out on the title mission. Benicio, Brad Pitt, and Dennis Farina deliver standout performances, within a context of the film's brutal aura that sometimes takes the form of violent action.

Traffic (Steven Soderbergh, dir.) *Traffic* is a state-of-the-art epic about drug dealing along the Mexican border, transcending all clichés, with Benicio a standout (and Oscar winner) among a cast that includes Michael Douglas, Catherine Zeta-Jones, Don Cheadle, and Dennis Quaid.

Samuel (Leroy) Jackson

Born December 21, 1948, in Washington, D.C. Samuel was raised in Chattanooga by his mother and grandmother, both of whom insisted that he follow the straight-and-narrow path, which included education as a means of advancement. Young Samuel excelled as an architecture major at Morehouse College, Atlanta, and he would have pursued a successful career in the field were it not for a stutter that plagued him since childhood. A speech therapist advised that he might control the situation by appearing in plays. No sooner had he landed a role in a college musical production than Jackson was hooked, changing his major. After winning a role in a regional TV commercial for a fast-food chain, Jackson used the money to finance his move to New York, where he found work with Shakespeare Festival and a Negro ensemble company. Future filmmaker Spike Lee caught Samuel's performance in *A Soldier's Story* (1981), and he hired S.L.J. once in a position to do so. Samuel starred in *School Daze* (1988), *Do the Right Thing* (1989), *Mo' Better Blues* (1990), and *Jungle Fever* (1991). Then, *GoodFellas* and *Jurassic Park* opened way for action-hero stardom.

ACTION FILMOGRAPHY

GoodFellas (1990); *Patriot Games* (1992); *Juice* (1992); *White Sands* (1992); *True Romance* (1993); *Menace II Society* (1993); *Hail Caesar* (1993); *Jurassic Park* (1993); *Pulp Fiction* (1994); *Kiss of Death* (1995); *Die Hard With a Vengeance* (1995); *The Long Kiss Goodnight* (1996); *Jackie Brown* (1997); *Sphere* (1998); *The Negotiator* (1998); *Star Wars Episode I: The Phantom Menace* (1999); *Deep Blue Sea* (1999); *Rules of Engagement* (2000); *Shaft* (2000); *Changing Lanes* (2002); *Star Wars Episode II: The Attack of the Clones*.

MUST-SEE

Die Hard With a Vengeance (John McTiernan, dir.). A marvelous entry in the ongoing franchise, Samuel L. plays an embittered man who finds himself accidentally joining supercop John McClane (Bruce Willis) in a crusade against a bomb-wielding terrorist (Jeremy Irons). A believable plot, effective direction, and spectacular stunts keep it on top.

Negotiator (Gary Gray, dir.). Jackson came into his own as an action star with his role as Lt. Danny Roman, a Chicago-based hostage expert who finds himself framed for crimes he didn't commit. Ironically, he is forced to take hostages himself in order to clear his name. Jackson's pairing with Kevin Spacey makes for a memorable mano-e-mano movie.

Rules of Engagement (William Friedkin, dir.). In his best action role so far, Jackson stars as a marine officer unjustly held responsible when a Middle

Eastern standoff turns violent. Action and drama intertwines as Tommy Lee Jones plays the defense attorney at S.L.J.'s court-martial.

Star Wars Episode I: The Phantom Menace (George Lucas, dir.). Jackson plays Mace Windu in the long-awaited, if slightly disappointing, follow-up to the beloved space-fantasy series. Way too much talk, not enough action, though the action *is* spectacular when it does occur.

Shaft (John Singleton, dir.). This should have put Jackson over the top as the next great action star. He's perfectly cast as the nephew of Richard Roundtree, but a so-so script and Singleton's lack of ease with such a genre film undermine the potential. Still, Samuel L. as Big John? You can dig it!

Jet Li (Li Lian Jie)

Born April 26, 1963, in Beijing, China. Jet Li grew up destitute following his father's death. To remove himself as an economic burden from his mother, Jet accepted an invitation to Beijing's sports academy, living free on the Asian

Jet Li in
The Enforcer.

equivalent of "scholarship." He quickly mastered the Wu Shu form of martial arts, becoming the international champ at age 11. A world tour brought him to America, where he met then-president Nixon. He was also introduced to film producers looking for a successor to Bruce Lee, the preteen then considered too young. He coached, earned more awards, and eventually starred in first chop-socky epic filmed in the People's Republic of China, *Shaolin Temple* (1979). He directed himself in *Born to Defend* at age 23. *Once Upon a Time in China* films made him a superstar throughout Asia. Jet Li's dream was to be an American box office sensation. He accepted the bad-guy role in Joel Silver's fourth *Lethal Weapon*. His first American starring vehicle was *Romeo Must Die*. Next, Luc Besson created *Kiss of the Dragon* for Jet. Jet's future possibilities include working with Silver on his next *Matrix* film and playing "Kato," if *The Green Hornet* is revived.

ACTION FILMOGRAPHY

Shaolin Temple (1979); *Shaolin Kids* (1983); *Born to Defend* (1986); *Arahan* (aka *Martial Arts of Shaoli*, 1986); *Dragon Fighter* (aka *Dragon Kickboxer*, 1988); *Dragons of the Orient* (1988); *The Master* (1989); *Swordsman II* (1991); *Once Upon a Time in China* (1991); *Once Upon a Time in China II* (1992); *Legend of Fong Sai-Yuk* (1993); *Kung Fu Master* (aka *Lord of the Wu Tang*, 1993); *Once Upon a Time in China III* (aka *The Invincible Shaolin*, 1993); *Last Hero in China* (1993); *Claws of Steel* (aka *Deadly China Hero*, 1993); *Tai Chi* (aka *Twin Warriors*, 1993); *Legend II* (1993); *Defender* (1994); *Shaolin Kung Fu* (1994); *Fist of Legend* (1994); *Legend of the Red Dragon* (1994); *Meltdown* (1995); *My Father Is a Hero* (aka *Jet Li's The Enforcer*, 1995); *Adventure King* (1996); *Black Mask* (1996); *Once Upon a Time in China 4* (1997); *Lethal Weapon 4* (1998); *Contract Killer* (aka *Hitman*, 1998); *Romeo Must Die* (2000); *Top Fighter* (2000); *Kiss of the Dragon* (2001); *The One* (2001); *Hero* (2002); *Cradle to the Grave* (2002); *About Face* (2002).

MUST-SEE

Once Upon a Time in China (Tsui Hark, dir.). A mid-1800s period piece about folk hero Wong Fei Hung, who opposes Western influences then invading his country and the local criminals who hope to profit from them. Handsome production values, top-flight fight scenes, though the low-humor comic relief does get a bit sticky.

Legend of the Red Dragon (Wong Jing, dir.). Strong vengeance-driven story with Li and his young son, whom he instructs along the way, on a journey to revenge deceased wife.

Black Mask (Danny Lee, dir.). Perhaps Jet's most appealing vehicle so far, with a touch of sci-fi, he (and enemies) have all been transformed into beyond belief super-fighters. Four fabulous Hong Kong fight sequences, though search for the 106-minute director's cut.

Kiss of the Dragon (Chris Mahon, dir.). A Luc Besson–inspired film gives us a more sophisticated Jet, as a Bond-like secret agent, romancing sultry call-girl Brigitte Fonda.

The One (James Wong, dir.). Offbeat sci-fi vehicle for Jet, realizing that we have a parallel universe, and his alter-ego (Li in a dual role) breaks through, trying to assume his life.

Brad (William Bradley) **Pitt**

Born December 18, 1963, in Shawnee, Oklahoma. The family moved to Springfield, Missouri, where Brad's father managed a trucking company. At Kickapoo High, Brad was successful in athletics, the debating team, student government, and the drama club. Major while attending University of Missouri, Journalism. Nonetheless, he found time to perform in fraternity shows, leaving college several credits short of graduation to pursue acting career in L.A. While waiting for break, Brad took any job that came his way, including hawking (in giant chicken costume) "el Pollo Loco." Cast as "J. D." in *Thelma and Louise* after William Baldwin deserted to do *Backdraft* (1991). Many early indie films—*Johnny Suede* (1991), *Cool World* (1992)—didn't click. Brad received the action-hero role in *Legends of the Fall*, then picked by Tarantino for brief but showy part in *True Romance*. Despite Robert Redford-like macho-preppie looks, he refuses to coast on charisma, searching out difficult, complex roles and portraying them with De Niro-ish intensity.

ACTION FILMOGRAPHY

No Man's Land (uncredited, 1967); *A River Runs Through It* (1992); *True Romance* (1993); *Legends of the Fall* (1994); *Se7en* (1995); *Twelve Monkeys* (1995); *The Devil's Own* (1997); *Fight Club* (1999); *Snatch* (2000); *The Mexican* (2001); *Spy Game* (2001).

MUST-SEE

True Romance (Tony Scott, dir.). A Tarantino script about a modern Bonnie and Clyde (Christian Slater and Patricia Arquette), given more main-stream/commercial tone by hit maker Scott. A flaked-out Pitt owns every scene he's in. Get the unrated version!

Se7en (David Fincher, dir.). Old cop (Morgan Freeman), young cop (Pitt) team find themselves facing the most horrific of serial killers imagina-ble (Kevin Spacey). Warmup for *Fight Club* by Fincher and Pitt neatly com-bines creepy suspense with edgy action.

Twelve Monkeys (Terry Gilliam, dir.). Chris Marker's "underground" cult classic *La Jetee* (1962), transformed into a first-rate Hollywood sci-fi/action flick. Pitt is fascinating as a seemingly harmless madman who may be planning to destroy the world unless time-traveler Bruce Willis can stop him. Imaginative and absorbing.

Fight Club (David Fincher, dir.). Quiet guy (Edward Norton) finds him-self drawn into a bizarre relationship with edgy Pitt, joining the title group for violent, illegal secret combats. Or so it would seem. ("First rule of Fight Club: You don't talk about Fight Club!") It either works for you or seems a pretentious mess.

Spy Game (Tony Scott, dir.). Often called "the young Robert Redford," Pitt and onetime mentor join up for a socko combination of thrills, spills, neat spy suspense, and sudden action. Not particularly original but great fun all the way.

Jean (Juan) Reno

Born July 30, 1948, in Casablanca, Morocco. Andalusian parents had fled to escape Franco's fascistic rule in Spain. Mother passed away in Africa. Other-wise, happy youth spent at beach, watching American action stars (John Wayne, William Holden) at the movies. Following aftermath of Six-Day War, Juan (17)—now "Jean"— relocated, this time in France to study acting. In the military (1968) he staged entertainments for the troops, avoiding typical soldier-style drudgery. After a bohemian life in Paris, further acting lessons, TV, and stage roles. Minor movie parts led to casting in films by Luc Besson, perfect director/actor combo as Reno's unique screen persona emerged: world-weary, yet possessing a hidden energy reserve that can suddenly

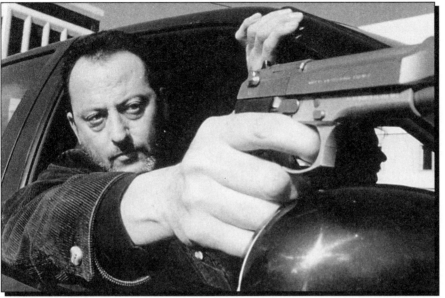

Jean Reno in *Ronin*.

explode. As a diver in *The Big Blue* (1988), he became an offbeat leading man. With *La Femme Nikita*, Jean transformed to an offbeat action hero of an existential, even nihilistic order. Still, some decisions questionable. Could have had role of "Agent Smith" in *Matrix*, but that would have meant passing up . . . *Godzilla!*

ACTION FILMOGRAPHY

The Final Combat (1983); *Subway* (1985); *La Femme Nikita* (1991); *The Professional* (1994); *Mission: Impossible* (1996); *The Jaguar* (1996); *Godzilla* (1998); *Ronin* (1998); *Rollerball* (2002).

MUST-SEE

The Final Combat (Luc Besson, dir.). We're back in *Blade Runner/Mad Max* territory, as strange individual (Pierre Jolivet) wanders the wasteland, searching for retribution, Jeanas "Brute," a killer encountered along the way. Moody film, sans dialogue; worth a glance.

 La Femme Nikita (Luc Besson, dir.). Small role for Jean as cold-blooded killer augments stylish film that introduced the hit-woman as pop-culture icon, played by Anne Parillaud. Drugged-out street girl turned into gorgeous gun-wielding babe by government agency, but her identity is taken away.

The Professional (aka, Leonard; Luc Besson, dir.). Reno's supporting character (more or less) from *Nikita,* given a film of his own, as an assassin locked with evil Gary Oldman in a death-duel, while romancing underage beauty (Natalie Portman). Mesmerizing if maniacal. Catch the director's cut at 133 minutes if you want it to make any sense.

Ronin (John Frankenheimer, dir.). The old chestnut about unsavory characters, unknown to each other, brought together by a mysterious bene-factor to pull a violent job, realizing there's a traitor in their midst. Onetime great director tries to liven up vehicle for Jean, De Niro, with a great car chase but little empathy for the characters.

Will(ard) (Christopher) **Smith, Jr.**

Born September 25, 1968, in Philadelphia, Pennsylvania, Will is the second of four children, whose father owned a refrigeration company. Middle-class boyhood in West Philly, nicknamed "Fresh Prince" long before TV show of that name owing to natural charm. No wait for success; he turned down an MIT scholarship and with "DJ Jazzy" Jeff Townes formed a musical group. On to great financial success following TV series *Fresh Prince of Beverly Hills* was created for Will, playing a thinly disguised variation of himself. Then more sophisticated comedy-drama film roles, including *Six Degrees of Sepa-ration* (1993) suggested he'd be the next Cary Grant, not a new Harrison Ford. Then, offbeat casting— having the 6-foot-2 talented good-looker play a rougher character in *Bad Boys*—paid off. With the critically drubbed *Inde-pendence Day*, Smith moved into super-stardom, a performer who can open a film in a big way, particularly during Hollywood's all-important early summer season.

ACTION FILMOGRAPHY

Bad Boys (1995); *Independence Day* (1996); *Men in Black* (1997); *Enemy of the State* (1998); *Wild Wild West* (1999); *Ali* (2001); *Men in Black II* (2002); *Bad Boys 2* (2003); *Sharkslayer* (2003).

MUST-SEE

Independence Day (Roland Emmerich, dir.). Deserved Oscar went to the F/X in this unofficial remake of *War of the Worlds*, only this was *not* written by H. G. Wells. Hokey dialogue occasionally makes this sound like a satire rather than serious actioner, as good soldier Will (modeling performance on Harrison Ford) fights off large-scale alien invasion.

Men in Black (Barry Sonnenfeld, dir.). Will and Tommy Lee Jones comprise a terrific team in smart-funny action-*cum*-F/X fest about two men assigned to oversee aliens who have quietly entered our society, finding themselves on one of those missions to save the world. Quirky, clever bits make this commercial filmmaking at its most enjoyable.

Enemy of the State (Tony Scott, dir.). More thriller than actioner, though there's plenty of that to go around, too. The decent Will goes up against corrupt Jon Voight, in a Washington battle of wits that only one will survive. Terrific supporting cast includes Gene Hackman, Jamie Kennedy, and (unbilled) Jason Robards.

Wesley Snipes

Born in Orlando, Florida, July 31, 1962. Snipes was raised in the Bronx and attended famed (thanks to film *Fame*) High School for the Performing Arts. Disappointed when mother moved family south before graduation. A year later he was back in New York, attending State University's Purchase campus, north of the city, known for its arts program. Success came early, with bit in a Goldie Hawn comedy *Wildcats* (1986). Martin Scorsese picked Snipes to play gang-leader menacing Michael Jackson in rock-video *Bad* (1987). Shortly, featured in varied roles, ranging from supporting part of jazz musician in Spike Lee's *Mo' Better Blues* (1990) to lead, a year later, as male half of an interracial couple (with Annabella Sciorra) in *Jungle Fever* (1991). Like most black actors, Wesley was sometimes faced with not working or playing street criminals, so he found an outlet, beginning with

Wesley Snipes in *Blade*.

Passenger 57, as a genre star, alternating between good and bad-guy roles. He found time for comedy (*To Wong Foo, Thanks for Everything*, 1995), as drag queen.

ACTION FILMOGRAPHY

Streets of Gold (1986); *King of New York* (1990); *New Jack City* (1991); *Passenger 57* (1992); *Rising Sun* (1993); *Demolition Man* (1993); *Boiling Point* (1993); *Sugar Hill* (1993); *Drop Zone* (1994); *Money Train* (1995); *Murder at 1600* (1997); *U.S. Marshals* (1998); *Blade* (1998); *The Art of War* (2000); *Zigzag* (2001); *Liberty Stands Still* (2001); *Blade 2* (2002).

MUST-SEE

New Jack City (Mario Van Peebles, dir.). The only strong film by the director/actor, this was the movie that revived "black-exploitation flicks" if in a more modern milieu. Snipes excels as an egomaniacal drug kingpin, relentlessly pursued by agents Van Peebles and Judd Nelson. Rapper Ice T also in cast.

Demolition Man (Marco Brambilla, dir.). Wesley's first over-the-top super-villain in futuristic action flick has him looking like Dennis Rodman, with shocking blonde hair, terrorizing populace of L.A. in 2032. Sylvester Stallone is deadpan cop awakened (barely) from cryogenic sleep to take him on, with inventive funny/furious fights galore.

Drop Zone (John Badham, dir.). Well-mounted action thriller, in the tradition of *Point Break* (borrowing one of that film's performers, Gary Busey), about a sky diving team that moonlights as hardened criminals. Airborne action scenes terrific.

Blade (Stephen Norrington, dir.). Adapted from popular Marvel comic book character created by Marv Wolfman, this is Snipes' best characterization in an action film so far. He's a part-vampire personage, relying on knowledge of the dark side to fight, in notably bloody if effectively staged battles, the worst vampire-menace since ol' Dracula.

Chow Yun-Fat (Jan Yun Faat)

Born in Lama Island in 1955, precise date not available. His move toward action-movie stardom began at age 16; family relocated on Kowloon Peninsula, where Chow/Jan found work as extra at TVB, hugely successful Hong

Kong TV production company. If the actors made so much money, he'd become one. Enrolled in theater classes, he became staple of Asian television with a regular role on *Shanghai Town*. Appeared in drama and comedy including *Story of Wu-Viet*, but no thought of becoming a genre star. When John Woo's first choice for *A Better Tomorrow* (Ti Lung) wasn't available, Chow was awarded the role. Shortly, he created a tough-guy persona, wielding a pair of pistols, American gunslinger style, while chewing on a toothpick. Woo played Leone/Kurosawa to Chow's Eastwood/Mifune. After the Tarantino revolution, Woo's violent thrillers were imported into the United States to cash in on craze for international action, bringing Chow U.S. stardom, leading to non-action roles as well, including *Anna and the King* (1999).

ACTION FILMOGRAPHY

Massage Girls (1976); *Hard Boiled Killers* (1980); *Kiss Kiss, Bang Bang* (1981); *God of Killers* (1981); *Blood Money* (1983); *Shanghai Beach* (1983); *Head Hunter* (1983); *Seventh Curse* (1986); *A Better Tomorrow* (1986); *Color of a Hero* (1986); *Hero* (1987); *City on Fire* (1987); *A Better Tomorrow 2* (1987); *Dragon and Tiger Fight* (1987); *Prison Turbulence* (1987); *Autumn's Tale* (1987); *Goodbye, Hero* (1988); *City War* (1988); *Tiger on the Beat* (1988); *Love and Death in Saigon* (1989); *Triads* (1989); *The Killer* (1989); *Once a Thief* (1990); *Hard-Boiled* (1992); *Full Contact* (1992); *Replacement Killers* (1998); *The Corruptor* (1999); *Crouching Tiger, Hidden Dragon* (2001); *Bulletproof Monk* (2003).

Chow Yun-Fat in *Crouching Tiger, Hidden Dragon*.

MUST-SEE

A Better Tomorrow 2 (John Woo, dir.). Rare case of the sequel being far superior to the original, mainly because Woo realized that Chow (who'd had the second lead in the first film) had star charisma, focusing on him this time. The two find their metier here!

The Killer (John Woo, dir.). Dynamite dramatic triangle between a dedicated cop (Danny Lee), the title character (Chow) he's obsessed with catching, and a club performer (SallyYeh) blinded by accident during one of the hit man's missions. Junk movie formulas lifted to the level of what some would call genius by the director who clearly inspired Tarantino.

Hard-Boiled (John Woo, dir.). A hero this time around, Chow is reunited with former co-star Leslie Cheung as a buddy-buddy team out to thwart the evil plans of dealers in illegal arms. Woo, who also wrote the script, plays a key role as a sullen bartender. There are five (count 'em!) dazzlingly staged fight sequences, each unique in its own way.

Crouching Tiger, Hidden Dragon: See chapter 2.

4
THE SHAPE OF THINGS
TO COME

Spiderman's record-breaking opening weeks ensure that a sequel be put into production a.s.a.p. Top-billed stars Tobey Maguire and Kirsten Dunst will be reunited with director Sam Raimi, having taken his time to decide whether he'd go the web route again. Likely, the second installment will (in the tradition of the 1990s' *Batman* movies) feature two villains, Mr. Lizard and Dr. Octopus. *Spiderman*'s long gestation period suggests there may be some truth to the old adage that good things come to those who wait. If so, producer Gale Ann Hurd may eventually have reason to rejoice. Her decade-long attachment to an *Incredible Hulk* film appears to be reaching fruition, with Ang Lee (*Crouching Tiger, Hidden Dragon*) set to direct. Erica Bana, of *Black Hawk Down,* and recent Oscar-winner Jennifer Connelly will play the leads. This time around, the title creature will be computer generated.

Doubtless, in due time there will be a computer-generated hero or heroine that "works" for audiences in a way that *Final Fantasy*'s action babe did not. Lest we forget, when *Tron*—the first major film to set action heroes in a computer-generated future-world—opened in 1982 to big hype and weak ticket sales, there were those who insisted (incorrectly, as it turns out) that this technique would never click with the public. Ten years later, when the bugs were all worked out, Steven Spielberg considered what George Lucas's state-of-the-art craftsmen had to offer, realizing that computer-generated dinosaurs would appear far more convincing than the Ray Harryhausen tabletop models he had originally dreamed of employing for *Jurassic Park*.

Not that human action heroes need worry. The immense opening spring weekend of *The Scorpion King* (and, more significant, its strong box-office legs) suggests that The Rock (aka, Dwayne Johnson) may be to the next generation what Arnold Schwarzenegger has represented for the previous two decades—The Reigning Action Hero. Up next is *Helldorado*, in which The Rock will scour the Amazon jungles as a state-of-the-art bounty hunter. As for Arnold, Sly, and others of their ilk, such aging action heroes are likely to become enshrined as well-loved living legends from our collective

"The Rock" in *The Scorpion King*, likely to be the next big action-film franchise.

action-movie past. Before that occurs, though, each remains active. Harrison Ford currently headlines *K-19: The Widowmaker*, a Cold War action adventure about a crippled Russian nuclear sub, while Arnold is in pre-production on *Terminator 3.*

Speaking of the past, the *least*-likely-to-continue trend is remaking famed films, the very titles of which were to guarantee automatic success. Though Tim Burton's *Planet of the Apes* redux did open huge in the summer of 2001, it sank as soon as word got out how bad the movie is. Other remakes, including *The Time Machine* and *Rollerball*, barely made a dent at the box office.

Audiences want something new, on the big screen if not to our collective unconscious. Which explains why so many comic books, familiar in print but not celluloid, are successfully being mined. One property shortly to join such existing franchises as *X-Men* is *Daredevil*, in which Ben Affleck (who this summer assumed the "Jack Ryan" role in Tom Clancy's relatively realistic CIA stories) will star as a costumed crime fighter. What a long way the action film has come! Glance backward to a half-century ago and recall that George Reeves and Adam West abruptly ended their "serious" careers when they agreed to appear in *Superman* and *Batman* in the fifties and sixties, respectively.

Now, Oscar-winning talent *wants* to be associated with such characters, rather than accepting those parts out of career desperation. Nicolas Cage, Academy Best Actor choice for the "serious" *Leaving Las Vegas*, is an admitted comic book fanatic who would like to appear either as The Man of Steel or, perhaps, the less reknown but fraught with potential hero of *Hellblazer*. Such action figures have come to be seen less as cartoon figures than the contemporary equivalent of what they always, for the comic book cogniscenti, were—Greek mythic heroes. Not every such superhero will be from Stan Lee and Marvel, though. Talk continues about a revival of DC's *Superman*, following the small-screen success of The WB's *Smallville*.

Not all future action films will offer an escape from reality. Having twice depicted Vietnam (*Platoon* and *Born on the Fourth of July*), A-list auteur Oliver Stone plans to complete a trilogy with *The Hunted*, telling the true story of captive soldier Bobby Garwood, possibly to be played by Hayden Christensen of *Star Wars*. Even those directors long associated with over-the-top action are, in the current political climate of revised patriotism, attracted to more down-to-earth tales. John Woo martial arts mayhem gave way to a more serious civil rights drama about ethnicity in the WWII military with *Windtalkers*.

Kung fu, however, is in no immediate danger of disappearing from sight. The success of *Crouching Tiger, Hidden Dragon* has reinvigorated the martial arts craze while making it more mainstream than ever. This has its downside, because many dreadful Asian chop-socky films starring Jet Li, Chow Yun-Fat, and other Eastern stars are flooding the market, not only in theaters, but also on DVD and video store shelves. Many are dreadful. One too many weak items may indeed leave viewers with a bad taste for the genre. With a little luck, though, there will be more masterpieces on the order of Ang Lee's contemporary classic.

What we don't need is anything else on the order of Peter Hyams's *Musketeer*, with its offensive anachronistic grafting of Asian action concepts on to historical costume drama. Far more effective was the inspired combination of F/X and vampire lore in *Blade II*, a rare case of the sequel rating as

Ewan McGregor in the ongoing *Star Wars* saga.

superior to the original. Positive response has put director Guillermo del Toro in a position to adapt the graphic novel *Hellboy*. If del Toro's first choice works out, Steve Buscemi will headline, while Wesley Snipes will likely continue with his now-proven series.

Other ongoing franchises are likely to continue, despite the prospect of diminishing returns for most all except the phenomenal *Men in Black*. Film six, chapter three of the *Star Wars* saga is already in production, with Ewan McGregor and Samuel L. Jackson again performing under George Lucas's direction, despite the fact that *Attack of the Clones* did not achieve what had been hoped for financially during its opening late spring 2002 weekend.

Likewise, there will be a *Lara Croft, Tomb Raider* sequel, though the film did not net nearly as much in the way of commercial (or, for that matter, critical) response as had been expected. The second and third installments of *Lord of the Rings* are already in the can, and there will be more *X-Men* and *Men in Black* features, carrying us through the remainder of the decade.

Action films currently in the planning stages run a wide gamut of subjects and possibilities. Though best known for high-tech action, Jerry Bruckheimer (*Top Gun, Black Hawk Down*) has a King Arthur epic in mind, though he'd want it to be as gritty as possible. Screenwriter David Franzoni (*Gladiator*) has been hired as the scribe. For fans of that unique sub-genre known as "the wussie western," a sequel to *Dances With Wolves* is currently in the works, though apparently without Kevin Costner. The first film's Oscar-winning director claims that Kevin Blake's novel *The Holy Road* "didn't speak to me the way the first one did."

Even the *Indiana Jones* franchise may get another go-around. George Lucas has written a story for which producer Kathleen Kennedy is currently searching for the right writer to transform into a script. Whether Spielberg would direct has not yet been announced. However, the world's most popular director is certainly not shying away from action these days, as *Minority Report* with Tom Cruise makes clear. Also clear is that the action movie, born during the earliest days of what came to be called cinema, has been both rediscovered and reinvented. Now, it has at last returned to what it once was—the essence of movies as a pop-culture experience. Considering the box office success of *XXX* during the late summer of 2002, expect overnight sensation Vin Diesel to play a significant role.

5

IF THEY MOVE, <u>KILL</u> THEM!: LEGENDARY ONE-LINERS

Macho artists from Ernest Hemingway to Howard Hawks know something every true action fan is on some level aware of: At their best, these films are not merely violent escapist fantasies but philosophic dramas, in which men attempt to resolve moral issues or assert deeply believed values through the only avenue open to them—combat. In the modern action film, such existential thinking usually expresses itself through some glib retort. Here are some of the most memorable.

"Hasta la vista, *baby*!"

—Arnold Schwarzenegger, *Terminator 2: Judgment Day* (1991)

"Do you feel lucky, punk? Well, do you?"

—Clint Eastwood, *Dirty Harry* (1970)

"I hate quiche!"

—Charles Bronson, *10 to Midnight* (1983)

"My style, you can call the art of fighting without fighting."

—Bruce Lee, *Enter the Dragon* (1973)

"It ain't over till it's over."

—Sylvester Stallone, *Rocky III* (1982)

"C'mon, baby, come to papa—and I'll kill your fuggin *dalmation*!"

—Bruce Willis, *Die Hard* (1988)

"Get your stinking paws off me, you damned dirty ape!"

—Charlton Heston, *Planet of the Apes* (1968)

"We deal in lead."

—Steve McQueen, *The Magnificent Seven* (1960)

**"I hate snakes!"
—Harrison Ford in
*Raiders of the Lost
Ark.***

"Live fast, die young."

—Sybil Danning, *Battle Beyond the Stars* (1980)

"Which bullet has my name on it, the first or the last?"

—Roger Moore (as "James Bond"), *The Spy Who Loved Me* (1977)

"Everybody gets dead."

—John Wayne, *Hondo* (1953)

"Everybody dies."

—John Garfield, *Force of Evil* (1948)

"Every man dies, but *not* every man really lives."

—Mel Gibson, *Braveheart* (1995)

"They're all dead—they just don't know it yet."

—Brandon Lee, *The Crow* (1994)

"Do you want to live forever?"

—Sandahl Bergman, *Conan the Barbarian* (1982)

"That which does not *kill* us makes us *strong*."

—Frederick Nietzsche, quoted in prologue,
Conan the Barbarian (1982)

"When you side with a man, you *stay* with him."

—William Holden, *The Wild Bunch* (1969)

"All for one, and one for all."

—Michael York, *The Three Musketeers* (1974)

"You gonna do something, or just stand there and bleed?"

—Kurt Russell (as "Wyatt Earp"), *Tombstone* (1993)

"Every so often, we have to let the general public know that we can still blow shit up."

—Philip Baker Hall, *Rush Hour* (1998)

"When you call me that . . . *smile!*"

—Gary Cooper, to Walter Huston who has just insinuated
that he's a son of a bitch; *The Virginian* (1929)

"*Smile*, you son of a bitch!"

—Roy Scheider, *Jaws* (1975)

"Fill your hand, you son of a bitch!"

—John Wayne (to Robert Duvall), *True Grit* (1969)

"Stay away from her, you *bitch!*"

—Signourney Weaver to the mother of all monsters, *Aliens* (1986)

"Sometimes you have to lose yourself before you can find anything."

—Burt Reynolds, *Deliverance* (1974)

"Don't think, *feeeeeeel*; it is like a finger pointing away to the moon."

—Bruce Lee, *Enter the Dragon* (1973)

"Trust in the force, Luke."

—Alec Guinness, *Star Wars* (1977)

"Hokey religions and ancient weapons are no match for a good blaster at your side."

—Harrison Ford, *Star Wars* (1977)

"Why doesn't someone just pull out a .45, and—BANG!—settle it?"

—Bruce Lee, *Enter the Dragon* (1973)

"A gun is a tool, no better or worse than the man using it."

—Alan Ladd, *Shane* (1953)

"Guns don't kill people; *people* kill people."

—DMX, holding a heavy-duty rifle on a crowd of potential victims in *Romeo Must Die* (2000)

"Do we get to win this time?"

—Sylvester Stallone, *Rambo: First Blood Part II* (1985)

"Pay-back time!"

—Jesse Ventura, *Predator* (1987)

"I'll need three coffins . . . mmmmmmmm . . . make that four."

—Toshiro Mifune, *Yojimbo* (1961)

"God, but I love the smell of Napalm in the morning."

—Robert Duvall, *Apocalypse, Now!* (1979)

"The horror! *The horror!*"

—Marlon Brando (final words), *Apocalypse, Now!* (1979)

Quentin Tarantino, the man who created the current wave of contemporary action films.

"Madness! *Madness!*"

> —James Donald (final words), *The Bridge on the River Kwai* (1957)

"I'm here to fight for truth, justice, and the American way."

> —Christopher Reeve, *Superman* (1978)

"Any one of you fuckin' pricks move, I'll execute every mother fuggin' last one of ya."

> —Honey Bunny, *Pulp Fiction* (1994)

"Any man who will stay, and fight to the death, cross over this line."

> —Richard Carlson (as "Colonel Travis") in *The Last Command* (1955)

"Yippie-kay-yay, motherfucker!"

> —Bruce Willis, *Die Hard* (1988)

"Your worst nightmare."

> —Sylvester Stallone to Charles Napier, who has just asked his identity over a two-way radio, *Rambo: First Blood Part II* (1985)

"Never take your eyes off your opponent, even when you bow."

> —Bruce Lee, *Enter the Dragon* (1973)

"I'm your huckleberry."

> —Val Kilmer (as "Doc Holliday," to "Johnny Ringo"), *Tombstone* (1993)

"In the desert, nothing's harmless unless it's dead."

> —Burt Lancaster, *The Professionals* (1966)

"We all end up dead—the question is, *how* and *why*."

> —Mel Gibson, *Braveheart* (1995)

"I'll be back."

> —Arnold Schwarzenegger, *The Terminator* (1985)

"Now I have a machine gun. Ho! Ho! Ho!"

> —Bruce Willis, celebrating Christmas Eve by killing terrorists, *Die Hard* (1988)

"Go ahead, make my day!"

> —Clint Eastwood, *The Enforcer* (1976)

"Stick around."

> —Arnold Schwarzenegger, speaking to the corpse of a terrorist he's just nailed to the wall with a knife, *Predator* (1987)

"A man's gotta do what a man's gotta do."

> —John Wayne (as "Davy Crockett"), *The Alamo* (1960)

A man don't go his own way, he's nothin'."

> —Montgomery Clift, *From Here to Eternity* (1953)

"When you draw a gun, kill a man."

—Walter Brennan, *My Darling Clementine* (1946)

"If it bleeds, we can *kill* it."

—Arnold Schwarzenegger, to his teammates in *Predator* (1987)

"If they move, *kill* them!"

—William Holden to his men as they prepare
to rob a bank in *The Wild Bunch* (1969)

6

ESSENTIALS: THE NINETIES

The common man as action hero, vividly portrayed by Bruce Willis in the *Die Hard* movies, was a concept that would continue to dominate during the early nineties. But the new face of action was largely determined by *Terminator 2: Judgment Day* (1991), with its mind-blowing special effects in place of the original's strong story. Fortunately, several filmmakers—Michael Mann, Mel Gibson—proved that, even in age of F/X popcorn flicks, thought-provoking action movies could still be made, from urban crime films to revived costume pictures. Then came Tarantino, redefining action via a final attack on middlebrow notions of "good taste." Films that had always been dismissed—Philippine prison pictures, Asian chop-socky films, 1940s' film noirs—were apotheosized in his work. Out of all this emerged a balance between state-of-the-art special effects and an intellectualized version of the action film, conveying metaphysical themes as well as big explosions—at its best, employing big explosions to convey metaphysical themes.

The Last of the Mohicans (1992)

CREDITS

Director, Michael Mann; screenplay, Mann and Christopher Crowe, from the novel by James Fenimore Cooper; producers, Mann and Hunt Lowry; original music, Ciaran Brennan, Randy Edelman, and Trevor Jones; cinematography, Dante Spinotti; running time, 113 min.; rating, R.

CAST

Daniel Day-Lewis (*Nathaniel,* aka *Hawkeye*); Madeleine Stowe (*Cora*); Russell Means (*Chingachgook*); Eric Schweig (*Uncas*); Jodhi May (*Alice*); Steven Waddington (*Duncan*); Wes Studi (*Magua*); Maurice Roëves (*Colonel Munro*).

THE FILM

The oft-filmed 1826 American classic was here brought to the screen as an Eastern counterpart to *Dances With Wolves*, though far superior to that over-rated fabrication about frontier life. Native American lifestyles are depicted with absolute accuracy rather than naïve idealization. Two Indian activists, Russell Means and Dennis Banks, were included in the cast. Mann actually listened to and took their advice, so the Indian "way" is presented in its true complexity: beautiful but also brutal. One flaw keeps Mann's film from rating as the perfect screen rendering of the book—the interracial love affair between the Mohican brave Uncas and Cora, younger daughter of Colonel Munro, so sensitively presented in Cooper's novel (and present in the fine 1936 version) was eliminated, though today one might have expected it to be emphasized. Hawkeye emerges as a supreme depiction (within the period-piece context) of the loner as anti-hero, who lives in the wilds and is contemptuous of authority, rejoining the human community in part to "do the right thing," in part because he's fallen in love.

Jurassic Park (1993)

CREDITS

Director, Steven Spielberg; screenplay, David Koepp and Michael Crichton, from the novel by Crichton; producers, Kathleen Kennedy and Gerald R. Molen; original music, John Williams; cinematography, Dean Cundey; running time, 126 min.; rating, PG-13.

CAST

Sam Neill (*Dr. Alan Grant*); Laura Dern (*Dr. Ellie Sattler*); Jeff Goldblum (*Dr. Ian Malcolm*); Richard Attenborough (*John Parker Hammond*); Bob Peck (*Robert Muldoon*); Martin Ferrero (*Donald Gennaro*); B. D. Wong (*Dr. Henry Wu*); Joseph Mazzello (*Tim Murphy*); Ariana Richards (*Lex Murphy*); Samuel L. Jackson (*Ray*).

THE FILM

Jurassic Park is the greatest dinosaur movie ever made, reviving the grand tradition that runs from Willis S. O'Brien's *The Lost World* to Merrian C. Cooper's *King Kong* to Ray Harryhausen's *Valley of the Gwangi*. Little in Michael Crichton's bestselling novel was retained, other than the essential

The T.-rex gets curious in *Jurassic Park*.

concept of DNA dinosaurs wreaking havoc on an isolated island where a theme park has been created—Westworld with flesh-and-blood beasts instead of cowboy cyborgs. The emergent film helped solidify the concept of a "theme-park movie," the viewing experience an approximation of a ride. This concept shortly became literal with the construction of the *Jurassic Park* features at Universal Studios. Carrying this further, every item of merchandise (lunch boxes, books, dinosaur toys, T-shirts, etc.) seen in the film's park Gift Shop were sold in stores in conjunction with its release. Importantly, this was the film that proved computer-generated graphics could be completely convincing. When Spielberg initially agreed to direct, he planned to use tabletop stop-motion dinosaurs, for at the time computer-created creatures appeared crude. However, when Spielberg saw the remarkable quality of ILM's computer-generated dinosaurs, he was overwhelmed. *Jurassic Park* was also the first to use DTS digital surround sound, which has since become essential to the modern moviegoing experience. Incidentally, Harrison Ford was the first choice for the hero in the hat who must rescue kids from monsters—Spielberg's recurring theme—but his hefty price tag would have necessitated the elimination of several species of dinosaurs; Universal was keeping a close eye on the budget, as no one realized what a phenomenon the film would become.

Tombstone (1993)

CREDITS

Directed, George P. Cosmatos; screenplay, Kevin Jarre; producers, Sean Daniel, James Jacks, and Bob Misiorowski; original music, Bruce Broughton; cinematography, William A. Fraker; running time, 128 min.; rating, R.

CAST

Kurt Russell (*Wyatt Earp*); Val Kilmer (*Doc Holliday*); Sam Elliott (*Virgil Earp*); Bill Paxton (*Morgan Earp*); Powers Boothe ("*Curly Bill*"); Michael Biehn (*Johnny Ringo*); Jason Priestley (*Billy Breckinridge*); Jon Tenney (*Sheriff John Behan*); Stephen Lang (*Ike Clanton*); Thomas Haden Church (*Billy Clanton*); Dana Delany (*Josephine Marcus*); Paula Malcomson (*Allie Earp*); Lisa Collins (*Louisa Earp*); Dana Wheeler-Nicholson (*Mattie Blaylock*); Joanna Pacula (*Kate Fisher*); Michael Rooker (*McMasters*).

THE FILM

The Disney Company was so convinced this film would be greeted with jeers by critics, they refused to screen it for reviewers in advance of the premiere. They were proven wrong by strong notices and box-office success. More accurate than most Wyatt Earp films (owing to a painstakingly researched script by Kevin Jarre), director George Cosmatos (*Rambo 2*) transformed the tale into an action film. If the costumes and settings were wild west, action-starved audiences made *Tombstone* a solid hit during the holiday moviegoing season. Russell proved a perfect choice for Earp, his star image precisely right for the man of few words. Val Kilmer provided the real acting, creating a Doc Holliday that's true both to history and legend, Doc nihilistic enough for a modern audience in search of great one-liners between bursts of violent action. Though the "war" between the Earps and the Clantons claimed, in actuality, only five lives all told, Cosmatos wisely set historical accuracy (very much present in the film's dramatic scenes) aside whenever the shooting started, turning this into *Rambo* on the range.

SEE
Pg. 67

The Crow (1994)

CREDITS

Director, Alex Proyas; screenplay, David J. Schow and John Shirley, from a comic book by James O'Barr; producers, Jeff Most, Edward R. Pressman, and Bob Rosen; original music, Phil Anselmo, Rex Brown, and Graeme Revell; cinematography, Dariusz Wolski; running time, 100 min.; rating, R.

CAST

Brandon Lee (*Eric Draven*); Ernie Hudson (*Sgt. Albrecht*); Michael Wincott (*Top Dollar*); David Patrick Kelly (*T-Bird*); Angel David (*Skank*); Rochelle Davis (*Sarah*); Ling Bai (*Myca*); Laurence Mason (*Tin Tin*).

THE FILM

This influential film set the pace for much that would follow, with its big-scale realization (and in the process legitimization) of the new edgy comics (now called graphic novels). *The Crow* took the "Dark Prince" concept from the revitalized *Batman* and ran with it, grafting on elements from the ever more popular Asian martial arts movies as well as old film noir shadow-world styles. This film's director, Alex Proyas, would eventually create *Dark City* (see chapter 21), which shares the vision of a ruined future-world (predecessors include *Blade Runner* and the "Harry Canyon" sequence of *Heavy Metal, The Movie*). *The Crow*'s box-office success set the pace for everything from *Spawn* with Wesley Snipes to TV's *Dark Angel*. The film was supposed to make a major star of Brandon (son of Bruce) Lee, and probably would have had he not been killed in a bizarre accident. The film was finished by employing modern technology—through digital sampling of existing footage, the filmmakers made it appear as if Lee had been on the set the entire time. Like Tim Burton's two *Batman* features, *The Crow*'s "look" draws heavily on classics of silent German expressionism, both in the graphic arts and such motion pictures as *The Cabinet of Dr. Caligari* (1919) and *Metropolis* (1926). Also essential, as the title suggests, is the deeply disturbing gothic vision of Edgar Allan Poe, whose raven was recycled for this tale's title figure—a black bird accompanies a murdered rocker as he rises from the grave on Halloween eve to enact a horrific revenge, including ritualistic torture, on gang members responsible for his, and his girlfriend's, death. And

John Milton is quoted, furthering the notion of modern action movies incorporating intellectual and spiritual sources of high literary art, without losing the audience.

Pulp Fiction (1994)

CREDITS

Directed by Quentin Tarantino; written by Tarantino and Roger Avary; producer, Lawrence Bender, Danny DeVito (exec. prod.); cinematography, Andrzej Sekula; running time, 154 min.; rating, R.

CAST

John Travolta and Samuel L. Jackson in *Pulp Fiction*.

John Travolta (*Vincent Vega*); Samuel L. Jackson (*Jules Winnfield*); Uma Thurman (*Mia*); Harvey Keitel (*Wolf*); Tim Roth (*Pumpkin*); Amanda Plummer (*Honey Bunny*); Maria de Medeiros (*Fabienne*); Ving Rhames (*Marsellus Wallace*); Eric Stoltz (*Lance*); Rosanna Arquette (*Jody*); Christopher Walken (*Captain Koons*); Bruce Willis (*Butch Coolidge*); Quentin Tarantino (*Jimmie*).

THE FILM

If *Reservoir Dogs* had served as his cinematic equivalent of a first novel, then *Pulp Fiction* emerged as Quentin Tarantino's epic. Combining elements that hail back to 1940s' film noir (the boxer asked to throw a big fight) with ultra-contemporary street smarts, throwing in elements from every sort of déclassè film genre he'd loved on home video, adding bits and pieces of conversations he'd heard and remembered, Tarintino here redefines popular movies in general, action films in particular. His semi-surreal cross between a Drive-In junk movie and an ambitious art film includes a fractured time frame that makes incredible demands on an audience. An ever-edgier Hollywood played to an emerging audience; everything that was best (but which had, by the fast disappearing middle-of-the-road moviegoer, been considered worst) about lowbrow and highbrow entertainment converged, providing a knock-out taste of things to come. The film won the coveted Palme d'Or at the Cannes Film Festival. At the Oscar ceremonies, filmdom's Establishment—still not knowing quite what to do with Tarantino—awarded him only the (shared) statuette for Best Screenplay. Robert Zemeckis won best director for *Forrest Gump*, also a Best Picture Oscar winner. Just as most filmmakers of the 1950s cite *Citizen Kane* as the film that inspired them, so did *Pulp*—not *Gump*—send a group of would-be Tarantinos running off to film school, where they composed nihilistic postmodern action scripts. Tarantino relished mixing and matching the actors he had most enjoyed watching over the years with newcomers whom he felt had great potential. Appearing in *Pulp* was as much as a status symbol for such performers as being awarded a part in a Woody Allen movie (and working for scale) was to a totally different breed of actor. The movie, shot for just under $8 million by the then-gutsy Miramax indie outfit, grossed more than $100 million on its initial run.

Heat (1995)

CREDITS

Written and directed by Michael Mann; producers, Mann and Art Linson; executive producers, Pieter Jan Brugge, Arnold Milchan, and Kathleen M. Shea; original music, Michael Brook, Brian Eno, Elliot Goldenthal, and Terje Rypdal; cinematography, Dante Spinotti; running time, 172 min.; rating, R.

CAST

Al Pacino (*Vincent Hanna*); Robert De Niro (*Neil McCauley*); Val Kilmer (*Chris Shiherlis*); Jon Voight (*Nate*); Tom Sizemore (*Cheritto*); Diane Venora (*Justine Hanna*); Amy Brenneman (*Eady*); Ashley Judd (*Charlene Shiherlis*); Mykelti Williamson (*Sgt. Drucker*); Wes Studi (*Detective Casals*); Dennis Haysbert (*Breedan*); Natalie Portman (*Lauren*).

THE FILM

Alter-egos Robert De Niro and Al Pacino had never played a scene together before this teaming. Though they co-starred in *The Godfather, Part II* (1974), they were kept separate by their characters' differing time periods. Michael Mann brought them together in a brutal but provocative contemporary crime film, balancing its bloody street battles between cops and criminals with strong characterizations. Particularly interesting are the two principals, a mastermind thief named McCauley and a loner cop, Hanna, who finds himself involved in a complex relationship with the man he's tracking that far exceeds anything else in his sterile personal life. Though this gambit can be traced back to earlier crime films, it has rarely if ever been played with such intensity or originality as here. Writer-director Mann made familiar material feel fresh by his intelligent (if also bone-crushing) treatment. Also impressive is the non-stereotypical depiction of women. Though Hanna's wife cheats on him, she's never reduced to the slut caricature. Likewise, Eady offers McCauley his one chance for escape from what criminals call "the life," yet she's never reduced to a cliché of the simple good girl. The interpersonal scenes are written with conviction and played in an understated manner, allowing them to serve as effective preludes to the film's pièce de rèsistance, the daylight shoot-out after the heist goes wrong, as if the filmmaker had decided to show us in vivid detail the very sequence Quentin Tarantino chose to leave out of *Reservoir Dogs*. Downtown L.A. believably becomes a state under siege with the extended fight, flight, and pursuit, in truth similar to others that have appeared in other urban action flicks, though not only bigger but better. While serving as a prime example of this type of film, *Heat* also manages to transcend its genre, a deeply moving motion picture about modern human beings, isolated and alienated from society until the next blast of gunfire.

Braveheart (1995)

CREDITS

Director, Mel Gibson; screenwriter, Randall Wallace; producers, Gibson, Bruce Davy, and Alan Ladd, Jr.; original music, James Horner; cinematography, John Toll; running time, 177 min.; rating, R.

CAST

Mel Gibson (*William Wallace*); Sophie Marceau (*Princess Isabelle*); Patrick McGoohan (*Longshanks*, aka *King Edward I*); Angus Mac-Fadyen (*Robert the Bruce*); James Robinson (*Young William*); Sean Lawlor (*Malcolm Wallace*); James Cosmo (*Campbell*); Sean McGinley (*MacClannough*); Tommy Flanagan (*Morrison*); Brian Cox (*Argyle Wallace*); Jeanne Marine (*Nicolette*); Peter Hanly (*Prince Edward*); Catherine McCormack (*Murron*).

THE FILM

Winner of the Best Picture Oscar for 1995, as well as best director for Gibson, *Braveheart* proved (to the surprise of many) that an old-fashioned *Spartacus*-type historical epic could not only get made, but also score at the box office, even in an age of high-tech futuristic action movies. The film does recall Kirk Douglas's 1960 spectacular, here transplanted to thirteenth-century Scotland, about a bold (and fact-based) rebel leader who defies the corrupt Establishment of his time. To make the film financially feasible, Gibson employed state-of-the-art computer graphics, quadrupling the number of extras in the elaborate fight sequences. Animal rights activists originally refused to believe that horses destroyed during battle scenes were in fact computer generated. Other protesters included loyal followers of Robert the Bruce—generally considered one of Scotland's great heroes but here envisioned as a medieval sleaze—and gay rights activists, who felt the swishy portrayal of England's prince and his "consort" was degrading, though their relationship was historical. Attention was paid to the accuracy of weaponry, as had been the case with the Kirk Douglas film, which had been seen and loved by Gibson in his youth.

The Matrix (1999)

CREDITS

Directed and written by Andy and Larry Wachowski (aka "The Wachowski Brothers"); producer, Joel Silver; executive producer, Bruce Berman; original music, Paul Barker; cinematography, Bill Pope; running time, 136 min.; rating, R.

Larry Fishburn,
Keanu Reeves, and
Carrie-Anne Moss in
The Matrix.

CAST

Keanu Reeves (*Thomas A. Anderson/Neo*); Carrie-Anne Moss (*Trinity*); Joe Pantoliano (*Cypher/Mr. Reagan*); Larry Fishburn (*Morpheus*); Hugo Weaving (*Agent Smith*); Gloria Foster (*Oracle*); Marcus Chong (*Tank*); Julian Arahanga (*Apoc*); Matt Doran (*Mouse*); Belinda McClory (*Switch*).

THE FILM

The Wachowski brothers made their reputation with the post-Tarantino cult-classic *Bound* (1996), employing its limited success as a springboard to their first big-budget project. On the surface, *The Matrix* focuses on Neo, an ordinary guy—legally employed in the software industry, secretly a computer hacker—going through the unexciting motions of his life in a hazy near-future. His doldrums are broken when Trinity appears on his monitor, ushering in Morpheus, a seeming savior from ennui. This powerful if menacing presence introduces Neo to The Matrix, a complex realm of existence beyond the everyday. The Matrix is a scientific, computer-age rendering of the metaphysical, existing just beyond our world, unseen and at best dimly understood. Morpheus also informs Neo he is "the chosen one," a champion who must be trained to fight evil forces menacing the cosmos. In time, Neo grasps that "everyday reality" is not real at all, rather a construct created for man by forces that view people as chess pieces to be manipulated. *Matrix* succeeded beyond anyone's wildest expectations, both critically and financially, making clear that the contemporary audience would accept a heady blend of traditional sci-fi, innovative cyberpunk concepts, hard-edged violent action, state-of-the-art special effects, martial arts mayhem, and dazzling visuals, all within the framework of an essentially intellectual vision, so long as the filmmakers never allow their ideas to diminish the movie's roller-coaster ride appeal.

Three Kings (1999)

CREDITS

Director, David O. Russell; screenplay, Russell and John Ridley (story); producers, Bruce Berman, Paul Junger Witt, and Edward L. McDonnell; original music, Carter Burwell; cinematography, Newton Thomas Sigel; running time, 115 min.; rating, R.

CAST

George Clooney (*Maj. Archie Gates*); Mark Wahlberg (*Sgt. Troy Barlow*); Ice Cube (*Chief*); Spike Jonze (*Conrad Vig*); Nora Dunn (*Adriana Cruz*); Jamie Kennedy (*Pvt. Walter Wogaman*); Saïd Taghmaoui (*Captain Said*); Brian Bosworth (*Action Star*).

THE FILM

A next-millennium redux of one of Clint Eastwood's few box-office failures, *Kelly's Heroes*, this dark comedy includes the kind of absurdist attitude toward war that had been introduced in the water-ski sequence in Coppola's *Apocalypse Now*. Here, the viewing experience is enhanced by state-of-the-art special effects, rewriting the book on action films for the upcoming decade. *Three Kings* tells a story much like the one in the Eastwood film (U.S. soldiers become unofficial mercenaries as they attempt to claim an enemy treasure for themselves), *Kings* also nods in reference to John Ford's *Three Godfathers* (1947), in which outlaws become saviors under extreme pressure. In *Kings*, a quartet of soldiers go into Operation Desert Storm hoping to save the world. Then, realizing the true and dark implications of their mission, they drop community values and opt for rugged individualism. The anti-heroes attempt to grab $23 million in gold Saddam Hussein's troops had lifted from Kuwait. Like *The Matrix, Fight Club,* and other modern action films, this movie does not offer an escape from intellectual ideas, but conveys them via rip-roaring violence undercut by glib anti-war (and anti-authority) messages.

Remarkable F/X literally allow the viewer to follow bullets out of guns and into people's bodies, as well as the cavity created in a body by that bullet gradually filling with bile. Such moments are followed by anti-Bush (the elder) diatribes worthy of an Oliver Stone film, though the garish depiction of death comes closer to Tarantino. Though some critics claimed such stuff to be only a variation on the pornography of violence, others sensed this is the logical extension of what Peckinpah had been up to in *The Wild Bunch*— a highly moral work *about* amoral violence.

Rush Hour (1998)

CREDITS

Director, Brett Ratner; screenplay, Jim Kouf and Ross LaManna, from a story by LaManna; producers, Roger Birnbaum, Arthur Sarkissian, and Jonathan Glickman; original music, Lalo Schifrin and Michael Jackson ("Another Part of Me"); cinematography, Adam Greenberg; running time, 98 min.; rating, PG-13.

CAST

Jackie Chan (*Det. Inspector Lee*, HKPD); Chris Tucker (*Det. James Carter*, LAPD); Elizabeth Peña (*Tania*); Philip Baker Hall (*Capt. Diel*); Chris Penn (*Clive Cod*); Tom Wilkinson (*Juntao*); Ken Leung (*Sang*); Tzi Ma (*Consul Han*); Julia Hsu (*Soo Yung*).

THE FILM

Jackie Chan's first huge Hollywood hit plays off a conventional premise— the fish out of water. A by-the-book straight-laced Hong Kong hero gets mismatched with an L.A. streetwise "character," at first a seemingly impossible

Chris Tucker and Jackie Chan in *Rush Hour*.

choice for partner. In time, they work together and bring in the bad guys, kidnappers of a Chinese consul's daughter. This buddy-buddy concept had been done to death, in films as varied as the appealing *Tango and Cash* and the disastrous *Black Rain*. Yet *Rush Hour* proved irresistible, due to the infectiously charming persona of Chan, who as actor and stunt coordinator brilliantly conceived and dazzlingly realized elaborate action sequences. Unlike the cliché pairings of previous buddy movies, *both* heroes here are minorities, the Asian Chan and African American Chris thus offering a new dynamic. The film's huge financial success both in the United States ($120 domestic theatrical gross) and abroad made it clear that the commercial cinema in general, the action movie in particular, had truly come of age, and that vast audiences willing to attend a multi-cultural movie so long as the stars were appealing, the action fast and furious. Ironically, Chan's longtime following expressed disappointment. What they most loved—complex displays of martial arts, grandly choreographed—were played down to make room for conventional comedy-drama and large-scale action set-pieces, such as vertigo-inspiring leaps and falls from high buildings.

7

SOMETIMES AN ACTION HERO: STARS WHO "SWING" BOTH WAYS

Bogart was one of the first Hollywood personalities to strike a deal between being an action star and achieving status as a "serious" actor. For every shoot-'em-up saga (*High Sierra*, *The Roaring Twenties*, *The Oklahoma Kid*) and each trench coat yarn (*Casablanca*, *The Maltese Falcon*, *The Big Sleep*), there'd be a straight role, comedy, or drama (*In a Lonely Place*, *The Caine Mutiny*, *Sabrina*). Audiences either accepted him in both guises or chose between the two Bogarts the one that appealed to them. Many performers to follow have opted for such an approach. Here are the key figures from 1960 to 2000.

Nicolas (Kim) Cage (Coppola)

Born January 7, 1964, in Long Beach, California, raised in a literary home. Father August (one of Francis Coppola's brothers) an English professor, (German) mother, Joy Vogelsang, dancer/choreographer. As Uncle Francis came to fame, Kim made the decision *not* to capitalize on family name. He's absent, then, from most of Coppola's output, only exception being the coming-of-age drama *Rumble Fish* (1983). Earned a part in *Fast Times at Ridgemont High* (1982), with no one involved aware of his bloodline. Despite such non-action roles, the name "Cage" was lifted from his favorite action comic book. His mother's severe bouts of depression and the subsequent divorce of his parents caused Nic to head for San Francisco, where he studied at the American

Nicolas Cage in *Gone in Sixty Seconds*.

65

Conservatory. Back in L.A., unable to win roles, he worked behind the candy counter at Fairfax Theatre. Appealing part in youth-film *Valley Girl* (1983). Shortly, opposite Cher in *Moonstruck* (1987), he eventually won an Oscar for *Leaving Las Vegas* (1995). No sooner established as dramatic/comic performer than he switched predominantly to action films.

ACTION FILMOGRAPHY

Fire Birds (1990); *Deadfall* (1993); *Kiss of Death* (1995); *The Rock* (1996); *Con Air* (1997); *Face/Off* (1997); *Snake Eyes* (1998); *8 MM* (1999); *Gone in Sixty Seconds* (2000); *Windtalkers* (2000); *Constantine* (2002).

MUST-SEE

The Rock (Michael Bay, dir.). Unnerving action flick with Cage as an intellectual, teamed with Connery—the only man ever to escape from Alcatraz—heading for title place in order to capture mad military man ensconced there. Lots of explosions, little sense to story line.

Con Air (Simon West, dir.). Hardened criminals aboard the title plane stage a mid-air takeover, with morally questionable Cage having to decide which way to go. John Malkovich, Ving Rhames, and John Cusack work hard to overcome fabricated script.

Face/Off (John Woo, dir.). Cage's best action flick to date, as he and John Travolta experience identity crisis within the sort of shoot-out situation director Woo is so expert at mounting. Title refers to bizarre plot that has Travolta taking Cage's face, while Cage "becomes" Travolta. Clever and exciting.

Kevin (Michael) Costner

Born on January 18, 1955, Lynwood, California, third child of ditch digger. Sang in Baptist choir, fashioned canoe, and traveled rivers Lewis and Clark had navigated. Solid athlete in high school, college (Cal. State Fullerton, business major). Married then-girlfriend, Cindy Silva, accepted marketing job, and took acting lessons. Chance meeting with Richard Burton, who insisted Kevin "go for it." In Hollywood, roles didn't come. He drove a truck and took tourists on stars' homes tour. Appeared in softcore porn film, then he received a key role in *The Big Chill* (1983) as a suicidal Yuppie, the part cut from final print. When roles finally came, he was at his best when playing contemporary laid-back version of Henry Fonda, particularly in appealing baseball films *Bull Durham* (1987) and *Field of Dreams* (1989).

Costner won an Oscar for Best Director (over Martin Scorsese) for vastly overrated *Dances With Wolves*. Later directorial projects proved unbearably pretentious. Infuriated when producers cut frontal nude scene from *For Love of the Game* (1999) after preview audiences howled with laughter at the sight.

ACTION FILMOGRAPHY

The Gunrunner (1984); *Silverado* (1985); *Fandango* (1985); *Shadows Run Black* (1986); *The Untouchables* (1987); *No Way Out* (1987); *Dances With Wolves* (1990); *Robin Hood: Prince of Thieves* (1991); *The Bodyguard* (1992); *A Perfect World* (1993); *Wyatt Earp* (1994); *Waterworld* (1995); *The Postman* (1997); *Dragonfly* (2002); *Open Range* (2003).

MUST-SEE

Silverado (Lawrence Kasdan, dir.). Ambitious, amiable attempt to make a "big" western in the Ford/Hawks tradition mostly works. Costner, Danny Glover, Kevin Kline, and Scott Glenn make a formidable team, some truly spectacular stuntwork involving big-scale cattle stampede.

The Untouchables (Brian De Palma, dir.). Strong if overrated retelling of the Eliot Ness versus Al Capone saga in Roaring Twenties' Chicago, Costner occasionally overshadowed by Robert De Niro's scenery-chewing Scarface. Sean Connery won a deserved Best Supporting Actor Oscar. Shoot-out with gangsters on Canadian border is strong stuff.

Wyatt Earp (Lawrence Kasdan, dir.). Big-scale bio-pic is too long for audiences to handle, not long enough to do justice to the title character's fascinating life. Still, this is easily the most accurate Earp movie ever made, with Kevin authentically gruff and dour.

SEE PG. 55

Tom Cruise (Mapother IV)

Born July 3, 1962, in Syracuse, New York, though parents (ever on the go) were just passing through. Attended fifteen different schools by the time he was 14. A profoundly religious teenager, studied at Franciscan seminary, planning to dedicate life to God. First permanent home: Glen Ridge, New Jersey, where mother and second husband settled. There, dyslexic Cruise

**Tom Cruise in
Mission Impossible.**

became interested in acting, gave up dream of priesthood, headed for Manhattan. First film: *Endless Love* (1981), bit part in a Brooke Shields tearjerker. Early on, appeared to be more interested in "serious" acting than superstardom, with edgy roles in offbeat films—*The Color of Money* (1986), *Rainman* (1988)—though action parts beckoned with *Top Gun*. Still, likes to balance heroic epics with less mainstream work, including excellent portrayal in *Jerry Maguire* (1996), *Magnolia* (1999). Married to actress Mimi Rogers, 1987–1990. In 1990, Tom turned his back on Catholicism in favor of Dianetics and wed Nicole Kidman; their union lasted eleven years.

ACTION FILMOGRAPHY

Taps (1981); *Legend* (1985); *Top Gun* (1986); *Born on the Fourth of July* (1989); *Days of Thunder* (1990); *Far and Away* (1992); *Mission: Impossible* (1996); *Mission: Impossible II* (2000); *Minority Report* (2002).

MUST-SEE

Legend (Ridley Scott, dir.). Intriguing misfire, Cruise young mythic-hero out to stop deadly villain (Tim Curry). Great looking, but hopelessly loopy.

Longer European cut, with Jerry Goldsmith score instead of Tangerine Dream New Age music, far superior to American theatrical version.

Top Gun: See chapter 9.

Born on the Fourth of July: See chapter 19.

Mission: Impossible (Brian De Palma, dir.). Appealing update of the old TV action suspenser just misses being a modern classic. Cruise brings the team together for a high-tech adventure, with Jean Reno and Ving Rhames along for the ride. Best feature is the final chase, a marvel of moviemaking magic. Worst moment: revelation of the villain.

Minority Report (Steven Spielberg, dir.). In a confused future-world worthy of Terry Gilliam's *Brazil*, a cop (Cruise) who arrests violent criminals before they can strike realizes that he himself has been picked by the computers as an upcoming killer. Ambitious if over-long sci-fi actioner in which great scenes shine.

Robert De Niro

Born August 17, 1943, raised on borderline between mean streets of Little Italy and artistic avenues of Greenwich Village. Nicknamed "Bobby Milk" by local goodfellas owing to his unhealthy complexion. Father an acclaimed artist, mother edited literary journal. They divorced when he was 10. Robert pursued acting at P.S. 41, playing cowardly lion in school production of *The Wizard of Oz*. Alternately ran with tough street gang, studied at The New School. Off-Broadway debut in *One Night Stands of a Noisy Passenger* with Shelley Winters, studied with Lee Strasberg. Intense method approach, reknown for never doing the same type of character twice and totally disappearing into roles. Worked in late-1960s indie-commercial films for Brian De Palma (*Hi, Mom!*, 1969), then hitched up with Martin Scorsese, realizing they'd vaguely known each other in boyhood. Then, cast by Coppola in *Godfather II*, won Oscar for younger version of Brando, who earlier won an Academy Award for the role. Recently, drifting more and more into action vehicles.

ACTION FILMOGRAPHY

Bloody Mama (1970); *Mean Streets* (1973); *The Godfather, Part II* (1974); *Taxi Driver* (1976); *The Deer Hunter* (1978); *Raging Bull* (1980); *Once Upon a Time in America* (1984); *The Mission* (1986); *The Untouchables* (1987); *Midnight Run* (1988); *GoodFellas* (1990); *Backdraft* (1991); *Cape Fear* (1991);

Heat (1995); *Cop Land* (1997); *Jackie Brown* (1997); *Ronin* (1998); *Men of Honor* (2000); *15 Minutes* (2001); *The Score* (2002).

MUST-SEE

Mean Streets (Martin Scorsese, dir.). Cross between European arthouse item (i.e., Fellini's nostalgic/autobiographical youth-movie *I Vitteloni*) and vintage Hollywood noirs (Fritz Lang's *The Big Heat*) as young toughs wander NYC's tuff turf. Think Lucas's *American Graffiti*, only East Coast and violent. De Niro and Harvey Keitel make an incredible team.

    The Godfather, Part II (Francis Ford Coppola, dir.). Oscar-winning Best Picture follow-up to Oscar-winning Best Picture of two years earlier is even better, if not so easily accessible to mainstream audiences. De Niro, as young Corleone, delivers sly, subtle performance, winning his first Oscar. Vivid shoot-outs in context of epic American drama.

    Taxi Driver (Martin Scorsese, dir.). The reinvention of serious American cinema, with De Niro the title character, alienated in nighttime Manhattan, his repressed violence rising to the surface. Surreal look at modern manias, assassinations, and so forth, becomes more significant with each passing year. Final shoot-out makes *The Wild Bunch* look like a Sunday school picnic.

    The Deer Hunter: See chapter 19.

    Raging Bull: See chapter 22.

    Once Upon a Time in America (Sergio Leone, dir.). De Niro and James Woods as boyhood pals who rise to power in the Jewish Mob during the Depression, then are divided by misunderstanding (and possible betrayal) for many years. Brilliant displays of violent action from the late master. High recommendation applies *only* to full 227-min. cut.

    Midnight Run (Martin Brest, dir.). De Niro as a modern-day bounty hunter, competes with fellow pro (John Ashton) and crime boss (Dennis Farina) to bring in a bail jumper Charles Grodin (who steals the show). Bobby's first foray into comedy-action is pretty much perfect, with great gags, incredible stunts, intriguing characters.

    GoodFellas (Martin Scorsese, dir.). The life of a Mafia "street soldier," as seen through the eyes of an arrogant jerk (Ray Liotta) who rats on his pals (De Niro, Joe Pesci, Paul Sorvino). The greatest gangster movie since *The Godfather*. Harsh, authentic all the way.

Michael (Kirk) Douglas

Born September 25, 1944, in New Brunswick, New Jersey. Son of Kirk Douglas and his first wife Diana (Dill). Graduated from University of California, Santa Barbara, 1968. Roomed with Danny De Vito while both struggled to make it in New York theater. Self-conscious decision to avoid the kinds of roles his father had played for fear of typecasting as "Jr." Early parts include hippie-era characters in *Hail, Hero!* (1970) and *Summertree* (1972). First action role as young cop on TV's *Streets of San Francisco* with Karl Malden. As a producer, he received Best Picture Oscar for *One Flew Over the Cuckoo's Nest* (1975). Produced and took supporting role in *The China Syndrome* (1979) with Jane Fonda and Jack Lemmon. Eventually felt confident enough in his own image to play Kirk-like role in *Romancing the Stone*, a huge hit, commercial and critical. Oscar-winning Best Actor for *Wall Street* (1987) as evil ("Greed is good!") "Gordon Gekko." Often accepts action roles now.

ACTION FILMOGRAPHY

The Star Chamber (1983); *Romancing the Stone* (1984); *The Jewel of the Nile* (1986); *Black Rain* (1989); *Shining Through* (1992); *Falling Down* (1993); *The Ghost and the Darkness* (1996); *The Game* (1997); *Traffic* (2000).

MUST-SEE

Romancing the Stone: See chapter 9.

The Ghost and the Darkness (Stephen Hopkins, dir.). Michael as a mentor this time around, playing big game hunter who aids young would-be hero (Val Kilmer) as they try to stop two man-eating lions that threaten to close down a railway project in Africa. Strong action, thanks to William Goldman's first-rate script and Hopkins's moody direction.

The Game (David Fincher, dir.). On his way to such modern classics as *Se7en* and *Fight Club*, the contemporary auteur of intellectual action movies almost carries us through a provocative plot, marred only by a dishonest letdown ending, as a slick businessman gets a gift from his brother (Sean Penn) and enters into an ever more threatening "game."

Traffic: See "Benecio Del Toro" in chapter 3.

Brendan Fraser in
The Mummy.

Brendan Fraser

Born December 3, 1969, in Indianapolis, Indiana. Canadian father was a travel industry agent, moved young Brendan constantly. Parts of youth spent in Ottawa, Detroit, Seattle, Rome, and London. In that latter city, his fascination with theater began, the famed West End right around the corner. Back in the states, attended Cornish Institute in Seattle, majoring in drama. Landed a small role in *Dogfight* (1991) starring River Phoenix. Next, in *Encino Man* (1992), playing unearthed Neanderthal; formulaic comedy, yet Fraser impressed reviewers with ability to endow his incoherent character with sincerity, intelligence. First dramatic lead as a Jewish youth who "passes" to avoid prejudice in *School Ties* (1992). Veered between silly comedy (*George of the Jungle*, 1997) and intense drama (*Gods and Monsters*, 1998). More recently, reaches for top-level of stardom with performance as soldier-of-fortune in new *Mummy* movies, his persona highly reminiscent of the young Duke Wayne.

ACTION FILMOGRAPHY

The Mummy (1999); *The Mummy Returns* (1992); *The Quiet American* (2002).

MUST-SEE

The Mummy (Stephen Sommers, dir.). Well-staged action sequences—ranging from big battles on desert to shoot-outs deep in the catacombs of a mummy's tomb—combined with Fraser's appealing persona made this a huge hit. The direction is unsophisticated at best, and the gag lines mostly fall flat. Still, a lot of fun.

The Mummy Returns (Stephen Sommers, dir.). More of the same, but not nearly so good. Has its moments, though, some terrific, as Fraser and female lead from first film (Rachel Weisz) touch the forbidden tomb, causing all hell to (literally) break loose. Never boring.

Eddie Murphy in
Beverly Hills Cop.

Eddie (Regan) Murphy

Born April 3, 1961, in Brooklyn, New York. Following his father's death, Murphy was raised by his mother who worked at the telephone company, and stepfather, an ice cream plant foreman. After catching Richard Pryor's act, inspired to become comedian, performing when and where he could land a gig. Work at Manhattan's Comic Strip led to *Saturday Night Live*, swiftly moving from also-ran to top attraction. *Trading Places* (1982) for John Landis, co-starring with *SNL* alum Dan Aykroyd, proved his charisma could transfer to big screen. Then, *48 Hours*, his first action film, allowed Eddie to be funny *and* tough, more than holding his own against Nick Nolte. Interested in becoming full collaborator, worked on script and production for such films as *Coming to America* (1988), and he directed as well as wrote *Harlem Nights*. Superstardom came with the *Beverly Hills Cop* franchise, though flops—*The Golden Child, Boomerang* (1992)—resulted when strayed too far from the charming smart-ass people loved to see him play.

ACTION FILMOGRAPHY

48 Hrs. (1982); *Beverly Hills Cop* (1984); *The Golden Child* (1986); *Beverly Hills Cop II* (1987); *Harlem Nights* (1989); *Another 48 Hrs.* (1990); *Boomerang* (1992); *Beverly Hills Cop III* (1994); *Metro* (1997); *Mulan* (1998); *Bowfinger* (1999); *Shrek* (2001); *Showtime* (2002); *I Spy* (2002); *The Adventures of Pluto Nash* (2002); *The Incredible Shrinking Man* (2003).

MUST-SEE

48 Hrs. (Walter Hill, dir.). Clever action-comedy pits streetwise Eddie against wary partner Nick Nolte as they track down a dangerous criminal. The mix of humor and violence clicks this time around, thanks largely to Murphy's hipster presence, unleashed energy, and knowing glances.

Beverly Hills Cop (Martin Brest, dir.). "Fish out of water" action-comedy originally intended for Sly Stallone. A wiseass Detroit detective heading for pseudo-sophisticated L.A. to solve a crime. Daniel Petrie, Jr.'s smart script keeps violence from becoming too mean-spirited. First-rate supporting cast (John Ashton, Paul Reiser, Jame Russo) adds to fun.

Harlem Nights (Eddie Murphy, dir.). Impressive if uneven debut as writer/director/star. Murphy's childhood idol Richard Pryor joins him in a period piece about nightclub owners who find themselves menaced by the Mob during the 1930s. Jasmine Guy makes a great "shady lady."

Paul (Leonard) Newman

Born January 26, 1925, in Shaker Heights, Ohio. Father owned a successful sporting goods store. Happy home life. Began acting in grade school, did a brief stint in the Navy, then on to Kenyon College, later Yale Drama School. In New York, he trained at Actor's Studio, soon perceived as the Jewish Marlon Brando owing to intense method style. Broadway debut in *Picnic* (1953), much small-screen work including *Bang The Drum Slowly* (1956) during "golden age" of drama. Film work during 1950s generally undistinguished, though *Cat On a Hot Tin Roof* (1958) opposite Liz Taylor proved his superstar appeal. Early 1960s, Newman found his own unique niche in *The Hustler* (1961) and *Hud* (1963) as amoral contemporary anti-hero. In real life, precisely the opposite. Married to Joanne Woodward, both active in varied liberal causes. Found a new creative outlet in directing, beginning with vehicle for actress-wife, *Rachel, Rachel* (1968). Newman won belated Oscar for *The Color of Money* (1986). As great a guy as he is an actor.

ACTION FILMOGRAPHY

The Silver Chalice (1954); *Somebody Up There Likes Me* (1956); *The Left Handed Gun* (1958); *Exodus* (1960); *The Outrage* (1964); *Harper* (1965); *Hombre* (1967); *Cool Hand Luke* (1968); *The Secret War of Harry Frigg* (1968); *Winning (1969); Butch Cassidy and the Sundance Kid* (1969); *Sometimes a Great Notion* (1971); *The Life and Times of Judge Roy Bean* (1972); *The Towering Inferno* (1974); *The Drowning Pool* (1975); *Buffalo Bill and the Indians* (1976); *Slap Shot* (1977); *When Time Ran Out* (1980); *Fort Apache, the Bronx* (1981); *Twilight* (1998).

MUST-SEE

Harper (Jack Smight, dir.). "The Moving Target" by Ross Macdonald (wherein the anti-hero was named "Archer"), rethought (by William Goldman) as a detective vehicle for Old Blue Eyes. Appreciated in its time as a throwback to the Bogart type detectives in an era when ever more awful spy capers were prevalent. Mystery with much action wears well.

 Hombre (Martin Ritt, dir.). Plight of Native Americans underlies fabulous action western with Paul (a half-Indian here), attempting to remain a rugged individualist, gradually drawn into the human community when varied stagecoach passengers are menaced by gun crazy villain (Richard Boone). Crackling good job all around, final shoot-out exciting and memorable.

 Butch Cassidy and the Sundance Kid: See chapter 11.

 Fort Apache, the Bronx (Daniel Petrie, Sr., dir.). Arguably the best urban crime drama of the past quarter-century, Paul was never better than playing tough cop with a solid conscience and a fair mind, dealing with escalating slum problems. Brings the viewer down emotionally, but well worth the ride.

(Charles) **Robert Redford, Jr.**

Born August 18, 1937, in Santa Monica, California. Father was an accountant for Standard Oil. Mother's death was a traumatic event. As a troubled youth he stole hubcaps; then, lost college sports scholarship (baseball, University

Robert Redford in Butch Cassidy and the Sundance Kid.

of Colorado) owing to drunken behavior. He studied art at Pratt Institute, acting at American Academy of Dramatic Arts. In between, Bob bummed around Europe, painting. Tried acting—good looks undercut preppie-ish "golden boy" with tacit masculinity. Could have had lead in *The Graduate* (1967) but felt he was too old for the part. Yuppie role opposite Jane Fonda, *Barefoot in the Park* (1967), made him a star; teaming with Paul Newman in *Butch Cassidy and the Sundance Kid* and *The Sting* (1973) a superstar. Redford possesses rare ability to be both matinee idol for women and macho hero to men. Oscar-winning director, *Ordinary People* (1980). Dedicated to environmental issues, cinema art, formed Sundance Institute, Utah, its film festival now a major annual event.

ACTION FILMOGRAPHY

War Hunt (1962); *Butch Cassidy and the Sundance Kid* (1969); *Tell Them Willie Boy Is Here* (1969); *Little Fauss and Big Halsy* (1970); *Jeremiah Johnson* (1972); *The Great Waldo Pepper* (1975); *A Bridge Too Far* (1977); *The Electric Horseman* (1979); *The Last Castle* (2001); *Spy Game* (2001).

MUST-SEE

Butch Cassidy and the Sundance Kid: See chapter 11.

Jeremiah Johnson: See chapter 12.

The Last Castle (Rod Lurie, dir.). Exciting yarn about military prisoners staging a major revolt, with TV's James Gandolfini (*The Sopranos*) making easy transition to the big screen. Action well staged by director Lurie, who also guides Redford through his most intense and convincing performance in years.

Keanu (Charles) Reeves

Born September 2, 1964, in Beirut, Lebanon, his name means "cool breeze." His mother was a showgirl, father a geologist. Their relationship faltered,

Mom moving with Keanu and sister Kim to New York. Stepfathers included theater director, rock promotor, hairstylist. Biological father jailed owing to drugs. Nicknamed "The Wall" thanks to abilities as hockey goalie while living in La Salle. Keanu retains Canadian citizenship. Appeared in tenth-grade production of *Romeo and Juliet*, realized acting was life's calling. Pursued "serious" drama in *The River's Edge* (1986), but goofy comedy *Bill and Ted's Excellent Adventure* (1989) made him a star. To prove acting chops, Reeves took small, showy role of villain in Kenneth Branagh's *Much Ado About Nothing* (1993). Critics divided on whether his performance was unique or affectation, as happened when he did *Hamlet* in Canadian summer stock company, turning down big bucks for *Speed 2*. Became superstar thanks to superior actioners, most notably *The Matrix*.

ACTION FILMOGRAPHY

Youngblood (1986); *Point Break* (1991); *Speed* (1994); *Johnny Mnemonic* (1995); *Chain Reaction* (1996); *The Matrix* (1999); *The Replacements* (2000); *The Watcher* (2000); *Hardball* (2001); *Matrix Reloaded* (2002/03).

MUST-SEE

Point Break (Kathryn Bigelow, dir.). Keanu is part of gang that pulls off bank robberies using surfing *and* sky diving. Actually, he's a government agent who infiltrates the group. Plot is so far-out that it has to be taken as a surrealist gag to be enjoyed. On that level, a stylish stunt-laden hoot.

   Speed (Jan De Bont, dir.). Over-the-top villain Dennis Hopper (who else?) hijacks bus, driven by gorgeous girl (Sandra Bullock); top cop Keanu tries to disengage bomb set to go off if the bus slows down. Strong blending of suspense, stunt action, best of its type.

   The Matrix: See chapter 6.

John (Joseph) Travolta

Born February 18, 1954, in Englewood, New Jersey, the youngest of six siblings. Everyone in his large, loving family obsessed with show business. Dropped out of high school to search for roles in stock productions and dinner theater, learning tap dance from Gene Kelly's brother. Early love of his life was Diana Hyland, eighteen years his senior, whom he met while filming a TV movie. Her death from cancer devastated John. Won pivotal role in popular mid-1970s' TV-series *Welcome Back, Kotter*. Swiftly catapulted into

John Travolta in *Broken Arrow*.

first rank of Hollywood leading men with one/two punch of *Saturday Night Fever* (1977) and *Grease* (1978). Career faltered after starring opposite Lily Tomlin in *Moment by Moment* (1978), an attempt to portray a more "sensitive" character, followed by unwise High Camp dance routines in *Staying Alive* (1983). Lightning struck twice when Quentin Tarantino bounded on to the scene, transforming John into top action hero, beginning with *Pulp Fiction*.

ACTION FILMOGRAPHY

Urban Cowboy (1980); *Pulp Fiction* (1994); *Get Shorty* (1995); *Broken Arrow* (1996); *Face/Off* (1997); *Mad City* (1997); *The Thin Red Line* (1998); *Battlefield Earth* (2000); *Swordfish* (2001); *Domestic Disturbance* (2001); *Basic* (2002).

MUST-SEE

Pulp Fiction: See chapter 6.

Broken Arrow (John Woo, dir.). Travolta's the action *villain* this time, chewing the scenery as a crazed pilot who skyjacks a plane carrying nuclear weapons, demanding a huge payment or he'll blow up the country. Christian Slater is the hero who opposes him. Woo picks up where Tarantino left off, re-establishing John's career in exciting action hit.

Face Off: See "Nicolas Cage" in chapter 7.

Swordfish (Dominic Sena, dir.). One more big, violent heist in a style that crosses early Quentin Tarantino with later David Fincher. Hey, you get to see Halle Berry topless, so don't complain.

Denzel Washington

Born December 28, 1954, Denzel grew up in integrated Mt. Vernon, New York. Father worked two jobs and was also a Pentecostal preacher. Traditionalist upbringing, those values remaining with him. Shattered when at age 14 his parents divorced. He grew surly, even though his dedicated mother, a former gospel singer, used her beauty parlor proceeds to get her son a private school education. On to Fordham University. Then, working as summer camp counselor in Connecticut, he staged the "big show," sensed this is what he loved best. Back at college, played lead in *Emperor Jones*, left journalism studies to pursue acting. Earned part in TV movie *Wilma*, met musician/actress Pauletta Pearson, later wife and mother of his children. Further training at American Conservatory Theater in Frisco led to TV roles, notably

Denzel Washington in *Glory*.

"Dr. Chandler" on acclaimed *St. Elsewhere*. Achieving stardom, occasionally plays African Americans (*Malcolm X*, 1992). More often, he pursues parts that are not necessarily written for a black man.

ACTION FILMOGRAPHY

The Mighty Quinn (1989); *Glory* (1989); *Ricochet* (1991); *Crimson Tide* (1995); *Devil in a Blue Dress* (1995); *Virtuosity* (1995); *Courage Under Fire* (1996); *Fallen* (1998); *The Siege* (1998); *The Bone Collector* (1999); *The Hurricane* (1999); *Remember the Titans* (2000); *Training Day* (2001); *John Q* (2002).

MUST-SEE

Glory (Edward Zwick, dir.). Fact-based Civil War story about an African American unit, commandeered by white officer (Matthew Broderick), in training and then in combat. Lavishly staged battle sequences jell beautifully with civil rights statement. Denzel won Best Supporting Actor Oscar for his performance as an individualistic recruit.

   Crimson Tide (Tony Scott, dir.). Old-time commander (Gene Hackman) orders young officer (Denzel) to fire sub's atomic torpedoes at a Soviet ship, but is stunned when the lieutenant refuses. Possible mutiny follows, with non-stop thrills and fine action.

   Courage Under Fire (Edward Zwick, dir.). Sturdy drama, well performed, as career soldier Denzel investigates life of deceased hero (Meg Ryan) for possible Congressional Medal of Honor. Fierce fighting would've been more believable in Vietnam than the Gulf War.

   The Siege (Edward Zwick, dir.). Frightfully predictive of 9/11, a thinking-person's action movie about terrorist strike against New York. Problems escalate as a general (Bruce Willis) goes out of control, spars with rational FBI agent (Denzel). Formidable.

   The Hurricane: See chapter 22.

   Training Day (Anton Fuque, dir.). Denzel's a cop again, though— surprise!—this time, he's the corrupt one, attempting to lure young recruit Ethan Hawke into his criminal paterns. An okay urban-action, bolstered by Denzel's bravura Oscar-winning performance.

8

THE FAMILY HOUR: ACTION FILMS TO WATCH WITH YOUR KIDS

So you want to introduce your young son to the action genre, but the wife will not be happy if the bouncin' boy-o begins his "education" with, say, *The Wild Bunch*? Don't get depressed, dude—here's a selection of the greatest action films made for the entire family to watch together. Hey, the little woman may join you!

Adventures of the Wilderness Family, The (1975). Stewart Raffill, dir. Robert F. Logan, Susan Damanate Shaw. At the height of the back-to-nature movement during the 1970s, this family-oriented action film proved to be a huge surprise success at the box office. An ordinary family turns away from civilization, heads out to survive in the wild Rockies.

Bear, The (1989). Jean-Jacques Annaud, dir. Tcheky Karyo, Andre Lacombe. Exciting environmentalist treatise—transformed into an enjoying fable—about a baby bear and his endless mishaps in the wilds. Non-condescending treatment of animals will recall the great Disney Nature Films, only this is a bit more brutal, particularly when hunters close in.

Dark Crystal, The (1983). Jim Henson, Frank Oz, dirs. Kiran Shah, Kathryn Mullen. Yet another hero-quest, as brave souls search for a missing talisman, in this case the title object. The difference this time around is that the creatures encountered along the way all come from the beloved Muppet Factory. Exciting yarn packs a strong moral.

Davy Crockett, King of the Wild Frontier (1955). Norman Foster, dir. Fess Parker, Buddy

Fess Parker in *Davy Crockett, King of the Wild Frontier*.

Ebsen, Kenneth Tobey. From the backwoods of Tennessee to the last stand at San Antonio's Alamo, this Disney film (recut from three TV shows) offers surprisingly realistic fight scenes with Creek Indians, fistfights, an inspiring final defense of the doomed fort.

Doc Savage: The Man of Bronze (1975). Michael Anderson, dir. Ron Ely, Pamela Hensley, Robyn Hilton. Before Spielberg and Lucas began the revival for pulp-fiction heroes from the 1940s, this ahead-of-its-time (and sadly neglected) little film brought back such a guy, in the guise of a former Tarzan. Producer George Pal's final family fantasy.

Dragonslayer (1981). Matthew Robbins, dir. Peter McNicol, Caitlin Clarke, Ralph Richardson. Perhaps the least-seen of all post–*Star Wars* fantasies, this marvelous epic, produced with children and teenagers in mind, proved a bit horrific for the younger kids, particularly when the all-too-real-looking creature appears to menace a pretty princess.

Fantastic Voyage (1966). Richard Fleischer, dir. Raquel Welch, Stephen Boyd, Arthur Kennedy, Donald Pleasance. A submarine (including crew) is shrunk to miscroscopic size, then injected into a human body where they must kill off an evil virus. Oscar-winning F/X, state-of-the-art in their time, appear dated today, but that only adds a curious charm.

Gumball Rally, The (1976). Chuck Bail, dir. Michael Sarrazin, Gary Busey. The same basic story that was shot on a huge budget as *The Cannonball Run*, and as a B-movie as *Cannonball*, here told in a family-friendly way. Numerous whackos enter into a cross-country race, leading to more wild car pileups than Mack Sennett could have imagined.

Hatari! (1962). Howard Hawks, dir. John Wayne, Red Buttons, Elsa Martinelli. The "Duke" and buddies trap wild animals in the African bush, bringing 'em back alive for zoos. Their pursuit of a rhino inspired the similar dinosaur chases in Spielberg's *Jurassic Park 2*. Kids will love baby elephant march finale, which inspired a memorable Henry Mancini tune.

Incredible Shrinking Man, The (1957). Jack Arnold, dir. Grant Williams, April Kent. From the pen of gifted sci-fi/fantasy writer Richard Matheson comes one of the best F/X fests of the 1950s, as a normal man passes through a cloud of atomic dust, then finds himself growing ever smaller. Fight scenes involving the family cat and a horrific spider can still give you the chills today.

Jason and the Argonauts (1963). Don Chaffey, dir. Todd Armstrong, Nancy Kovack, Nigel Green. Second only to *The 7th Voyage of Sinbad* (see chapter 24) in the canon of Ray Harryhausen's renderings of ancient mythology. Title character and Hercules search for the Golden Fleece. The dazzling fantasies include Hydra, Poseidon, and the skeleton army.

Greek heroes ward of Ray Harryhausen's skeleton creatures in *Jason and the Argonauts*.

Mighty Joe Young (1949). Ernest B. Schoesdack, dir. Terry Moore, Ben Johnson, Robert Armstrong. From the folks who gave you *King Kong* comes the first great all-family action film of the postwar era. Showman discovers oversized gorilla in Africa, brings him stateside, where he breaks loose, fights lions. A modern fairy tale, and quite fabulous.

Mulan (1998). Tony Bancroft, Barry Cook, dirs. Ming-Na Wen, Eddie Murphy, Lea Salonga (voices only). Feminist fable, drawn from ancient Asian tale, has young woman disguising herself as boy in order to fight for her country. Contemporary Disney artists have done an impressive job of remaining truthful to Chinese legends and graphics.

NeverEnding Story, The (1984). Wolfgang Petersen, dir. Noah Hathaway, Barret Oliver, Moses Gunn. From a filmmaker who would shortly thereafter graduate to the "big leagues" of Hollywood action, a terrific adventure tale about a little boy riding off to action on a flying creature-companion and another child who reads the other's story.

One Million Years B.C. (1966). Don Chaffey, dir. Raquel Welch, John Richardson, Martine Beswick. All kids love dinosaurs and, up until *Jurassic Park*, no one did them better than F/X wizard Ray Harryhausen. While kids are enjoying the marvelous tabletop models, dads can ogle the young Welch and Beswick in animal-skin bikinis.

Return of the Jedi (1983). Richard Marquand, dir. Harrison Ford, Mark Hamill, Carrie Fisher. Third (and final) entry in the original *Star Wars* series is the most kid-friendly, in large part owing to the Ewoks, adorable creatures who come off like a cross between schnauzers and midgets, joining Luke, Han, and Leia to fight the Evil Empire.

Shrek (2001). Vicky Jenson, Andrew Adamson, dirs. Cameron Diaz, Michael Meyers, Eddie Murphy (voices only). An appealing computer-generated animation funfest, which kids and adults will love equally if in different ways. The ancient romantic fables about a princess in sore need of rescuing—as well as every Disney film ever made—come under satiric scrutiny.

Sidekicks (1993). Aaron Norris, dir. Chuck Norris, Beau Bridges, Jonathan Brandis. Here's a trimmed-down (for the better!), child-accessible version of *The Last Action Hero*, and the one Chuck Norris film that can truly be rated as family-friendly. A little boy, picked on by bullies, idolizes the star, who teaches him the art of defensive action.

Spy Kids: See "Antonio Banderas" in chapter 3.

Squanto: A Warrior's Tale (1994). Xavier Koller, dir. Adam Beach, Eric Schweig. Here's a chance to teach your kids something about Native Americans as they really were before the white man arrived, as a young brave enjoys his natural surroundings until kidnapped and dragged back to Europe. High adventure with a serious undercurrent.

Story of Robin Hood and His Merrie Men, The (1952). Ken Annakin, dir. Richard Todd, Joan Rice, Peter Finch. We're not forgetting the Michael Curtiz/Errol Flynn 1936 Warner Bros. super-production when we make the claim that this is the best version of the Robin Hood story ever filmed, shot entirely on English locations.

Swiss Family Robinson (1960). Ken Annakin, dir. John Mills, Dorothy McGuire. Wonderful Disney film of the Johann Wyss classic scuttles most of the book's lugubrious prose, offering instead a series of hair-raising adventures as the title family is stranded on a miraculous animal-infested island. Great stunt work in final shoot-out with pirates.

Tarzan (1999). Chris Buck, Kevin Lima. Glenn Close, Minnie Driver, Tony Goldwyn (voices only). In many respects, the finest Tarzan film since the first two produced by MGM in the early 1930s, with an eye toward children yet never for one moment any condescending attitude. The jungle comes vividly alive in modern-classic animation.

3 Ninjas (1992). Jon Turteltaub, dir. Michael Treanor, Victor Wong, Max Elliott Slade. Every little kid's fantasy: Those martial arts lessons that cost Mom and Pop so much actually pay off big time, as the junior set employs its defensive arts to defeat the routine bad guys menacing the community. If your kids see it, they'll want lessons, too!

Time Bandits (1981). Terry Gilliam, dir. Sean Connery, John Cleese, Michael Palin. A little boy finds himself swept up by the seven (minus one) dwarfs, then thrust through a time tunnel, meeting (among others) the Greek warrior-king Agamemnon (Connery). Try and imagine a *Monty Python* film for the family audience and you've got it. Zany fun.

Time Machine, The (1961). George Pal, dir. Rod Taylor, Yvette Mimieux. Delightful adaptation (by George Pal) of H. G. Wells's sci-fi story, toned down for family audiences as Victorian-age hero zips into future, encounters lovely Eloi, evil Morlocks, and wages a one-man war for the good of mankind. Taylor is terrific in his first action-hero role, and Mimieux is gorgeous.

Treasure Island (1950). Byron Haskin, dir. Robert Newton, Bobby Driscoll. From the magic pen of Robert L. Stevenson, by way of the Disney studios at the height of their powers, comes this ripping yarn of pirates, hidden gold, and a bitter (and notably bloody) fight between good and evil on an uncharted isle. Far outclasses any other version of the tale.

9

ESSENTIALS:
THE EIGHTIES

The eighties were the Reagan era, both in life and on film. The rugged individualist—already reintroduced during the second half of the seventies as America, struggling with its identity and reaching back to a more conservative image of itself—emerged as the key figure in popular culture. Shortly, Mel Gibson, Arnold Schwarzenegger, and Tom Cruise would become representative stars, joining Harrison Ford and Sylvester Stallone who had arrived a few years earlier. This was also a time of healing, as the country—polarized since the late sixties—slowly became a community once more. No longer did films appeal to young or old, as had been the case in the prevous decade's early years, but to *everyone*. Lucas and Spielberg would continue to rise in status, with their mytho-poetic approach to action. Even more characteristic of the decade would be the Simpson-Bruckheimer and Joel Silver superproductions, more often than not directed by Tony Scott and John McTiernan, respectively. For them, style rules supreme over substance, as simplistic stories—and values—were projected in the most vivid imagery imagineable for an audience hungry for a return to traditions that bring with them peace of mind.

Raiders of the Lost Ark (1981)

CREDITS

Director, Steven Spielberg; screenplay, Lawrence Kasdan, from a story by Philip Kaufman and George Lucas; producers, Howard Kazanjian, Frank Marshall, and Lucas; original music, John Williams; cinematography, Douglas Slocombe; running time, 115 min.; rating, PG.

CAST

Harrison Ford (*Dr. Henry Jones, Jr.*); Karen Allen (*Marion Ravenwood*); Paul Freeman (*Rene Belloq*); Ronald Lacey (*Toht*); John Rhys-Davies (*Sallah*); Alfred Molina (*Sapito*); Denholm Elliott (*Marcus Brody*).

Harrison Ford in
*Raiders of the Lost
Ark.*

THE FILM

In the 1970s, George Lucas had pioneered the retro-adventure with the first
Star Wars film, a homage to the 1930s' *Buck Rogers* and *Flash Gordon* outer
space serials he'd seen on TV as a kid. To his redux, Lucas added an intellec-
tual/metaphysical dimenson derived from reading Joseph Campbell's schol-
arly work on mythology. Simultaneously, Steven Spielberg had begun
mounting his own contemporary popcorn-movie entertainments, an alternative to the serious *new cinema* introduced by Martin Scorsese and Francis
Coppola. *Raiders* marked the first collaboration of these boy-geniuses, a

natural coming together of like minds. Lucas provided the dazzling concept, allowing Speilberg to bring Indiana Jones to full fruition on-screen. Building not only on *Star Wars* but also the then-recent revival of *Superman*, the Indy trilogy unconsciously reflected the mind-set of Reagan-era America. Indy resembles several characters Reagan played during the 1940s, and the growing nostalgia for that supposedly simple era—when we were good, the Nazis bad—served as an appreciated model for a country that had temporarily lost its faith in itself. The film offers an aesthetic redemption of what had long been considered déclassè pop culture—comic books, Saturday morning serials, etc.—as what had formerly been relegated to B-budget arenas, now produced on a grand scale. No better example exists than the film's opening sequence in which Indy attempts to escape with a precious object from a cave. Everything that occurs is lifted directly from "The Prize of Pizarro" in *Uncle $crooge* (nr. 26, June–August 1959), a comic book by Carl Banks, in which Don and his three nephews must avoid a succession of traps identical to the ones Indy must survive.

The Road Warrior (1981)

CREDITS

Director, George Miller; screenplay, Miller, Brian Hannant, and Terry Hayes; producer, Byron Kennedy; original music, Brian May; cinematography, Dean Semler; running time, 94 min.; rating, R.

CAST

Mel Gibson ("*Mad" Max Rockatansky*); Bruce Spence (*Gyro Captain*); Mike Preston (*Pappagallo*); Max Phipps (*Toadie*); Vernon Wells (*Wez*); Kjell Nilsson (*Humungus*); Emil Minty (*Feral Kid*); Virginia Hey (*Warrior Woman*); Harold Baigent (*Narrator; voice only*).

THE FILM

The original *Mad Max* (see chapter 21) proved a surprise hit, despite its small budget. This larger epic extension of the story became one of the seminal movies of the early eighties. Set in a ruined future, populated by villains in punk regalia, the film's hero is initially the sort of rugged individualist we'd watched throughout the seventies. Here, though, he gradually accepts his place in a community. The film was shot in Australia, with a star from that

Mel Gibson in *The Road Warrior*.

country, even as "down under" became chic. Wild car chases across a barren landscape were inspired by the classic pursuit of the title item in John Ford's *Stagecoach*, also the inspiration for the extended chase sequences in the first and third Indiana Jones films. Max himself is modeled on a key character from another of the legendary Ford/Wayne films, *The Searchers* (1956). Like Ethan Edwards, he's a wanderer/warrior of the wasteland, severed from home and family, a Lost Dutchman drifting from one temporary way station to the next in a barren, unhospitable world.

Conan the Barbarian (1982)

CREDITS

Director, John Milius; screenplay, Milius and Oliver Stone, from stories by Robert E. Howard; producers, Dino and Raffaella De Laurentiis, Buzz Feitshans, and Edward R. Pressman; original music, Basil Poledouris; cinematography, Duke Callaghan; running time, 129 min.; rating, R.

CAST

Arnold Schwarzenegger (*Conan*); James Earl Jones (*Thulsa Doom*); Max von Sydow (*King Osric*); Sandahl Bergman (*Valeria*); Ben Davidson (*Rexor*); Gerry Lopez (*Subotai*); Mako (*The Wizard*); Valérie Quennessen (*The Princess*); William Smith (*Conan's Father*); Leslie Foldvary (*Sacrificial Snake Girl*); Nadiuska (*Conan's Mother*); Kiyoshi Yamazaki (*Sword Master*); Cassandra Gava/Gaviola (*The Witch*).

**Arnold Schwarzenegger
in *Conan the Barbarian*.**

THE FILM

If the term "rugged individualism" hadn't already existed, it would have had to be created to describe Arnold's Conan, in terms of the character's physique and his value system. *Conan* was co-written and directed by John Milius, an odd duck in the seventies being a macho-man in an age of peace-and-love proseletyzing. In the eighties, however, a meaner mood appeared in life and prevailed on film. Big John was the right man at the right moment. Like his colleagues, Milius adored old movies, drawing his metier from them, particularly John Wayne's action epics and sand-and-sandal mini-spectacles, imported from Italy during the 1960s. *Conan* allowed him to mount a homage to such work on a grand scale. If *Star Wars* was Lucas's dream vision of what the *Flash Gordon/Buck Rogers* serials could have been with a bigger budget, *Conan* did the same for the violent, sexual, tawdry imports about characters named Atlas, Ursus, and Machiste. Robert E. Howard's pulp novels had long held spellbound a loyal, mostly male cult of readers. Milius drew on those stories, also on the comic book illustrations by Ron Cobb, in which the perfectly sculpted hero deals swiftly and surely with fantasy women and monstrous incarnations of evil. All this came together as, on a misty medieval realm of pagan myth, Milius imposed a post-Nietzsche sensibility, beginning with the film's opening quote from that modern philosopher: "That which does not kill us makes us strong!"

Romancing the Stone (1984)

CREDITS

Director, Robert Zemeckis; screenplay, Diane Thomas and (uncredited) Lem Dobbs, Treva Silverman, and Howard Franklin; producers, Jack Brodsky and Joel and Michael Douglas; original music, Alan Silvestri; cinematography, Dean Cundey; running time, 105 min.; rating, PG.

CAST

Michael Douglas (*Jack Colton*); Kathleen Turner (*Joan Wilder*); Danny DeVito (*Ralph*); Zack Norman (*Ira*); Alfonso Arau (*Juan*); Manuel Ojeda (*Zolo*); Holland Taylor (*Gloria*); Mary Ellen Trainor (*Elaine*); Kymberly Herrin (*Angelina*).

THE FILM

As the eighties neared mid-decade, the great complaint about action films argued that they were told from the male point of view, excluding women—other than for intense sex without romance—thereby turning off half the country to the genre. *Romancing the Stone* turned that convention around, for the lead character is (despite Douglas's top billing) the female bodice-ripper novelist (Turner) who enjoys the ultimate romantic thrill—immersed in an adventure every bit as exciting as any experienced by her fictional alter-ego, "Angelina." These include a love affair with an adventurer who, on the surface, resembles the idealized ones she creates in her paperback books. This being "real life," the results are ironically different. The film had enough action to satisfy male viewers, yet women flocked to it as well, *Stone* emerging as the perfect combination of chick-flick and guy-movie, thus the great date film of its era. The antics in the Colombian jungle are played with verve thanks to the guiding hand of director Zemeckis, best known for *Back to the Future*, here creating his first full-throttle action film. The intense violence and, more notable, vivid sex scenes between Turner and Douglas pushed the limit of the PG rating and, in truth, beyond.

The Terminator (1984)

CREDITS

Director, James Cameron; producer, Gale Anne Hurd; screenwriters, Cameron and Hurd, with additional dialogue by William Wisher, Jr., inspired by stories by Harlan Ellison; original music, Joe Dolce, Brad Fiedel, and Tane McClure; cinematography, Adam Greenberg; running time, 108 min.; rating, R.

CAST

Arnold Schwarzenegger (*The Terminator*); Linda Hamilton (*Sarah Connor*); Michael Biehn (*Kyle Reese*); Paul Winfield (*LAPD Det. Ed Traxler*); Lance Henriksen (*Det. Vukovich*); Rick Rossovich (*Matt*); Bess Motta (*Ginger Ventura*); Earl Boen (*Dr. Silberman*); Dick Miller (*Pawn Shop Clerk*); Shawn Schepps (*Nancy*); Bruce M. Kerner (*Desk Sgt.*); Bill Paxton (*Punk with Blue Hair*).

THE FILM

If *Conan* established Schwarzenegger as a major action star, *The Terminator* took him to the superstar level. Though shot on a low budget, the film established itself as a box-office sensation, advancing the then-marginal careers of producer Hurd and director Cameron. The story itself is essentially an old *Twilight Zone* adventure—the title character is sent back in time to kill a woman before she can give birth to the son who, in the future, may save the world from deadly cyborgs. Another time traveler, Reese, also searches for Sarah to protect her. Happily, Sarah does not merely scream for help but fights alongside Reese as an equal. In the sequel, she would emerge as even more of an action heroine, pumped up for further confrontations. Viewed today, the film may seem surprisingly minimalist in light of the 1991 sequel, which introduced the F/X concept of "liquid metal," so mind blowing in its time if quickly reduced to a visual cliché after being employed in countless TV commercials. The original is a far finer film, relying on clever dialogue and believable if fantastical situations. A pervasive sense of threat during the nearly nonstop chase makes the film as effective on a thriller level as a sci-fi actioner. To say that *The Terminator* influenced future films of the genre is a gross understatement.

Rambo: First Blood Part II   (1985)

CREDITS

Director, George P. Cosmatos; screenplay, Sylvester Stallone and James Cameron, from a story by Kevin Jarre; producers, Buzz Feitshans and Andrew G. Vajna; original music, Jerry Goldsmith; cinematography, Jack Cardiff; running time, 95 min.; rating, R.

CAST

Sylvester Stallone (*John Rambo*); Richard Crenna (*Col. Samuel Trautman*); Charles Napier (*Marshall Murdock*); Steven Berkoff (*Lt. Col. Podovsky*); Julia Nickson (*Co Bao*); Martin Kove (*Ericson*).

THE FILM

During the production of *First Blood* (1982), Sylvester Stallone argued endlessly with director Ted Kotcheff over the tone and conceptualization of the central character. Kotcheff wanted a relatively realistic story about a Vietnam

Sylvester Stallone in *Rambo*.

vet who becomes the victim of small-town prejudice. Stallone hoped to mount a mini-epic in which John Rambo emerges as a one-man army, an incarnation of the rugged individualist. The result was an incongruous blend of the two, leaving neither man satisfied. The film, however, scored at the box office, allowing Sly to seize control of the inevitable sequel. Here, he was able to create another alter-ego (and ongoing franchise) on the order of Rocky Balboa—John Rambo, an adolescent's vision of the undefeatable man of valor from ancient myth, brought into the present as a means of exorcising the lingering psychic demons of Vietnam. The film is a simplistic if effective diatribe, its hero returning to Southeast Asia to rescue POWs still held captive. The Vietcong (and, significantly, their Russian allies) are cardboard villains who fire endless rounds at Rambo, somehow always missing, as in a B-action flick for kids in bygone years, now marketed to adults. As despised as the actual enemy are petty bureaucrats and self-serving politicians (Charles Napier chief among them here) who succumb to the numbing complexity of rules and paperwork, thwarting Rambo from striking quickly and effectively. Ironically, the film played more effectively with people who, like Stallone, did not serve in Vietnam. Instead of cheering Rambo on, many combat vets felt this cartoon-like depiction was an insult to the far more complex war in which they'd participated.

Aliens (1986)

CREDITS

> Director, James Cameron; screenplay, Cameron from a story by Cameron, David Giler, and Walter Hill; producer, Gale Anne Hurd; original music, James Horner; cinematography, Adrian Biddle; running time, 137 min.; rating, R.

CAST

> Sigourney Weaver (*Lt. Ellen Ripley*); Michael Biehn (*Cpl. Dwayne Hicks*); Paul Reiser (*Carter Burke*); Lance Henriksen (*Bishop*); Carrie Henn (*Rebecca "Newt" Jorden*); Bill Paxton (*Pvt. Hudson*); William Hope (*Lt. Gorman*); Jenette Goldstein (*Pvt. Vasquez*); Al Matthews (*Sgt. Apone*).

THE FILM

Alien, Ridley Scott's excellent suspense thriller set in space, had been a huge hit for 20th Century-Fox during the late 1970s, so a sequel was inevitable. The great danger was that it might turn out to be a second-rate redux. Wisely, Fox executives decided to go another route entirely. They retained the concept of the alien, as well as the surviving character Ripley, placing them not only in a new story but another genre entirely—the action film. This allowed Weaver to incarnate an early example of what would become an increasingly significant character over the next two decades, the action babe who can hold her own with (or even outdo) the men. This occurred on screen even as feminist concepts, introduced into society and considered radical during the 1970s, were a decade later absorbed into mainstream entertainment. Here, Ripley—having been in a state of hibernation for fifty-seven years—is revived and persuaded against her better judgment to return to the planet where she encountered the creature, this time as advisor to a group of space soldiers searching for missing colonists. Once there, she finds herself again facing off with an alien (indeed, a society of aliens) and protects a child who becomes her virtual adopted daughter. Typical of eighties' films is an intriguing balance between 1960s' group-action efforts and 1970s' rugged-individualist style. Ripley is at first a part of a group, including (in this more enlightened age) women and men, minorities as well as Anglos—but in the end must wage a one-person war against the creature.

Top Gun (1986)

CREDITS

Director, Tony Scott; screenplay, Jim Cash and Jack Epps, Jr.; producers, Jerry Bruckheimer and Don Simpson; original music, Harold Faltermeyer, Giorgio Moroder, and (uncredited) Otis Redding; cinematography, Jeffrey L. Kimball; running time, 87 min.; rating, PG-13.

CAST

Tom Cruise (*Lt. Pete "Maverick" Mitchell*); Kelly McGillis (*Charlotte "Charlie" Blackwood*); Val Kilmer (*Lt. Tom "Iceman" Kazanski*); Anthony Edwards (*Lt. Nick "Goose" Bradshaw*); Tom Skerritt (*Cmdr. Mike "Viper" Metcalf*); Michael Ironside (*Lt. Cmdr. Heatherly "Jester"*); John Stockwell ("*Cougar*"); Barry Tubb ("*Wolfman*"); Rick Rossovich ("*Slider*"); Tim Robbins ("*Merlin*"); Meg Ryan (*Carole*).

THE FILM

"Let's rock 'n' roll" took on a new meaning here, forever leaving behind the hippie-era notion that the new music had something to do with an enlightened mind-set. Thanks to an incessant, blaring score by noted producer Giorgio Morodor, rock now became associated with the latter-day cowboy, carrying his conservative values into the wild blue yonder on a sophisticated aircraft rather than a horse, both guns still blazing. Producers Simpson and Bruckheimer began shooting with a mere forty pages of script, well aware the film's inevitable success had nothing to do with plot, character, or theme. The screenplay serves as only a skeleton on which director Scott would graft its dense identity—rapidly edited, exciting images of high-tech activity, intense romance (within the bounds of a PG-13 rating to ensure a large audience), and plenty of wiseass one-liners for the young leads to quip. The film was "about" state-of-the-art hardware, male-model-type actors, and the conquest of women by rugged guys who show a lot of beefcake when not tearing through the sky. Some critics objected to the pro-war attitude, particularly the final aerial combat scene in which flyboys decimate Libyan jets to the great pleasure of an ecstatic audience, making it clear that any remaining peace and love karma from the sixties was officially over—the youth of Reagan-era America made love *and* war.

Lethal Weapon (1987)

CREDITS

Director, Richard Donner; screenplay, Shane Black; producer, Donner and Joel Silver; original music, Eric Clapton and Michael Kamen; cinematography, Stephen Goldblatt; running time, 110 min.; rating, R.

CAST

Mel Gibson (*Sgt. Martin Riggs*); Danny Glover (*Sgt. Roger Murtaugh*); Gary Busey (*Mr. Joshua*); Mitch Ryan (*Gen. McAllister*); Tom Atkins (*Michael Hunsaker*); Darlene Love (*Trish Murtaugh*); Traci Wolfe (*Rianne Murtaugh*); Jackie Swanson (*Amanda Hunsaker*); Damon Hines (*Nick Murtaugh*); Don Gordon (*Cop*).

THE FILM

The buddy-buddy film, so prominent during the late sixties and early seventies, returned with a vengeance thanks to a sharp Shane Black script. That writer would, with this film's success, become the flavor of the month among action scribes during the late eighties. Producer Joel Siegel was particularly fond of this type of edge-of-your-seat, gut-wrenching action laced with wild comedy, and expert marketing of such testosterone films for *real* men allowed Siegel to rise to the top of the Hollywood heap. What made the premise work here was the remarkable chemistry between the film's two stars. Gibson was able to dispel any questions as to whether he was merely a rugged pretty boy via an all-out (but never over-the-top) performance as a near-crazy detective. Danny Glover perfectly complements Mel as his more sedate side-kick. Much appreciated, too, is the anti-racist attitude; the black man is the refined, solidly middle-class officer here. Donner, who had done such an effective job with the first *Superman* film, proved to be one of the few older directors who could comfortably survive in the new youth-oriented climate of state-of-the-art Hollywood. Terrific set pieces—wild leaps from high buildings, roaring car chases, spectacular shoot-outs—all work since the audience really did care about the characters, who rise above the level of cliché.

Die Hard (1988)

CREDITS

Director, John McTiernan; screenplay, Steven E. de Souza and Jeb Stuart, from the novel *Nothing Lasts Forever* by Roderick Thorp; producers, Joel Silver, and Charles and Lawrence Gordon; original music, Michael Kamen; cinematography, Jan de Bont; running time, 131 min.; rating, R.

CAST

Bruce Willis (*Det. John McClane*); Bonnie Bedelia (*Holly Gennero McClane*); Reginald Vel Johnson (*Sgt. Al Powell LAPD*); Paul Gleason (*LAPD Chief Dwayne Robinson*); De'voreaux White (*Argyle*); William Atherton (*Dick Thornburg*); Hart Bochner (*Harry Ellis*); James Shigeta (*Joe Y. Takagi*); Alan Rickman (*Hans Gruber*); Alexander Godunov (*Karl*).

THE FILM

With this film, Willis achieved action-hero superstardom, creating the contemporary concept of relatively realistic—rather than over-the-top super-hero—suspense-action as a loner takes on terrorists. In Willis's own words at the time of *Die Hard*'s release, the protagonist is "an ordinary man who rises to extraordinary heroism while under extreme pressure." Though in less able hands the story line might have degenerated into routine action, John McTiernan continued his climb in status by alternating edge-of-your-seat sequences—depending more for their impact on thriller techniques than for graphic violence—with the high-tech action that became popular after *The Terminator*'s release. McClane becomes a one-man army though, unlike Stal-

Bruce Willis (sheltering Bonnie Bedelia) in *Die Hard*.

lone and/or Schwarzenegger, we are constantly in doubt as to whether he can accomplish what he sets out to do, thereby drawing in viewers emotionally rather than allowing us to watch from a detached position. The blue-collar guy is without notable refinement, yet hangs on to an old-fashioned value system and, in the end, prevails. The film is filled with conservative ideas, implied without being directly stated. The upscale Yuppie-slime hostage (Hart Bochner) is almost as reprehensible as the terrorist leader, while the representative of the media (William Atherton) likewise comes off as despicable. Foreigners in general are not treated with great respect, Russian dancer Alexander Gudonov playing a thickly accented, monstrously menacing German heavy, while the boss of Mrs. McClane's company is Japanese. This stereotype plays into the suspicion that Japan—before its current economic crisis—was in the process of co-opting the United States. In the end, right wins out and viewers are left with the impression that the once-endangered patriarchal structure has been reaffirmed when McClane wins back his formerly liberated, independent wife, as she realizes a *real* man is what she *really* needs.

10

THE PANTHEON: WORLD'S GREATEST ACTION STARS (1960–1995)

Ah, stardom! They put your name on a star in the sidewalk on Hollywood Boulevard and you find a pile of dog manure on it. That tells the whole story.

—Lee Marvin

These are the top performers who between 1960 and 1995 established themselves in our public imagination as The Tough Guys. When asked, shortly before he died, if he had any regrets, Steve McQueen answered in his typically blunt manner, "I live for myself and I answer to nobody." He might as well have been speaking for all the members of the *Pantheon* and the image each embodies—the man of action as Existential anti-hero.

Charles Bronson (Charles Buchinsky)

Born November 3, 1921, in Ehreneld, Pennsylvania. Like his father, worked in coal mines. First member of family to graduate high school. Stint as a tail gunner during World War II allowed him to continue his education under the G.I. Bill. Followed a brief stay at Philadelphia art school with study at Pasadena Playhouse, leading to bits in action films owing to rugged demeanor. Won a supporting part in Katharine Hepburn/Spencer Tracy comedy *Pat and Mike* (1952) as well as monstrous assistant to Vincent Price in 3-D classic *House of Wax* (1953). Changed name to "Bronson" after accepting first of many Native American roles. Appeared in brief-lived TV series as tough-guy news photographer, *Man With a Camera*; led to leads in B-budget items, then scene-stealing parts in great group-action films of the sixties. Turned down lead in Sergio Leone's spaghetti westerns to play wagonmaster on TV's *The Travels of Jamie McPheeters*. Finally worked for Leone in *Once Upon a Time in the West*, then on to European action pics, becoming superstar in Third World countries, listed on marquees as "El Brute." Returned to America for *Death Wish*, the series that transformed him

**Charles Bronson
in *Chato's Land*.**

into a controversial icon for vigilante justice on the mean streets of modern cities. Unfortunately, often paired with Michael Winner, dreadful director, in films co-starring wife Jill Ireland, whom he'd won away from then-husband David McCallum while filming *Great Escape*. Jill's long bout with breast cancer and his unswerving support brought the macho man new sympathy. Lack of prestigious action projects in favor of schlock items caused Bronson (unlike Eastwood, who always chose top directors before helming his own projects) to gradually lose status.

ACTION FILMOGRAPHY

Battle Zone (1952); *Torpedo Alley* (1953); *Crime Wave* (1954); *Vera Cruz* (1954); *Riding Shotgun* (1954); *Drum Beat* (1954); *Apache* (1954); *Target Zero* (1955); *Big House, U.S.A.* (1955); *Jubal* (1956); *Run of the Arrow* (1957); *Showdown at Boot Hill* (1958); *When Hell Broke Loose* (1958); *Machine Gun Kelly* (1958); *Gang War* (1958); *Never So Few* (1959); *The Magnificent Seven* (1960); *X-15* (1961); *A Thunder of Drums* (1961); *The Great Escape* (1963); *Four for Texas* (1964); *Battle of the Bulge* (1965); *The Dirty Dozen* (1967); *Guns for San Sebastian* (1968); *Villa Rides* (1968); *Once Upon a Time in the West* (1969); *You Can't Win 'Em All* (1970); *The Family* (1970); *Red Sun* (1971); *Chato's Land* (1971); *The Valachi Papers* (1972); *The Mechanic* (1972); *Chino* (1973); *The Stone Killer* (1973); *Mr. Majestyk* (1974); *Death Wish* (1974); *Breakout* (1975); *Hard Times* (1975); *Breakheart Pass* (1975); *St. Ives* (1975); *From Noon Till Three* (1976); *Raid on Entebbe* (TV, 1977); *White Buffalo* (1977); *Telefon* (1977); *Love and Bullets* (1979); *Caboblanco* (1980); *Borderline* (1980); *Death Hunt* (1981); *Death Wish II* (1982); *10 to Midnight* (1983); *The Evil That Men Do* (1984); *Death Wish 3* (1985); *Murphy's Law* (1986); *Death Wish 4: The Crackdown* (1987); *Assassination* (1987); *Messenger of Death* (1988); *Kinjite: Forbidden Subjects* (1989); *Death Wish 5: The Face of Death* (1994); *Family of Cops* (1999).

MUST-SEE

Run of the Arrow (Samuel Fuller, dir.). Bronson's only outing with action expert Fuller has him cast as a Lakota chief who accepts Rod Steiger into the tribe. Brutal, unforgettable western, and an inspiration for the better known but less satisfying *Dances With Wolves*.

The Magnificent Seven: See chapter 18.

The Great Escape: See chapter 18.

The Dirty Dozen: See chapter 18.

Once Upon a Time in the West (Sergio Leone, dir.). Arguably the greatest western ever, though emphasis is on theme, character, and style over action. Still, occasional violent scenes (particularly opening shoot-out between Bronson, Jack Elam, and Woody Strode) are remarkable. Bronson has lead over Henry Fonda, Jason Robards, and Claudia Cardinale.

The Family (Sergio Sollima, dir.). Shot in Italy as *Citta Violenta*, though not so much a Mafia movie as Mickey Spillane–like action thriller, pitching hit-man Bronson into battle with equally ugly adversary (Telly Savallas), taking on all comers, vulnerable only to a beautiful blonde (Ireland) who betrays him at every turn. Stylish and substantial.

Death Wish (Michael Winner, dir.). Fascinating if highly manipulative moral fable that effectively played on mid-seventies' audience's fears about escalating street crime. Average guy decides to eliminate all druggie-scum after wife is raped and murdered. Still potent.

Jackie Chan (Kong-sang Chan)

Born in Hong Kong, April 7, 1954, to destitute parents employed as domestic servants at the U.S. Embassy. As a child, was literally indentured to Chinese Opera Research, received strict training in mime, music, acting, dance, and martial arts for complete body control. Loving the latter, he sought work in burgeoning action-film industry. First employed as a stuntman in *Fist of Fury* (aka *The Chinese Connection*), working under such talents as Long Cheng and Sing Lung. Stole thunder from star Bruce Lee by performing highest fall in movie history. Succession of small parts, acting and performing dazzling stunts for John Woo. Half-dozen projects for director Lo Wei failed to ignite excitement, with Chan forced into Bruce Lee image as replacement for the deceased star. Broke off on own, announcing his heroes were Buster Keaton and Harold Lloyd—Chan's emerging screen persona of a similar comic order. Known for performing his own stunts, his career soared throughout Asia, thanks to revitalization of the chop-socky genre with *Half a Loaf of Kung Fu, Drunken Master*. Opting for total control over projects, refused to sign long-term contract with Golden Harvest until guaranteed he'd co-write and produce. Jackie insisted he also be allowed to sing the title song over opening credits. His big challenge was to break into American market, achieving at best modest success with *The Big Brawl*. Formed own production company Golden Way; created coterie of stuntmen when many professionals refused to work on Chan films owing to the huge accident rate. Achieved superstardom thanks to Tarantino, who insisted MTV bestow a Lifetime Achievement Award.

ACTION FILMOGRAPHY

The Chinese Connection (1971); *Ten Fingers of Death* (1971); *Kung Fu Girl* (1971); *Iron Hand* (1972); *Return of the Dragon* (1972); *Lady Kung Fu* (1972); *Fist of Anger* (1973); *Young Tiger* (1974); *Hand of Death* (1975); *New Fist of*

Fury (1976); *Story of Drunken Master* (1978); *Eagle's Shadow* (1978); *Karate Ghostbuster* (1978); *Dragon Fist* (1979); *Fearless Master* (1980); *The Big Brawl* (1980); *Cannonball Run* (1981); *Dragon Strike* (1982); *Project A* (1983); *Two in a Black Belt* (1984); *Spartan X* (1984); *Target* (1985); *Ninja Thunderbolt* (1985); *First Mission* (1985); *Police Force/Story* (1985); *Armour of God* (1986); *Cyclone Z* (1987); *Police Story Part 2/Police Force II* (1988); *Jackie Chan's Police Story* (1988); *Black Dragon* (1989); *Operation Condor* (1990); *Twin Dragons* (1992); *Police Story III* (1992); *City Hunter* (1992); *Crime Story/Hard to Die* (1993); *Once a Cop* (1993); *Drunken Fist II/Drunken Master 2/Legend of the Drunken Master* (1994); *Dead Heat* (1995); *Rumble in the Bronx* (1996); *First Strike* (1996); *Mr. Nice Guy* (1998); *Who Am I?* (1998); *Rush Hour* (1998); *Accidental Spy* (2001).

MUST SEE

Police Story (Jackie Chan, dir.). Jackie insisted on total control and the results paid off big time, resulting in one of the most exciting, enjoyable martial arts action movies ever made. Hardcore genre fans love it, but so do more mainstream audiences.

Operation Condor (Jackie Chan, dir.). Off to Europe and Africa on a wild mission, Jackie's accompanied by a virtual *Charlie's Angels* team of beautiful babes. Silly stuff, but loads of fun, showing off Jackie's electric personality at its best. Great fights.

Legend of the Drunken Master (Lau Kar Leung, dir.). Belated sequel to Chan's first commercial hit is by a far more skillful director, who also fights Chan in key scene. Jackie's best Hong Kong film to date—impressive and original action, strikingly executed stunts.

Rumble in the Bronx (Stanley Tong, dir.). It's off to America (Vancouver subbing for Manhattan) as Jackie bursts on to the scene, charms gorgeous ladies (Anita Mui and Francoise Yip), whacks the daylights out of bad guys, all the while maintaining that great smile.

Rush Hour: See chapter 6.

Sean Connery

Born August 25, 1930, in Edinburgh, Scotland. He dropped out of school at age 13 and enlisted in British Navy three years later. Got two tattoos on right arm before embarking for sea: "Scotland forever" and "Mum and Dad." Bleeding ulcers forced him to abandon career in merchant marine, became a nude nodel for Edinburgh Art College. A weight lifter, in 1953 he entered Mr. Universe Contest, placing third in tall man's division (he's 6-foot-1). Studied dance with Yat Malmgren while working as coffin polisher and milk delivery man. First movie: *Lilacs of the Spring* (1954). Began going bald, age 21. He decided to wear toupee for 007 roles, though in person always appears in natural state. Producer Harry Saltzman cast him as Bond when his first choice, Cary Grant, declined. Eventually left role not because (as reported) that he hated it, only wanted to stretch as an actor. Awkward period in late sixties, early 1970s, then gradually emerged as superstar. The balder, grayer, craggier he became, the sexier people found him. Voted "Sexiest Man Alive" by *People* magazine, 1989; October, 1997, *Empire* magazine (England) ranked him No. 14 among "The Top 100 Movie Stars of All Time"; "Sexiest Man of the Century" by *People,* 1999. Knighted by Queen Elizabeth, New Year's Eve, 1999. Married to actress Diane Cilento (*Tom Jones*) 1962–1974, and Micheline Roquebrune, 1975–present. Lives in Marbella, Spain, his home purposefully located near golf course so he can play daily when not filming.

ACTION FILMOGRAPHY

Hell Drivers (1957); *Action of the Tiger* (1957); *Tarzan's Greatest Adventure* (1959); *Operation Snafu* (1961); *The Longest Day* (1962); *Dr. No* (1962); *From Russia With Love* (1963); *Goldfinger* (1964); *The Hill* (1965); *Thunderball* (1965); *You Only Live Twice* (1967); *Shalako* (1968); *The Molly Maguires* (1970); *The Red Tent* (1971); *Diamonds Are Forever* (1971); *Zardoz* (1974); *The Terrorists* (1975); *The Wind and the Lion* (1975); *The Man Who Would Be King* (1975); *Robin and Marian* (1976); *The Next Man* (1976); *A Bridge Too Far* (1977); *The Great Train Robbery* (1979); *Meteor* (1979); *Time Bandits* (1981); *Outland* (1981); *Never Say Never Again* (1983); *Sword of the Valiant* (1985); *Highlander* (1986); *The Untouchables* (1987); *Indiana Jones and the Last Crusade* (1989); *The Hunt for Red October* (1990); *Robin Hood: Prince of Thieves* (1991); *Highlander II: The Quickening* (1991); *Rising Sun* (1993); *First Knight* (1995); *Dragonheart* (voice only, 1996); *The Rock* (1996); *The Avengers* (1998); *Entrapment* (1999); *The League of Extraordinary Gentlemen* (2003).

MUST-SEE

Dr. No (Terence Young, dir.). Connery's breakthrough, creating new anti-heroic action star, in comic bookish settings but heightened violence and sexuality, establishing pace for most of what was to come for action films in the 1960s and beyond! Gorgeous Caribbean settings, ravishing Ursula Andress in then-daring bikini, Joseph Wiseman as the evil genius.

From Russia With Love: See chapter 17.

Goldfinger: See chapter 18.

Thunderball (Terence Young, dir.). Sean's fourth go-round as 007. Not as well remembered as *Goldfinger*, but in truth the film is as fine. Knockout action sequences, including an incredible underwater fight-finale. Gadgets particularly good in this go-round. Lucianna Paluzzi is hot stuff as black-leather biker-babe villainess.

The Wind and the Lion: See chapter 15.

The Man Who Would Be King (John Huston, dir.). Wondrous mounting of Kipling tale with Christopher Plummer in cameo as the author. Two soldiers of fortune (Connery and terrific cockney Michael Caine) stumble into an uncharted kingdom, play God, wish they hadn't. Old-fashioned Hollywood action entertainment in finest sense of the term.

The Untouchables: See "Kevin Costner" in chapter 7.

Indiana Jones and the Last Crusade: See "Harrison Ford" in chapter 10.

The Hunt for Red October (John McTiernan, dir.). More suspense than action, but near-great film all the same. Russian sub commander Connery faces off Americans as perestroika is becoming a reality.

Clint Eastwood

Born May 31, 1930, in San Francisco. Flyer during the Korean War, survived plane crash over the Pacific. After swimming to an island, he was befriended by Martin Milner and David Janssen. Later achieving Hollywood success, they insisted Clint join them, despite his having never considered acting. A Universal Studios contract led nowhere; he was dumped owing to the size of his Adam's apple, which was regarded as too large for a star. Dug swimming pools for a living, visited friends at CBS, where he was spotted by a producer of the upcoming *Rawhide* series. Received an offer to become Sergio Leone's Man With No Name only after a dozen others "passed." Even after that success, cast in *Dirty Harry* only when Wayne, Sinatra, and Newman turned the role down. Director Don Siegel became a mentor. Clint dedicated *Unforgiven* (Oscar-winning Best Picture, Director) to Siegel and Sergio, both deceased. Ability to direct and star in films made him a virtual combination of John Ford and John Wayne. Still, career hampered somewhat owing to inexplicable fascination with talentless Sondra Locke, his leading lady on- and off-screen for over a decade. Like Wayne, long dismissed as artless redneck by eastern Establishment, owing to traditional values. Such criticism

Clint Eastwood in
The Dead Pool.

has recently waned, as his body of work, including many misfires, came to be seen as more than the sum of its parts. Growing respect came his way, particularly when Clint combined his three great loves—directing, jazz, and civil rights—in *Bird* with Forest Whitaker as musician Charlie Parker. Now, growing older with great dignity.

ACTION FILMOGRAPHY

Away All Boats (1956); *Lafayette Escadrille* (1958); *Ambush at Cimarron Pass* (1958); *Fistful of Dollars* (1964); *For a Few Dollars More* (1966); *The Good, the Bad, and the Ugly* (1967); *Hang 'em High* (1968); *Coogan's Bluff* (1968); *Where Eagles Dare* (1968); *Two Mules for Sister Sara* (1970); *Kelly's Heroes* (1970); *Dirty Harry* (1972); *Joe Kidd* (1972); *High Plains Drifter* (1973); *Magnum Force* (1973); *The Eiger Sanction* (1975); *The Outlaw Josey Wales* (1976); *The Enforcer* (1976); *The Gauntlet* (1977); *Firefox* (1982); *Sudden Impact* (1983); *City Heat* (1984); *Pale Rider* (1985); *Heartbreak Ridge* (1986); *The Dead Pool* (1988); *The Rookie* (1990); *Unforgiven* (1992); *In the Line of Fire* (1993); *True Crime* (1999); *Space Cowboys* (2000).

MUST-SEE

Fistful of Dollars: See chapter 21.

For a Few Dollars More (Sergio Leone, dir.). More intensely violent action, offbeat humor, moral complexity textured throughout this sequel, which scores big time by adding Lee Van Cleef as friendly adversary of Eastwood's mule-riding, cigar-chomping anti-hero.

The Good, the Bad, and the Ugly: See chapter 18.

Dirty Harry: See chapter 12.

The Outlaw Josey Wales (Clint Eastwood, dir.). Curious western, alternately brutal and poetic. Overrated on release, though not without interest. Clint plays former member of Quantrill-like guerrilla outfit, trying to create a peaceful commune in postwar west.

Unforgiven (Clint Eastwood, dir.). One-time gunslinger (Clint) comes out of retirement, goes up against town marshal (Gene Hackman) with a strong resemblance to Wyatt Earp, portrayed in less-than-positive terms. Morgan Freeman and Richard Harris lend great support in anti-glamorous, darkly lyric masterpiece. Oscar winner for Best Picture and Director.

In the Line of Fire (Wolfgang Petersen, dir.). Cat-and-mouse game between cold-hearted killer (John Malkovich), intending to assassinate a current president, and Clint as the agent who failed to protect Kennedy, sees this as his chance for redemption. A knockout!

Harrison Ford

Born July 13, 1942, in Chicago, Illinois, to an Irish Catholic father and Russian-Jewish mother. He excelled at neither scholastics nor athletics at Park Ridge high school, but did try broadcasts for school's new radio station. Dropped out of Ripon College, Wisconsin, owing to weak grades. There, however, he first tried acting. Drifting to Hollywood, signed a contract with Columbia Pictures. His argumentative attitude was considered unacceptable, so Ford was swiftly dropped. Subsequent studio-contract with Universal led to roles on series-TV, minor movies. While casting low-budget *American Graffiti* (1973), "movie brat" writer-diretor George Lucas rediscovered Ford, who was working as a carpenter. Francis Coppola then cast Harrison in a taut thriller, *The Conversation* (1974). Back working as a carpenter when Lucas called again, this time for *Star Wars*. Series might have led to dead end (consider Mark Hamill) if not for "Indiana Jones." Third franchise came Ford's way when Alec Baldwin dropped out of Tom Clancy's Jack Ryan movies following the first. Always hoping to stretch, with romantic comedy (*Working Girl*, 1988; *Sabrina*, 1995) and serious drama (*Regarding Henry*, 1991; *Random Hearts*, 1999), turning down prestigious action films (*Perfect Storm, The*

Patriot). Ford believes performance in little-seen *Mosquito Coast* (1986) to be his best work. Regarded by public as top action hero, particularly after becoming one in real life, when on July 31, 2000, Harrison piloted private helicopter down in Wyoming to rescue a lost hiker.

ACTION FILMOGRAPHY

A Time for Killing (1967); *Journey to Shiloh* (1968); *Star Wars* (1977); *Force 10 From Navarone* (1978); *Apocalypse Now* (1979); *The Frisco Kid* (1979); *Hanover Street* (1979); *The Empire Strikes Back* (1980); *Raiders of the Lost Ark* (1981); *Blade Runner* (1982); *Return of the Jedi* (1983); *Indiana Jones and the Temple of Doom* (1984); *Witness* (1985); *Indiana Jones and the Last Crusade* (1989); *Patriot Games* (1992); *The Fugitive* (1993); *A Clear and Present Danger* (1994); *Air Force One* (1997); *Six Days Seven Nights* (1998); *K-19: The Widowmaker* (2001).

MUST-SEE

Star Wars: See chapter 12.

Raiders of the Lost Ark: See chapter 9.

Blade Runner (Ridley Scott, dir.). Dazzling near-future action thriller. Ford is the dogged agent tracking down runaway cyborgs in Asian-dominated L.A., where black rain never relents, when he falls for lovely target (Sean Young). Highly influential, leading to many imitations. Be sure to catch Director's Cut (at 117 min.), which omits the cloying narration.

Indiana Jones and the Last Crusade (Steven Spielberg, dir.). Big improvement over second installment, almost as terrific as *Raiders*. Father (Sean Connery)/son (Ford) relationship neatly balanced with some of the most memorable action sequences ever staged. Ford and Connery are in memorable competition for gorgeous Nazi Alison Doody.

Patriot Games (Philip Noyce, dir.). Ford assumes role of Jack Ryan, seeming far more at home than Alec Baldwin in *Hunt for Red October* (1990); Sean Bean is a standout as an Irish terrorist on vengeance trail, Polly Walker also notable as a glamorous killer, Samuel L. Jackson strong in a supporting role. Dynamite final-chase sequence!

The Fugitive: See "Tommy Lee Jones" in chapter 14.

Air Force One (Wolfgang Petersen, dir.). Ford is the U.S. President, only his action-movie ways haven't been left behind. Non-stop thrills as motley group of hijackers assume control of title plane in mid-air, not reckoning on toughest president since Teddy Roosevelt.

Mel (Columcille) **Gibson**

Born in Peekskill, New York, January 3, 1956. The entire family (eleven kids in all) moved to Australia when father, a railroad breakman and devout Catholic, decided this was best way to keep his boys from being drafted for Nam. Mel hoped to be a journalist. His sister, believing he had star quality, filled out an application to Sydney's National Istitute of Dramatic Art. Accepted, Mel felt it would be a betrayal of loyal sibling if he didn't attend. Nervous about being onstage, was unable to remain standing for initial performance, played the entire show sitting. Overcoming stage fright, he won roles in minor movies, then joined South Australia Theater Company. Director George Miller picked him for upcoming low budget sci-fi action film, *Mad Max*. A huge hit down under, the film hardly made a stir in the United States. Bigger, better sequel *Road Warrior* caught on internationally, catapulting Mel to action-icon status. Proved his "serious" dramatic abilities in *The Year of Living Dangerously* (1982) and *Man Without a Face* (1993), also directing latter. Acclaimed as a comedy performer in *What Women Want* (2000). Despite such success, he remains in the minds of most viewers an an action hero, first and foremost, owing to the incredibly successful *Lethal Weapon* franchise, and period action films (*Braveheart, The Patriot*). Even his performance as the title character in Franco Zeffirelli's *Hamlet* (1990) emphasized action aspects of the story. Gibson remains true to his father's traditional values; he is still married to his first wife, raising seven children. Mel always taking the family on location with him, afterwards retreating en masse to their isolated home in Australia.

ACTION FILMOGRAPHY

Mad Max (1979); *The Road Warrior* (1981); *Gallipoli* (1981); *Attack Force Z* (1982); *The Bounty* (1984); *Mad Max Beyond Thunderdome* (1985); *Lethal Weapon* (1987); *Tequila Sunrise* (1988); *Lethal Weapon 2* (1989); *Bird on a Wire* (1990); *Air America* (1990); *Lethal Weapon 3* (1992); *Maverick* (1994); *Braveheart* (1995); *Ransom* (1996); *Conspiracy Theory* (1997); *Lethal Weapon 4* (1998); *Payback* (1999); *The Patriot* (2000); *We Were Soldiers* (2002).

MUST-SEE

Road Warrior, The: See chapter 9.

    Gallipoli (Peter Weir, dir.). World War I film for the arthouse crowd, though even diehard action fans will be moved to tears by final shot. Mel and Mark Lee play Australian runners who join British army to do their duty, only to find their athletic skills tested at title battle.

Lethal Weapon: See chapter 9.

Lethal Weapon 2 (Richard Donner, dir.). A rare case of the sequel measuring up to the original, this one really flies! Super addition of love story for Mel, with Patsy Kensit a perfect choice for leading lady. Scene-stealer Joe Pesci adds to the fun. Director's cut runs 119 min. and is worth seeking out.

Braveheart: See chapter 6.

Ransom (Ron Howard, dir.). Well-crafted Hollywood product neatly transforms from suspense flick to action thriller, as millionaire Gibson goes after baddies who kidnapped his son. Underappreciated actors Gary Sinese and Delroy Lindo add to the fireworks.

We Were Soldiers: See chapter 19.

Bruce Lee (Lee Yuen Kam)

Born in San Francisco, November 27, 1941. At age 3 months, Bruce made his stage premiere at Cantonese Opera Company where his father was a performer. Family returned to Kowloon in Hong Kong, Lee became a successful child actor in Asian film industry as "Lee Siu Lung." At age 13, he was badly

Bruce Lee (with Chuck Norris) in *Return of the Dragon*.

beaten by a street gang, began taking "wing chun" lessons with master Sifu Yip Man. Five years later, he won 1958 boxing championships but he ran afoul of the law due to street fights. The family sent then 19-year-old to America. Soon, Lee was teaching martial arts and studying philosophy at the University of Washington. Fell in love (with Anglo Linda Emery). Opened Jun Fan Kung-Fu academy, insisted on teaching students of any race, a slap in the face to "closed" Asian tradition. Controversial for combining diverse forms (American boxing, Japanese karate, Thai kickboxing) into new venue called JKD (Jeet Kune Do), and unique "one-inch punch" (arm extended, hitting opponent by twitching shoulder muscle). Shortly thereafter, arrived in L.A., taught stars (McQueen, Coburn) when not appearing as sidekick "Kato" on *The Green Hornet*. Returned to Hong Kong with Coburn, researched martial arts film they hoped to make, discovered *Hornet* most popular show in Asia. Studios barraged Lee with offers. He wrote and starred in three movies, still deeply disappointed when lead role in ABC series *The Warrior* (conceived as a vehicle for Lee) went to David Carradine, retitled *Kung-Fu*. Three years later, Drive-In theaters began booking Asian martial arts movies and Lee became an overnight sensation. Suffered from chronic headaches, and on July 20, 1973, Lee died from cerebral endema. Doctor who examined Lee's body credited actor's demise to combative life. Was buried five days later in the traditional Chinese clothing he'd worn in his best film, *Enter the Dragon*.

ACTION FILMOGRAPHY

The Wrecking Crew (1969); *Marlowe* (1969); *The Big Boss* (aka *Fists of Fury*, 1971); *Fist of Fury* (aka *The Chinese Connection*, 1972); *Enter the Dragon* (1973); *Return of the Dragon* (aka *Way of the Dragon*, 1973); *Game of Death* (1976); *Fury of the Dragon* (1976); *Circle of Iron* (1979).

MUST-SEE

Fists of Fury (Lo Wei, dir.). This second collaboration between director and star, released in the United States as *The Chinese Connection*, is far superior to first in terms of everything from quantity and quality of fight sequences to period-piece (1971) production values. A handsome showcase for Lee's unique brutal-ballet approach to martial arts.

   Enter the Dragon: See chapter 12.

   Return of the Dragon (Bruce Lee, dir.). With full control over script and direction, Lee finally solidified the approach he would have likely taken with future films. The classic confrontation with Chuck Norris in the Roman Colosseum remains Bruce's most famous fight sequence ever. Nice "fish out of water" approach, with wide-eyed Lee in Italy.

Game of Death (Robert Clouse, dir.). Bruce filmed a third of this, his most ambitious project, before his untimely death. Had he completed movie, this may have proven to be his masterpiece. Finished by others, uneven though pros far outweight cons. An incredible cast includes Chuck Norris and Kareem Abdul-Jabbar.

Lee Marvin

Born February 9, 1924, in New York City, Lee was the direct descendent of American aristocracy (Washington, Jefferson). His father was in advertising, mother a fashion journalist. As a youth, expelled from posh prep schools for fighting. He joined the marines and received a Purple Heart for a wound suffered during the June 1944 battle at Saipan. Later claimed he learned to act while trying to appear unafraid as shells landed. A severed sciatic nerve caused Lee to be labeled an invalid on return. He took a job as a plumber's apprentice. Arriving at a local theater to repair a broken toilet, he appeared precisely the right size (6-foot-3) to stand in for sick actor, realized by evening's end that he'd found his calling. Studied in New York, won parts off-Broadway and a small role in *You're In the Navy Now* for he-man director Henry Hathaway. Sensing the prematurely graying performer's potential, H.H. encouraged Marvin to improvise, expanded bit to supporting character. Shortly, found work in both TV and films, typecast—owing to large frame, lumbering gait, laconic manner—as a villain. Lee won lead on NBC's *M Squad* (1957–1959) when producers dared cast against type, Lt. Frank Ballinger meaner than the criminals. Took supporting roles in big action westerns during the late fifties/early sixties, his "serious" dramatic potential realized with scene-stealing role in Stanley Kramer's message movie *Ship of Fools* (1965). When Kirk Douglas turned down dual roles of old lawman and drunken gunfighter in *Cat Ballou*, Lee accepted and won Best Actor Oscar. Finally, he became an A-list action superstar. Such status proved surprisingly brief, owing to poor career choices: Marvin turned down Spielberg's offer to play "Quint" in *Jaws* to do an awful B-western, *The Spikes Gang*. Passed away from a heart attack on August 29, 1987.

ACTION FILMOGRAPHY

You're in the Navy Now (1951); *Hangman's Knot* (1952); *Eight Iron Men* (1952); *Duel at Silver Creek* (1952); *The Glory Brigade* (1953); *The Big Heat* (1953); *Seminole* (1953); *The Stranger Wore a Gun* (1953); *Gun Fury* (1953); *The Wild One* (1954); *The Caine Mutiny* (1954); *The Raid* (1954); *Bad Day at Black Rock* (1955); *Violent Saturday* (1955); *Shack Out on 101* (1955); *I Died a Thousand Times* (1955); *Seven Men From Now* (1956); *Attack* (1956); *Pillars of the Sky* (1956); *The Comancheros* (1961); *The Man Who Shot Liberty Valance* (1962); *Donovan's Reef* (1963); *The Killers* (1964); *Cat Ballou* (1965); *The Professionals* (1966); *The Dirty Dozen* (1967); *Point Blank* (1967); *Hell in the Pacific* (1968); *Monte Walsh* (1970); *Prime Cut* (1972); *Emperor of the North Pole* (1973); *The Spikes Gang* (1974); *The Klansman* (1974); *The Great Scout and Cathouse Thursday* (1976); *Shout at the Devil* (1976); *Avalanche Express* (1979); *The Big Red One* (1980); *Death Hunt* (1981); *Dog Day* (1984); *Delta Force* (1986).

MUST-SEE

Donovan's Reef (John Ford, dir.). Though the work of Ford, this action comedy seems more in line with Howard Hawks. Marvin—in his first big role in a major film—and John Wayne face off as friendly enemies in Hawaii. Fun and fighting, deftly blended.

The Killers (Don Siegel, dir.). Fast, smart version of Hemingway's oft-told short story. Lee and Clu Gulager play the title roles, with Ronald Reagan in his final action film and Angie Dickenson a latter-day femme fatale.

The Professionals: See chapter 18.

The Dirty Dozen: See chapter 18.

Point Blank (John Boorman, dir.). Donald E. Westlake's novel *The Hunter* becomes the great urban crime movie of the sixties. Marvin survives a double-cross on deserted Alcatraz Island, then goes on a vengeance trail with ironic results. Classic film noir story, successfully updated for era's psychedelic filmmaking style.

The Big Red One: See chapter 27.

Steve (Terence) McQueen

Born March 24, 1930, in Beech Grove, Indiana. On-screen persona directly drawn from his own life—a self-destructive rebel always walked his own lonely path, right or wrong. Survived a deeply troubled youth, incarcerated in the Chino home for bad boys, then served a stint in the Marines. Was accepted to Carnegie Institute, expelled after roaring through College of Fine Arts building on a motorcycle. Impressed everyone as a cool, charismatic actor. In 1955, he and Martin Landau were the only two among 2,000 hopefuls accepted by Lee Strasberg to the Actor's Studio. Having been ignored to point of anonymity as child, Steve could compensate only by becoming a superstar, winning the entire world's love. Beginning with the Broadway play *A Hatful of Rain*, Steve combined Richard Widmark's cocky tough guy with James Dean's sensitive youth. This led to a three-year stint on a TV western *Wanted, Dead or Alive*. Despite numerous box-office flops— *The Honeymoon Machine* (1961), *Soldier in the Rain* (1963), *Baby the Rain Must Fall* (1965)— Hollywood believed in this south-paw's potential. Eventually, he

Steve McQueen in *Bullitt*.

became the highest paid actor of the 1960s, particularly after concentrating on action roles. Was most effective when playing a quiet loner who appears to harbor no loyalty to anyone but himself, then achieves heroic proportions through unexpected last-minute self-sacrifice. A devotee of karate, he studied with Bruce Lee, served as a pallbearer at Lee's funeral. Turned down the great role that went to Robert Redford in *Butch Cassidy and the Sundance Kid*, refusing to accept second billing to Paul Newman. Steve eventually took thankless role of fire chief in *The Towering Inferno* because he'd receive billing over Paul. Passed away on November 7, 1980, while hoping to find a radical cure for an advanced case of lung cancer.

ACTION FILMOGRAPHY

Somebody Up There Likes Me (uncredited, 1956); *The Blob* (1958); *Never So Few* (1959); *The Great St. Louis Bank Robbery* (1959); *The Magnificent Seven* (1960); *Hell Is for Heroes* (1962); *The War Lover* (1962); *The Great Escape* (1963); *Nevada Smith* (1966); *The Sand Pebbles* (1966); *Bullitt* (1968); *Le Mans* (1971); *Junior Bonner* (1972); *The Getaway* (1972); *Papillon* (1973); *The Towering Inferno* (1974); *Tom Horn* (1979); *The Hunter* (1980).

MUST-SEE

The Magnificent Seven: See chapter 18.

The Great Escape: See chapter 18.

The Sand Pebbles (Robert Wise, dir.). Perhaps McQueen's best performance, playing an American sailor on board a Navy vessel cruising the Yangtze River in mid-1920s, the crew finding themselves in the middle of a violent political outbreak. Terrific supporting work by Richard Crenna, Richard Attenborough and Mako. Intelligent, upscale historic action flick.

Bullitt (Peter Yates, dir.). Perhaps the best of the 1960s' urban-cop films, McQueen is perfectly cast as loner-detective who hates his boss (Robert Vaughn) worse than the criminals. Editor Frank Keller, who devised the dazzling mid-movie chase sequence through San Francisco, won a much-deserved Oscar. Solidified S.M.'s supercool image.

The Getaway (Sam Peckinpah, dir.). Old Sam's least discussed film happens to be one of his best. McQueen is surprisingly understated as "Doc," who robs a bank, then spends the rest of the film fighting his way to border. Only liability: New York fashion-plate Ali MacGraw (S.M.'s then-girlfriend), hopelessly miscast as a white trash Texas babe.

Toshiro Mifune

Born April 1, 1920, Japan's greatest movie star was raised in Tsintao (now Qingdao/Shandong), China, to missionary parents. When World War II broke out, Mifune left Manchuria and joined the Imperial Air Force, stationed in Kyushu. Became interested in aerial photography while in service, afterward drifting to Tokyo, hoping to land a job as a still photographer. An

Toshiro Mifune in _Hell in the Pacific_.

old service friend recommended Misfune visit Toho studio and try for an assistant cameraman job, mistaken on arrival for an aspiring actor. Elderly director Kajiro Yamamoto noticed deep inner anger in Mifune's presence that he considered appropriate for a new kind of postwar star, suggested that colleague Senkichi Taniguchi test Toshiro for the upcoming _Shin Baka Jidai_ (1947). Won role and did his own stunts, saving the company the cost of hiring professionals. This led to a meeting with Akira Kurosawa, who'd penned the script. Together, they became the John Ford/John Wayne team of Japan. _Yoidore Tenshi_ (1948) was the first, _Akahige_ (1965) the last of sixteen collaborations, when their relationship ended in a personal feud while shooting the latter project. During a decade and a half, the duo redefined Asian cinema by incorporating elements of Hollywood westerns and gangster films into Japanese situations, transforming the legendary "samurai" into Eastern equivalent of America's action-film tough guy/loner.

Their films, in turn, won a worldwide following, greatly impacting on the new internationalized notion of westerns and other action flicks. Mifune eventually found fame in America thanks to impressions by John Belushi on _Saturday Night Live_, who lovingly mimicked Mifune's samurai mannerisms. Toshiro passed away on December 24, 1997, in Mitaka City, Tokyo, the result of organ failure.

SELECTED ACTION FILMOGRAPHY
(BASED ON CURRENT AMERICAN AVAILABILITY)

Rashomon (1950); *Seven Samurai* (1954); *Master Swordsman* (1954); *Swords of Doom* (1955); *Underworld* (1956); *Throne of Blood* (aka, *Castle of the Spider's Web*, 1957); *Ninjitsu* (1957); *The Hidden Fortress* (1958); *Big Boss* (1959); *Samurai Saga* (1959); *The Bad Sleep Well* (1960); *Last Gunfight* (1960); *Yojimbo* (aka, *The Bodyguard*, 1961); *Kamikazi* (1961); *Sanjuro* (1963); *Cushingura* (1962); *High and Low* (1963); *Legacy of 500,000* (1963); *Sugata Sanshiro* (1965); *Samurai* (1965); *Sword of Doom* (1966); *Grand Prix* (1966); *Samurai Rebellion* (1967); *Hell in the Pacific* (1967); *Red Lion* (1969); *Red Sun* (1971); *Midway* (1976); *Shogun Samurai* (1978); *Winter Kills* (1979); *1941* (1979); *Bloody Bushido Blade* (1979); *Inchon* (1981); *Sword of the Ninja* (1982); *Shadow of the Wolf* (1992).

MUST-SEE

Seven Samurai (Akira Kurosawa, dir.). The original *Magnificent Seven* borrows ideas from American westerns, including those of John Sturges. When this film premiered on the American arthouse circuit, the impact influenced Sturges to mount an internationalized remake. Fine as that one is, it can't compare to the poetic and philosophical choreography of violence encountered here.

Throne of Blood (Akira Kurosawa, dir.). Shakespeare's "Macbeth," reset in medieval Japan. When Birnham wood is supposed to come to Dunsinane Castle, it does so via a flurry of arrows. Highly stylized, almost surreal approach to mythic action adventure.

Hidden Fortress, The (aka *Hidden Castle*): See chapter 15.

The Bad Sleep Well (Akira Kurosawa, dir.). Shakespeare's "Hamlet" done in the style of American gangster film from the thirties, though set and shot in Japan. Mifune realizes his father did not die a natural death and heads out on a vengeance trail. Without this seminal movie, John Woo and Quentin Tarantino could have achieved what they later did on film.

Yojimbo (Akira Kurosawa, dir.). A loner wanders out of a desolate landscape and into a mean little town where two families feud violently. He plays each off against the other, destroying both dynasties and walking away the winner. The inspiration for Sergio Leone's *Fistful of Dollars*, though the original is even better.

Hell in the Pacific (John Boorman, dir.). Mifune and his American counterpart (Lee Marvin) find themselves stranded on a deserted island during World War II. They can't decide whether to kill each other or cooperate in order to survive. Occasionally a bit too heavy-handed as pacifist allegory. Still, a little-seen movie that deserves an audience.

Burt Reynolds

Born February 11, 1936, Burt was, in his early life, a living embodiment of the good ol' country boy cliché, though he is in fact part Cherokee. He attended Florida State University on a football scholarship, emerged as an acclaimed running back. A six-footer, Burt was drafted by the Baltimore Colts, a promising sports career sidelined by a knee injury. Immediately thereafter cast in minor movies and TV action shows—*Riverboat, Gunsmoke, Hawk, Dan August*. Then, everything came together at once. Heston and Brando turned down the role of "Lewis Medlock" in *Deliverance*, Burt (umpteenth choice) received the part by default. Simultaneously, he appeared as *Cosmopolitan*'s first male centerfold, as a result chosen to guest host *Tonight Show*. Burt arrived in black leather and effectively mocked own macho image. This train of events transformed long-time also-ran into a sudden superstar. Like lifelong hero Burt Lancaster, Reynolds attempted to alternate film genres—action movies for one portion of the audience, sophisticated comedies and dramas (e.g., *Starting Over*, 1979) for highbrow clientele. Once too often made horrible choices—Burt agreed to do awful Peter Bogdanovich musical *At Long Last Love* (1975) but turned down James L. Brooks's *Terms of Endearment* (1983). Invested heavily in Dinner Theater (Jupiter, Florida), its failure leading in part to bankruptcy. His comeback film was *Boogie Nights* (1997), though Burt—ever his own worst enemy—fired the agent who nabbed him that part, complaining it had ruined his career. Shortly thereafter, he finally received a long-hoped-for Oscar nomination for his work. Serious illnesses and long-term depression were widely mistaken by the public for AIDS. Wives include Judy Carne (1963–1965), Loni Anderson (1987–1993); significant others, Dinah Shore (apprx. 1968–1972) and Sally Field (apprx. 1973–1979).

ACTION FILMOGRAPHY

Armored Command (1961); *Operation C.I.A.* (1965); *Navajo Joe* (1966); *Sam Whiskey* (1969); *100 Rifles* (1969); *Impasse* (1969); *Shark!* (1969); *Run, Simon, Run* (1970); *Fuzz* (1972); *Deliverance* (1972); *Shamus* (1973); *The Man Who Loved Cat Dancing* (1973); *White Lightning* (1973); *The Longest Yard* (1974);

Hustle (1975); *Gator* (1976); *Smokey and the Bandit* (1977); *Semi-Tough* (1977); *Hooper* (1978); *Smokey and the Bandit II* (1980); *The Cannonball Run* (1981); *Sharky's Machine* (1981); *Stroker Ace* (1983); *Smokey and the Bandit 3* (cameo, 1983); *Cannonball Run II* (1984); *City Heat* (1984); *Stick* (1985); *Heat* (1987); *Malone* (1987); *Rent-a-Cop* (1988); *The Crew* (2000); *Driven* (2002).

MUST-SEE

Deliverance: See chapter 12.

The Man Who Loved Cat Dancing: see chapter 15.

White Lightning (Joseph Sargent, dir.). Good ol' boy outing about moonshiner Burt. First of his backwoods vehicles, and good of its kind. Bo Hopkins and Matt Clark provide laughs.

The Longest Yard (Robert Aldrich, dir.). Brilliant resetting of *The Dirty Dozen* (from the same director) in a prison. A football game between prisoners and the guards provides terrific opportunities for sports action. Burt's actual gridiron experience adds an extra touch of authenticity. His casual style of comic acting never worked so well as here.

Sharky's Machine (Burt Reynolds, dir.). Burt in top form, both as an action hero and project director. A top-flight police team sets out to stop crime lord Vittorio Gassman, Reynolds ironically falls for his enemy's high-priced hooker (Rachel Ward). Bolstered by strong cast—Brian Keith, Henry Silva, Charles Durning—and well-staged action.

Smokey and the Bandit (Hal Needham, dir.). America's mid-seventies' country-outlaw craze reached its height with this near-perfect update of the old Mack Sennett slapstick comedies about speeding cars and incompetent cops. Jackie Gleason pursues good ol' Burt and Sally Field cross-country. Superb action comedy, directed by a top stuntman. Believe it or not, Alfred Hitchcock's favorite film!

Hooper (Hal Needham, dir.). Burt and Sally Field, then an item, portray virtual renderings of themselves in an action comedy about making action comedies. Jan Michael Vincent plays a young hotshot stuntman, Brian Keith appears as real-life actor/stuntman Jocko Mahoney, Sally Field's father in real life and in the film.

Arnold Schwarzenegger

Born July 30, 1947, in Graz, Austria, the son of a destitute police chief. Arnold recalls absence of indoor plumbing, refrigerator, and telephone, though no lack of love. He hoped to join school soccer team but couldn't be admitted until adding bulk—this marked the beginning of his lifelong fascination with weight lifting. At age 15, Arnie joined the army to ensure strict discipline and decent diet. To enter Mr. Junior Europe contest, he went AWOL, winning the title, then spending a year in the brig. A big believer in the American Dream, he set his sights on fame and financial success in the United States. During the next decade, Arnie won Mr. Universe title five of six years, was named Mr. Olympia six years in a row. Lead in a low-budget comedy, *Hercules Goes to New York* (1970) brought in money which he invested in real estate, making him wealthy. Film roles included the following: The tough guy in Robert Altman's *The Long Goodbye* (1973) and a scene-stealing weight lifter opposite Sally Field, *Stay Hungry* (1976). His display of body-building expertise in the acclaimed documentary *Pumping Iron* (1977) made Arnie a household name. Swiftly became a top international action star, beginning with *Conan*. Also branched out to other roles, with comedies, some successful—*Twins*

Arnold Schwarzenegger in *Commando*.

(1988), *Kindergarten Cop* (1990)—others less so—*Junior* (1994), *Jingle All the Way* (1996). Maintained long-term marriage with Maria Schriver, of liberal Kennedy clan, while remaining a staunch Republican conservative. As the century turned, several physical problems hit. This, and box-office setbacks—beginning with *The Last Action Hero*—took some of the edge off his status. Now returning to popular franchises—a third *Terminator* and second *Total Recall* are both currently in the works.

ACTION FILMOGRAPHY

The Villain (1979); *Conan the Barbarian* (1982); *Conan the Destroyer* (1984); *The Terminator* (1984); *Red Sonja* (1985); *Commando* (1985); *Raw Deal* (1986); *Predator* (1987); *The Running Man* (1987); *Red Heat* (1988); *Total Recall* (1990); *Terminator 2: Judgment Day* (1991); *The Last Action Hero* (1993); *True Lies* (1994); *Eraser* (1996); *Batman and Robin* (1997); *End of Days* (1999); *The 6th Day* (2002).

MUST-SEE

Conan the Barbarian: See chapter 9.

The Terminator: See chapter 9.

Predator (John McTiernan, dir.). Fabulous combination of group-action and alien-invasion genres, as a guerrilla task force headed by A.S. wipes out its enemies, then is menaced by a transluscent stalker. Edge-of-your-seat thriller, with devastatingly violent action scenes, first-rate F/X. Supporting cast includes Carl Weathers, Sonny Landham, and Jesse Ventura.

Total Recall (Paul Verhoeven, dir.). Philip K. Dick's legendary sci-fi story *We Can Remember It for You Wholesale!* effectively expanded to a sci-fi action epic. Arnold and Sharon Stone perfectly matched for sharp-edged combat. Expert blending of intellectual premise with enough hardcore violence for genre fans, plus Arnie's top performance to date.

True Lies (James Cameron, dir.). Skillfully mounted tongue-in-cheek spy thriller from the *Terminator* team, Arnold as an agent whose clueless wife (Jamie Lee Curtis, quite terrific) must join him to fight a modern Dragon Lady (Tia Carrere) and her killer clan. Beautifully balances humor with expected action. Final chase over land and sea is a classic bit.

Sylvester Stallone

Born July 6, 1946, in Hell's Kitchen area of New York City to near destitute hairstylist father and a chorus girl mom. Facial and vocal deformities were the result of a difficult birth. A reclusive child, Sly gobbled up superhero comics and imitated their antics, leading to many broken bones. Unable to

Sylvester Stallone in Rocky IV.

conform, he was sent to a Pennsylvania home for delinquents, where athletic abilities were first recognized. This led to a scholarship at Switzerland's American College. While in attendance, Sly taught physical education to girls and also tried dramatics. Moved to New York, supporting himself as a writer (his first love) while picking up bit parts in Woody Allen's *Bananas* (1971), Neil Simon's *Prisoner of Second Avenue* (1974), as well as the lead in a porn film, *A Party at Kitty and Stud's* (1970), aka *Italian Stallion*. He desperately wanted a role (any role) in *The Godfather*, to no avail. Moved to L.A. and out of work, he decided to write a script for himself. Sly caught a boxing match between Ali and virtual unknown Chuck Wepner and set to work on *Rocky*, completing the first draft in four days. Studios offered to buy it if Burt Reynolds or Ryan O'Neal could star, but Sly held out, eventually finding backer for a low-budget film. *Rocky* swept the Oscars in 1976. Subsequent projects failed until *First Blood*, Sly transforming the relatively realistic character into a Nam-era superhero, modeled on those comic-book characters he'd worshiped as child, creating the modern action genre in the process. Four follow-ups to *Rocky* were all dismissed as hackwork. Later attempts to alter image with comedies—*Rhinestone* (1984), *Oscar* (1991), *Stop! Or My Mom Will Shoot* (1992)—failed dismally. Returned to action, with mixed results, until *Cop Land* won strong reviews. Tumultuous personal life, divorcing original wife from the rough times, marrying Glamazon actress Brigitte Nielsen, the relationship ending after numerous *National Enquirer* scandals.

ACTION FILMOGRAPHY

The Lords of Flatbush (1974); *Capone* (1975); *Death Race 2000* (1975); *Cannonball* (1976); *Rocky* (1976); *Paradise Alley* (1978); *Rocky II* (1979); *Nighthawks* (1981); *Victory* (1981); *First Blood* (1982); *Rocky III* (1982); *Rambo: First Blood Part II* (1985); *Rocky IV* (1985); *Cobra* (1986); *Over the Top* (1987); *Rambo III* (1988); *Tango & Cash* (1989); *Rocky V* (1990); *Cliffhanger* (1993); *Demolition Man* (1993); *The Specialist* (1994); *Judge Dredd* (1995); *Assassins* (1995); *Daylight* (1996); *Cop Land* (1997); *Get Carter* (2000); *Driven* (2001).

MUST-SEE

Rocky (John G. Avildsen, dir.). "Sleeper" hit of 1976 won three Oscars, including Best Picture, and deservedly so. A (pardon the pun) knockout in all respects, as Stallone's sad-faced street tough gains self-respect and a girlfriend named Adrian, played by Talia Shire, by fighting—and winning on his own terms—an Ali-like champ (Carl Weathers).

Nighthawks: See "Billy Dee Williams" in chapter 14.

First Blood (Ted Kotcheff, dir.). Sly's first hit after *Rocky*, the film suffers from conflict between Kotcheff's conception of Rambo as realistic victim and Stallone's notion of him as Nam-era superhero. Yet the film survives such turmoil, the chase strikingly played out in grand Pacific Northwest settings.

Rambo: See chapter 9.

Tango & Cash: See "Kurt Russell" in chapter 14.

Bruce (Walter) Willis

Born March 19, 1955, in Idar-Oberstein, West Germany. Army brat Bruce returned stateside when his dad left the service in 1957, taking a civilian job in New Jersey. Despite outgoing ways he suffered from a severe stutter. Refusing to let this restrict success, he ran for and won the presidency of his high school student body. Tried out for plays, realized he could control stutter while reciting dialogue. Drawn to a blue-collar lifestyle, Bruce took a job with the DuPont factory and might have remained there if not for a freak accident that claimed the life of a co-worker. Shaken, he drifted, half-heartedly pursuing career as a harmonica player. Recalling positive experience of theater, Bruce enrolled in Montclair State College, then headed for New York, attending every open audition. To pay bills, he waited tables at Café Central. In time, landed parts in Broadway play, Sam Shepard's *Fool for Love*, plus an ad for Levis 501 Jeans. This exposure brought an invitation to fly to L.A., read for *Desperately Seeking Susan*. Didn't get part, but heard about try-outs for *Moonlighting*. Though unknown, Bruce was picked for lead (opposite Cybil Shepherd) over hundreds of "name" actors when producer Glenn

Bruce Willis in
Die Hard.

Gordon Carol noticed a special spark, at once boyish and knowing. The show's success led to romantic comedy *Blind Date* (1987), with Kim Basinger. Film flopped, as did comedy-western *Sunset* (1988). Then, *Die Hard,* and with it action-hero superstardom. To escape typecasting, Bruce played a variety of roles: Notoriously unsuccessful *Bonfire of the Vanities* (1990), surprise hit *Nobody's Fool* (1994), and disastrous "personal" film, *Hudson Hawk* (1991). Tarantino to the rescue with a juicy part in *Pulp Fiction*, Bruce's career rebounding even as long-term marriage to Demi Moore failed.

ACTION FILMOGRAPHY

Die Hard (1988); *Die Hard 2* (1990); *The Last Boy Scout* (1991); *Billy Bathgate* (1991); *Striking Distance* (1993); *Pulp Fiction* (1994); *Die Hard With a Vengeance* (1995); *Twelve Monkeys* (1995); *Last Man Standing* (1996); *The Fifth Element* (1997); *The Jackal* (1997); *Mercury Rising* (1998); *Armageddon* (1998); *The Siege* (1998); *Bandits* (2001); *Hart's War* (2002).

MUST-SEE

Die Hard: See chapter 9.

Pulp Fiction: See chapter 6.

Twelve Monkeys: See "Brad Pitt" in chapter 3.

Die Hard With a Vengeance: See "Samuel L. Jackson" in chapter 3.

Fifth Element (Luc Besson, dir.). Incredibly appealing futuristic sci-fi. Bruce is a futuristic cabbie (shades of *Heavy Metal*'s "Harry Canyon"!), involved with beautific young woman (Milla Jovovich) out to save the world from total destruction. Satisfying blend of rugged action and offbeat ideas, comically presented in "smart" manner.

Armageddon (Michael Bay, dir.). Critics had a field day dismembering this engaging combination of sci-fi and action. Bruce heads up team that must fly into space and knock an asteroid off its course before it collides with Earth. Holds you from start to finish.

11

MOMENTS TO REMEMBER: CLASSIC ACTION SCENES

None of the following films fits neatly into the action genre. They are epics, biopics, period pieces, romantic adventures, and various other exercises in "serious" cinema. Each, however, contains at least one action sequence fans will want to catch.

Alamo, The (1960). John Wayne, dir. The Duke wanted this, his most personal project, to be the ultimate American epic. Action fans may not want to sit through the lengthy discussions, on every topic imagineable from Jeffersonian politics to the existence of God. But you'll not want to miss two assaults on San Antonio's mission-fortress by the Mexican army, Mexicans on San Antonio's mission-fortress, or an equally terrific counterattack by the Texans on a Mexican encampment during a raid for cattle.

Alexander the Great (1956). Robert Rossen, dir. One of the more thoughtful big-scale ancient-world spectacles Hollywood produced during the 1950s, this drags on too long (141 min.). While the story of Greece's conquering prince (Richard Burton) meanders to the point of tedium, there are four huge battle scenes, not to be missed by action buffs, as Alexander's forces take on diverse enemy armies, defeating them in unique ways.

Ben-Hur (1959). William Wyler, dir. Most of this 212-min. biblical epic is taken up with melodrama, history, and a spiritual message, combined effectively enough to win Best Picture of the Year and ten other Oscars. The two big action sequences are among the most remarkable ever filmed. First, during the battle at sea, the title character (Charlton Heston) saves Roman captain Jack Hawkins from pirates. Then, in the rightly famed chariot race, Ben-Hur competes with Messala (Stephen Boyd), his life-long enemy in a horse-drawn combat in the Colliseum.

Bonnie and Clyde (1967). Arthur Penn, dir. The film that changed everything in Hollywood, this combines elements of French New Wave arthouse items (particularly Jean-Luc Godard's *Breathless*, 1959) and déclassè Drive-In fare (notably, Roger Corman's *Machine Gun Kelly*, 1958), with such strong sexuality and violence that a Ratings-System had to be created to

Charlton Heston wins the chariot race (his stunt double for the trickier scenes was Joe Canutt, son of the film's second-unit director Yakima Canutt) in *Ben-Hur*.

accommodate it. As the title characters, Warren Beatty and Fay Dunaway shoot their way through the 1930s.

Butch Cassidy and the Sundance Kid (1969). George Roy Hill, dir. The same year that Sam Peckinpah surrendered to the darkness with *The Wild Bunch*, this sweet-spirited film arced in the other direction. Nonviolent outlaws (Paul Newman and Robert Redford) share gorgeous Etta Place (Katharine Ross). Action fans won't want to miss a railroad robbery, the leap over a waterfall, or the final shoot-out with the Mexican army in a small town.

Clash of the Titans (1981). Desmond Davis, dir. Ambitious attempt to visualize Greek mythology, as Zeus (Laurence Olivier) gazes down from Mount Olympus on Perseus (Harry Hamlin), first of the heroes. His quest is to rescue beautiful Andromeda (Judi Bowker) from a Ray Harryhausen sea monster. First, though, he stops off on a magical isle to fight the snake-haired Medusa, whose gaze can turn any man to stone.

Gene Hackman blasts a fleeing drug dealer in *The French Connection*.

Fall of the Roman Empire, The (1964). Anthony Mann, dir. Helmed by the man who gave us *El Cid,* it's difficult to grasp how such a lofty project could have turned out so dull. Centurion Stephen Boyd opposes both a crazed emperor (Christopher Plummer) and a barbarian chief (John Ireland). Why don't we care? Still, fine action sequences include a chariot race through the woods, a big battle in the snow, and great gladiatorial action.

French Connection, The (1971). William Friedkin, dir. Breaking all rules for a police procedural, Gene Hackman plays "Popeye" Doyle (based on an actual cop, Eddie Egan) as a nasty, bigoted s.o.b., rather than a conventional hero. Here, he goes up against a "sophisticated" international drug dealer (Fernando Rey). Not to be missed is the chase through New York streets, as the cop in a car pursues a criminal aboard a speeding train, with a devastating conclusion.

Godfather, The (1972). Francis Ford Coppola, dir. This intimate epic portrays America in transition during the mid-twentieth century, as seen through the eyes of a Mafia family. Standouts include Marlon Brando in the lead, Al Pacino and James Caan as his thoughtful and wild sons, respectively, and Sterling Hayden (in his last great role) as a mean-spirited Irish cop. Strong gunfire action amid the brilliant drama.

Greatest Show on Earth, The (1952). Cecil B. DeMille, dir. The old showman combined his cornball approach to gargantuan entertainment with that American institution, the Ringling Bros. Barnum and Bailey's circus. Charlton Heston is the tough road boss, and James Stewart plays a clown who uses his false face to conceal that he's actually a criminal. Numerous action scenes include the best train wreck ever filmed.

Helen of Troy (1955). Robert Wise, dir. This widescreen epic, loosely based on Homer's *Iliad*, suffers from a sentimentalization of the Helen-Paris story, star Rosana Podesta's lack of charisma, and a plodding first hour. Once Greece's thousand ships reach their destination, though, Wise offers two outstanding action sequences: The initial frontal assault on Ilium by Achilles (Stanley Baker) is *dynamite*, as is the Greek descent from the wooden horse and subsequent destruction of the city.

Henry V (1989). Kenneth Branagh, dir. The anti-Olivier, director/star Branagh understands that Gentle Will wasn't so gentle after all—he presented plays filled with as much sex and violence as today's films. Branagh recreates the story of England's sun king as an action epic with two stunning battles: Henry surrounding Harfleur castle, and his archers later devastating the French cavalry at the field of Agincourt.

King of Kings (1961). Nicholas Ray, dir. The story of Christ, treated by the director and star Jeff Hunter with reverence. Around this icon, the always-intriguing Ray built a flamboyant epic. Though much of the 168-min. running time will be of little interest to action fans, there are two incredible sequences in which Barabbas (Harry Guardino)—played here as a Spartacus-like revolutionary—fights the Romans in vividly staged combat. Early on, catch the guerrilla attack on the desert, and later on a full-scale siege on a Roman-controlled city concludes with his warriors all brutally massacred.

Lawrence of Arabia (1962). David Lean, dir. This Brit-produced epic takes an intelligent approach to the factual story of T. E. Lawrence (Peter O'Toole), who enters Araby during World War II and persuades nomadic tribes to join the Allies. The film transformed then-unknowns O'Toole and Omar Sharif (as his guide, "Ali") into superstars. Action sequences, best seen

Cary Grant flees a crop duster who fires machine-gun rounds in *North by Northwest*.

in widescreen, include Arab chieftan Anthony Quinn's cavalry attack and a strikingly rendered raid on an isolated train.

North by Northwest (1959). Alfred Hitchcock, dir. All thrillers contain a dollop of action, though few offer so much as this perfect chase movie. Cary Grant is the wrong man, pursued cross-country both by Russian spies and by American agents. There are two standout set pieces: first, an isolated Grant, menaced by a crop duster in the midwest; later, a battle of wits between Grant and Martin Landau atop Mt. Rushmore's gigantic presidential faces.

Pride and the Passion, The (1957). Stanley Kramer, dir. This elephantine epic (from C. S. Forester's novel, *The Gun*) concerns a British officer (Cary Grant) and a rebel leader (Frank Sinatra) overseeing transportation of an immense cannon to the fort where a military dictator (Theodore Bike)

BIKEL

?

awaits their attack. A fine second unit team under Yakima Canutt creates two excellent action sequences: The cannon's wild ride down a cliff and the assault on a seemingly impregnable fortress.

Searchers, The (1956). John Ford, dir. A towering combination of psychological drama and rugged epic. John Wayne and Jeff Hunter set out on a five-year search to reclaim a girl captured by Comanches. Numerous action scenes along the way, all superbly staged, include a river battle between outnumbered Texas Rangers, led by Ward Bond, and Chief Scar's warriors, as well as the final night attack on the Indian village.

Straw Dogs (1971). Sam Peckinpah, dir. How do you follow up *The Wild Bunch?* With this contemporary tale of an American intellectual (Dustin Hoffman) and his wife (Susan George) as they move to a rural area in England. Like *Deliverance,* this is an anti-romantic allegory—the locals taunt him, seduce his wife, and kill his cat, convinced the milquetoast will back down. Instead, he cleans his glasses for better eyesight, then grabs a gun and goes out to enforce the rules of territorial imperatives, knocking off every last one of them.

War and Peace (1956). King Vidor, dir. Despite the title, this Hollywoodization of Tolstoy's philosophic novel mostly concentrates on family and romantic events in early nineteenth-century Russia. But when Napoleon (Herbert Lom) invades, there follows a series of superb action sequences: The cavalry attack by Bonaparte's elite forces on a precarious Russian position has never been equaled, yet even this is topped by the counterattack, as the Russians wreak havoc on a retreating French division when they desperately attempt to cross a bridge to freedom during wintertime.

12

ESSENTIALS: THE SEVENTIES

In 1969, writer-director-actor Dennis Hopper explained the philosophy behind *Easy Rider*: "I don't believe in heroes anymore." That was understandable, considering our national mood. Two Kennedys and activist Dr. Martin Luther King had been assassinated. The country—from its poorest ghettos to the richest campuses—was aflame, in some cases literally. As a people, we had become more intensely divided than at any time since the Civil War. Yet when ultra-leftist author Eldridge Cleaver (*Soul on Ice*) left in disgust to visit Africa, he found conditions on that continent even *more* terrible for blacks than in America. Cleaver returned home and transformed into an ultra-conservative Republican.

Gradually, as our involvement in southeast Asia wound down, civil rights slowly but surely made progress, and Richard Nixon resigned in the wake of Watergate, a healing process began. As always, our movies reflected our mind-set. *Time* magazine had proclaimed, as the sixties ended, that *Easy Rider* was "the little film that killed the big films." In fact, counter-cultural films released in the wake of Hopper's movie failed dismally at the box office. On the other hand, as the 1970s began, *Airport* drew in old *and* young audiences with its huge scale. In it, old-timer Burt Lancaster saved the day from seeming disaster as he, Charlton Heston, and other traditional heroes had in the fifties and early sixties. Audiences cheered, needing to believe again that a single cowboy/knight could, as in earlier times, get the job done. Now, though, we were too worldly and jaded to accept a bygone notion of the hero. Nor could we if we wanted to. The filmmakers who had invented them for us—Ford, Hawks, Walsh, et al.—had retired. So Hollywood had to reinvent the action hero and, shortly, a group of "movie brats" would do just that.

At this decade's end, we would elect a former action star to the presidency. Ronald Reagan's staunchest supporters included many "radicals" from a decade earlier, including *Easy Rider*'s Hopper. Apparently, even *he* felt the need to believe in heroes again.

Dirty Harry (1971)

CREDITS

Director, Don Siegel; screenplay, Rita M. Fink, Dean Riesner, and John Milius (uncredited), from a story by Harry Julian Fink; producers, Siegel and Robert Daley; original music, Lalo Schifrin; cinematography, Bruce Surtees; running time, 102 min.; rating, R.

CAST

Clint Eastwood (*Callahan*); Harry Guardino (*Bressler*); Reni Santoni (*Chico Gonzalez*); John Vernon (*The Mayor*); Andy Robinson (*The Killer*); John Larch (*Chief*).

Clint Eastwood in *Dirty Harry.*

THE FILM

The early seventies introduced a new kind of cop film, so outrageous in conception that the first choices for the lead—Frank Sinatra, John Wayne, Paul Newman— turned this project down flat. Yet the movie would eventually be made, with Eastwood in the lead. *Dirty Harry* concerns an ultra-conservative rogue cop, pursuing a crazed serial killer. When Harry realizes the bureaucratic system will always stand in his way, he throws away his badge and— acting as judge, jury, and executioner—finds and kills his prey. In the process (and thanks to Don Siegel's mytho-poetic approach), "Dirty" Harry emerged as a larger-than-life legendary figure. Simultaneously, *The French Connection* (1971) redefined the "realistic" cop film (aka, "police procedural") for an upcoming era. Gene Hackman's "Popeye Doyle," anything but a "conventional" NYC detective hero, engaged the modern audience despite many unpleasant quirks—indeed, *because* of them. If we were no longer naïve enough to believe in perfect heroes, we could at least believe in *im*perfect ones. The revised supercop became a violent anti-hero. The opening reveals Eastwood, hot dog in one hand and his huge 44 Magnum ("the most powerful hand gun in the world") in the other, casually crossing a San Francisco street to face off with a would-be bank robber. In retrospect, the film seems less "fascist" (a term bandied about on initial release) than it once did. Eastwood's statements in interviews make clear he perceived this as a cautionary fable dramatizing what can happen if gun control *isn't* enacted. Yet it's important to recall the film was perceived as a "Law and Order" diatribe at a time when that divisive term implied total insensitivity to people of color. On closer inspection, it's obvious that Callahan is utterly oblivious to race. As another cop puts it, "Harry isn't prejudice—he hates *everybody!*"

Jeremiah Johnson (1972)

CREDITS

Director, Sydney Pollack; screenplay, John Milius and Edward Anhalt, from the novel *Mountain Man* by Vardis Fisher and the historical volume *Crow Killer* by Raymond W. Thorp and Robert Bunker, with additional (uncredited) contributions by David Rayfiel; producer, Joe Wizan; original music, Tim McIntire and John Rubinstein; cinematography, Duke Callaghan; running time, 116 min.; rating, PG.

CAST

Robert Redford (*Jeremiah Johnson*); Will Geer (*Bear Claw Chris*); Delle Bolton (*The Swan*); Josh Albee (*Caleb*); Joaquín Martínez (*Paints His Shirt Red*); Allyn Ann McLerie (*Crazy Woman Morgan*); Stefan Gierasch (*Del Gue*).

THE FILM

Having invented (uncredited) the character of "Dirty Harry," film school grad John Milius went on to pen a script that would eventually become *Jeremiah Johnson*, likewise redefining the western hero for a new kind of action movie. Instead of half a buddy-buddy team or part of a community of men, Johnson would (like Harry Callahan) perform as a loner, walking his own road. This is not the historical mountain man, rather a romanticized notion of trappers as uninterested in the profit motive, existing at one with Nature and respecting its unstated laws. Real-life mountain men were despoilers of the woodlands, blithely wiping out beaver and other fur-bearing animals to make money. This, though, was a decade during which "camping out" replaced the traditional family vacation at a motel, so history was altered to create a modern myth that fit the current sensibility. Redford also embodies the notion of a Vietnam veteran, returning from a war he has come to morally question; Jeremiah Johnson offers us history reinterpreted as drama for and about a specific moment in time—by implication, it is a movie about the seventies.

Enter the Dragon (1973)

CREDITS

Director, Robert Clouse; screenplay, Michael Allin; producers, Bruce Lee, Paul Heller, and Fred Weintraub; original music, Lalo Schifrin; cinematography, Gil Hubbs; running time, 97 min.; rating, R.

CAST

Bruce Lee (*Lee*); John Saxon (*Roper*); Kien Shih (*Han*); Jim Kelly (*Williams*); Ahna Capri (*Tania*); Robert Wall (*Oharra*) Angela Mao (*Su Lin Ying*); Bolo Yeung (*Yang Sze*); Betty Chung (*Mei Ling*); Jackie Chan (*Oharra Henchman*); Chuck Norris (*Messenger*); Sammo Hung Kam-Bo (*Shaolin*); Ching-Ying Lam (*Fighter*); Tony Liu (*Pigeon*); Wah Yuen (*Fighter*).

Bruce Lee in *Enter the Dragon.*

THE FILM

Shortly before this film's opening, Bruce Lee died. A cult formed after the film was rated as a financial hit. Critics likewise noted that Lee was not merely a violent brute (on the order of, say, Sonny Chiba) but a balletic/mime performer, employing his body for communication as well as killing. Shortly, his art was being compared to that of Charlie Chaplin, Gene Kelly, and Marcel Marceau. Much of *Enter the Dragon* was shot in Asia by an American director, Robert Clouse. Though his name would never become a household term, the filmmaker would guide numerous kung fu epics to the screen. The plot involves Lee, as an official agent of England, journeying to an isolated location, joining the international martial arts olympics, sponsored by crime lord Han (Shih Kien). Lee's assignment is to infiltrate the criminal organization, incurring the wrath of Han. The film alternates between kung fu demonstrations, Lee taking on one after another competitor and defeating them through brilliant displays of skill, and a James Bond–type thriller, as after hours Lee sneaks around the compound, battling guardsmen and romancing a statuesque blonde (Ahna Capri). The no-nonsense filmmaking created a cinematic equivalent to 1940s' pulp fiction, and the results exerted a huge influence on an evolving aesthetic that would eventually coalesce in the career of Quentin Tarantino.

Deliverance (1974)

CREDITS

Director, John Boorman; screenplay, James Dickey, from his novel; producer, Boorman; cinematographer, Vilmos Zsigmond; running time, 109 min.; rating, R.

CAST

Jon Voight (*Ed Gentry*); Burt Reynolds (*Lewis Medlock*); Ned Beatty (*Bobby Trippe*); Ronny Cox (*Drew Ballinger*); Billy Redden (*Lonny*); Bill McKinney (*Mountain Man*); Herbert "Cowboy" Coward (*Toothless Man*); James Dickey (*Sheriff*).

THE FILM

"This is the weekend they *didn't* play golf," the advertising claimed. Instead, four early-middle-aged Atlanta-area suburban male Yuppies decide to get in touch with Nature and exercise their machismo by riding the Appalachian rapids, divesting themselves of the suited/conformist lifestyle they're bogged down in. But this is an anti-romantic cautionary fable. Instead of having good-ol'-boy fun, they are attacked by a clan of crazed rednecks and must fight their way out. The survivors return home wiser, likely to play golf on future weekends. Released at the height of the back-to-nature craze, *Deliverance* provided a sobering antidote, as an intellectual (Jon Voight) and his pumped-up companion (Burt Reynolds) vie as to who might better resolve their dangerous situation. What begins as a community of men quickly breaks down, though the seeming rugged individualist (Reynolds) must step aside to let a Hamlet-like hero (Voight) test himself against the odds and get the job done. Director Boorman and screenwriter Dickey provided an emotionally riveting, adrenaline-pumping (if somewhat superficial) realization of the metaphysical novel's action-oriented story line. The film delivered an inspiration for *Iron John* and other works addressing the desire within each modern male's breast to come to terms, once again, with his savage heart-of-darkness.

The Three Musketeers (1974)

CREDITS

Directed by Richard Lester; screenplay, George MacDonald Fraser, from the novel by Alexandre Dumas (père); producers, Alexander and Ilya Salkind; original music, Michel Legrand; cinematography, David Watkin; running time, 105 min.; rating, PG.

CAST

Oliver Reed (*Athos*); Raquel Welch (*Constance*); Richard Chamberlain (*Aramis*); Michael York (*D'Artagnan*); Frank Finlay (*Porthos*); Christopher Lee (*Rochefort*); Geraldine Chaplin (*Anna of Austria*); Simon Ward (*Buckingham*); Faye Dunaway (*Milady de Winter*); Charlton Heston (*Cardinal Richelieu*); Jean-Pierre Cassel (*King Louis XIII*); Spike Milligan (*M. Bonancieux*); Roy Kinnear (*Planchet*).

THE FILM

In the years between *Easy Rider* (1969) and *Mean Streets* (1973), numerous observers of commercial cinema insisted that the old-fashioned costume picture was dead and gone. All that was wanting, however, was a film able to reinvigorate swashbucklers for the modern audience in the same way *The Wild Bunch* had the western. This occurred when Richard Lester, who helmed the beloved Beatle movies of the mid-sixties, was hired to bring this literary chestnut to the screen. The story remains the same: young D'Artagnan journeys to the French court in hopes of joining the musketeers, where he's taken under the wing of handsome Aramis, serious Athos, and plump Porthos. Together, the foursome fights guards employed by Cardinal Richelieu. But if the narrative remained unchanged, everything old was now new again. Earlier Hollywood versions tended to play down the royal affair between Queen

Anne and England's Buckingham, to maintain a Hays Office Seal of Approval. Made at the height of the sexual revolution, this version pulled no punches. Lester makes clear that Anne and Buckingham were indeed involved, and takes a devil-may-care attitude toward the scandal. The sword-fights were played with a post-Peckinpah sensibility toward violence, rather than the Old Hollywood's sanitized approach. The tale was shot on locations in Europe, rather than the backlot studio sets that now seem so over-obvious in MGM's 1948 version. At one point, when Richelieu listens in on a private conversation, the film appears to be informed by the Watergate scandal. The cast was wisely chosen, combining top young stars and old pros, as insurance that the public at large, rather than merely the youthful or older portion of it, would be drawn in. This film relates a great adventure for all times in accordance with the specific dictates of its own era.

Jaws (1975)

CREDITS

Director, Steven Spielberg; screenplay, Peter Benchley and Carl Gottlieb, and (uncredited) John Milius and Howard Sackler; from the novel by Benchley; producers, David Brown and Richard D. Zanuck; original music, John Williams; cinematography, Bill Butler and (underwater sequences) Rexford L. Metz; running time, 124 min.; rating, PG.

CAST

Roy Scheider (*Chief Martin Brody*); Robert Shaw (*Quint*); Richard Dreyfuss (*Matt Hooper*); Lorraine Gary (*Ellen Brody*); Murray Hamilton (*Mayor Vaughn*); Carl Gottlieb (*Ben Meadows*); Jeffrey C. Kramer (*Deputy Hendricks*); Susan Backlinie (*Chrissie*). Chris Rebello (*Michael Brody*); TV Interviewer (*Peter Benchley*).

THE FILM

Spielberg approached the traditional monster movie, particularly *Creature From the Black Lagoon* (1954), transforming an example of the once-déclassè genre into the first "summer blockbuster movie"—a film *everyone* wanted to see. Sixty-seven million Americans caught *Jaws*, making it the first film ever to earn more than $100 million on initial release. This changed the way Hollywood perceived the summer season, previously written off as a wasteland

Roy Scheider, Richard Dreyfuss, and Robert Shaw in *Jaws*.

for marginal features. Henceforth, summer would be more significant for major releases than even the Christmas holidays. The term "theme park movie" entered the language, indicating a motion picture (this was the first) that makes viewers feel as if they are actually on a ride. Universal, which released *Jaws*, installed a *Jaws* feature at their California park, leading to a synergy between various entertainment venues that would extend into and define the future of commercial movies. There were those who objected to the impact; for example, Pauline Kael of *The New Yorker* bemoaned an "infantilizaiton of the culture" as people turned their back on socially relevant films, seeking out ever-more-elaborate entertainments that combined comedy, thrills, special effects, and violent action. Yet *Jaws* did reflect (and helped to restore) a sense of community in an America that had become polarized in its pop culture as well as in its politics. Here was a film that spoke to everyone—even as the great Hollywood movies of the past had done—with its *Moby Dick*–like tale of three men in a boat, pursuing a shark that's menacing northeast beaches. Significantly, this being a 1970s' film, they attempt to form a makeshift community but fail, Police Chief Brody ultimately proving to be the rugged individualist who gets the job done.

The Spy Who Loved Me (1977)

CREDITS

Director, Lewis Gilbert; screenplay, Christopher Wood and Richard Maibaum, from the novel by Ian Fleming; producers, Albert R. Broccoli and William P. Cartlidge; original music, Marvin Hamlisch and (James Bond theme only) Monty Norman; cinematographer, Claude Renoir; running time, 125 min.; rating, PG.

CAST

Roger Moore (*James Bond*); Barbara Bach (*Major Anya Amasova*); Curt Jürgens (*Karl Stromberg*); Richard Kiel (*Jaws*); Caroline Munro (*Naomi*); Walter Gotell (*Gen. Gogol*); Geoffrey Keen (*Sir Frederick Gray*); Bernard Lee ("*M*"); Lois Maxwell (*Moneypenny*).

THE FILM

For the first time since *Goldfinger*, a Bond film offered a perfect combination of guns, girls, gadgets, and gimmicks. Moore's third time out worked better than earlier attempts, largely because the writers finally learned to flavor the film specifically for his more sophisticated, less intimidating conception. Everything clicked beautifully: Barbara Bach as the good girl, Hammer horror veteran Caroline Munro as the lethal lady; German actor Curt Jurgens as a less over-the-top supervillain than had recently been the case, and Richard Kiel as his 7-foot-2 steel-toothed (and very much over-the-top) henchman, "Jaws." Even Bond's choice of vehicle suggested that change was in the air, the famed Astin Martin giving way to a hipper white Lotus Esprit. The plot concerns the disappearance of a Royal Naval submarine, the *Polaris*, and Bond's attempt to retrieve it before nuclear warheads can be fired by the villains. Whereas earlier Cold War era films would have had the Soviets be the chief perpetrators, *Spy* allows Bond a working relationship with a beautiful "enemy" agent for the first time since *From Russia With Love* (1963). The Soviets, it turns out, have also lost a sub, so their most deadly (and attractive) agent joins 007, suggesting the dawn of *glasnost* was not all that far off. By this point, the Bond films had long since left any logic and/or connection to the "real" world of spying behind. What made the film work so well was that everyone involved played it as escapist entertainment without pushing the envelope too far.

Roger Moore and Barbara Bach in *The Spy Who Loved Me*.

Star Wars (1977)

CREDITS

Director, George Lucas; screenplay, Lucas; producers, Lucas and Gary Kurtz; original music, John Williams; cinematography, Gilbert Taylor; running time, 121 min.; rating, PG.

CAST

Mark Hamill (*Luke Skywalker*); Harrison Ford (*Han Solo*); Carrie Fisher (*Princess Leia Organa*); Peter Cushing (*Grand Moff Tarkin*); Alec Guinness (*Ben "Obi-Wan" Kenobi*); Anthony Daniels (*C-3P0*); Kenny Baker (*R2D2*); Peter Mayhew (*Chewbacca*); David Prowse (*Darth Vader*); James Earl Jones (*Darth Vader's voice*).

THE FILM

Like Spielberg, George Lucas revealed himself as an ardent film buff. His favorite movies include *Flash Gordon* and *Buck Rogers* cliffhangers, studio B-westerns with gunfighters shooting it out in cantinas, samurai epics (particularly *The Hidden Fortress*), and masterpieces of Russian montage. Lucas rolls them all up into a magnificent melange, creating the true *movie*-movie. *Star Wars* emerged as a virtual apotheosis for everything that ever enthralled a child at some half-forgotten Saturday matinee and, at a later point in that person's life, a film student at an eye-opening arthouse screening. But he had a loftier motive, slipping substance in under the entertaining surface, including the mythic conceptions of Joseph Campbell, who defined the two great hero figures: The enthusiastic hero who, like young Prince Arthur, believes himself to be of humble birth, eventually realizing he's noble while volunteering his services for a grand cause; and the reluctant hero, who does not choose to be bold but finds he can't escape his fate to become just that. These archetypes find new "faces" in the form of Luke and Han. Princess Leia is both modern feminist heroine and throwback to the tough-talking dames created by screenwriter Leigh Brackett for Howard Hawks. There is also, as in Campbell, a notion that metaphysical forces are at work in the universe, here "The Force." Ultimately, *Star Wars* proves less a superficial redux of old clichés than a modernist updating of what had formerly been written off as junk culture. A knowing humor permeates *Star Wars*, suggesting that we fully grasp that we are being conned (earlier audiences weren't aware of this while watching Hollywood entertainment) and loving every minute of it. *Star Wars*

**Harrison Ford in
*Star Wars.***

became a metaphor for our worldview, a modern incarnation of ancient myth that the American (and, in time, international) audience measured itself against. No wonder, then, that its invented idiom became a part of our language. For example, in the early eighties President Reagan chose to damn the Soviet Union, referring to it as "The Evil Empire." And, when he hoped to create a defense system in space, the president referred to that concept as "Star Wars."

Superman (1978)

CREDITS

Director, Richard Donner; screenplay, Mario Puzo, David and Leslie Newman, and Robert Benton, with (uncredited) Tom Mankiewicz, from the comic book by Jerry Siegel and Joe Shuster; producers, Richard Lester (uncredited) and Alexander and Pierre Salkind, and Pierre Spengler; original music, John Williams; cinematography, Geoffrey Unsworth; running time, 143 min.; rating, PG.

CAST

Marlon Brando (*Jor-El*); Gene Hackman (*Lex Luthor*); Christopher Reeve (*Superman*); Ned Beatty (*Otis*); Jackie Cooper (*Perry White*); Glenn Ford (*Pa Kent*); Trevor Howard (*First Elder*); Margot Kidder (*Lois Lane*); Jack O'Halloran (*Non*); Valerie Perrine (*Eve*); Maria Schell (*Vond-Ah*); Terence Stamp (*General Zod*); Susannah York (*Lara*); Jeff East (*Young Clark*); Marc McClure (*Jimmy Olsen*); Sarah Douglas (*Ursa*).

THE FILM

"You'll believe a man can fly!" That was the tag line used to promote this film, put into production after *The Three Musketeers* emerged as a box-office blockbuster. Producer Alexander Salkind sensed that if he salted old stereotypes with contemporary irony, audiences could and would cheer for simple heroes. And what could have been more "simple" than Superman who, in the 1930s, forties, and fifties, stood for truth, justice, and the American way? Superman was ripe for revival, if rethought for a generation halfway between the excesses of Woodstock and the neo-conservativism of Reagan. The tag line was important, since recent developments in F/X made it possible for flying sequences to appear believable, as compared with the crude (if charming) past approach that had George Reeves suspended by visible wires. The initial sequence, depicting the apocalyptic situation on Krypton, was rendered in a mythic manner, cementing the relationship between Superman and his antecedent, Hercules. Superman is a modern re-creation of that ancient legend, serving the same purpose for twentieth-century Americans: a fictional answer to real prayers for a demi-god with human emotions to arrive on the scene and deliver us from evil. No sooner has Clark Kent arrived in "Metropolis," finding work as a newspaper reporter, engaging in a love-hate relationship with Lois Lane, and going up against villain Lex

Luthor, than the tone altered to tongue-in-cheek entertainment. What had once been dismissed as B-budget stuff by parents and teachers was now "respectable" enough to be produced on an A-movie scale, the presence of Oscar winners Marlon Brando and Gene Hackman setting that concept in cement. The generation that came of age in the sixties refused to abandon the best-loved items of their youth, as previous generations had done. "Stay forever young," Bob Dylan instructed us, and the shift in popular entertainment made it abundantly clear that we had listened. Superman carries the American flag while flying, indicating that the pendulum had swung back again, fervent patriotism back in style.

Apocalypse Now! (1979)

CREDITS

Director, Francis Ford Coppola; screenplay, Coppola and John Milius, from the novella *Heart of Darkness* by Joseph Conrad; producers, Coppola and John Ashley; original music, Francis and Carmine Coppola and Mickey Hart; cinematography, Vittorio Storaro; running time, 150 min.; rating, R.

CAST

Marlon Brando (*Col. Walter E. Kurtz*); Robert Duvall (*Lt. Colonel William "Bill" Kilgore*); Martin Sheen (*Capt. Benjamin L. Willard*); Frederic Forrest (*Jay Hicks*); Albert Hall (*Chief Phillips*); Sam Bottoms (*Lance Johnson*); Larry Fishburn (*Tyrone*); Dennis Hopper (*Photo Journalist*); G. D. Spradlin (*Gen. Roger Corman*); Harrison Ford (*Colonel George Lucas*); Scott Glenn (*Capt. Richard Colby*).

THE FILM

Throughout the 1970s, Francis Coppola inhabited a unique niche among movie brats, creating movies with great social relevance (most notably, the *Godfather* films) at a time when most films, particularly action flicks, drifted into mindless/escapist territory. When his grand epic, in which he dared retell a Joseph Conrad classic in the framework of the Vietnam war, finally reached the screen (with a budget topping $32 million, then a near-record), there were those who wondered if an audience existed for such a movie. Fortunately, it did. Coppola dared tap into the still controversial Vietnam experience at precisely that time when the public was at last ready to confront its lingering demons, in part through motion picture representations (*Coming Home* and *The Deer Hunter* had approached the delicate subject two years earlier). In the eighties, Vietnam would be handled both romantically (*Rambo*) and realistically (*Platoon*). In addition to Conrad, Coppola—as influenced by legend as Lucas and Spielberg—had been studying *The Golden Bough* and other works of the ancient imagination. He expressed such ideas in visual terms while telling the tale of an American agent (Sheen) sent downriver with a skeleton crew to discover whatever happened to a brilliant officer, Kurtz (Brando), who had planned to raise up the lifestyle of primitive natives to a more civilized level. After numerous adventures, each anecdote presented in a more surreal style than the previous, the agent discovers Kurtz has "gone over," been dragged down, become a cannibal. Once a civilized man enters the heart of darkness, he will be absorbed by it rather than drag what he finds up into the light. The only sane reaction from civilized men to such an insane situation is expressed in Kurtz's dying words: "The horror! The horror!" John Milius, the man who all but defined the action film early in the decade, wrote the original screenplay. Some of his conceptions, dazzlingly realized by the director, have become associated with the essence of cinema, particularly the breathtaking sequence in which American aircraft swoop down on a native village to the ironic accompaniment of Wagnerian opera and the Rolling Stones.

13

SHAKE 'N' BAKE:
THE DISASTER FILMS

This was the hottest joke making the rounds in the mid-seventies—head for the nearest twin theaters, catch the early show of *Earthquake* at one, then rush over for the later show of *The Towering Inferno* at the other. Presto— Shake 'n' bake! In fact, this unique action subgenre dates back at least to *The Johnstown Flood* (1926). The Windy City went up in smoke during the last act of *In Old Chicago* (1938), everyone in India ended up soggy when *The Rains Came* (1939), and America's most infamous earthquake provided exciting conclusions for *San Francisco* (1936) and *Flame of the Barbary Coast* (1945). The best-known of all doomed ships went down on two occasions, *Titanic* (1953) and *A Night to Remember* (1958).

But those were old adventure films, so the excitement was mostly saved for the end. In modern action movies, the big event serves as the central subject. Besides, there was something about our shattered sensibility in the seventies—having survived the Vietnam war only to plunge directly into the Watergate scandal—that made us fear the very foundations of our society were falling apart, so seemingly unrelated stories served as allegories for what was tearing us apart at the time. All of the following are rated from a low of one star to a high of five in terms of their appeal for today's action fans.

Airport (1970). George Seaton, dir. This is where the genre started. Burt Lancaster (replaced by Charlton Heston in future films) deals with a myriad of possible traumas at a snowed-in airport. Highly enjoyable all the way. ★★★★

Airport 1975 (1974). Jack Smight, dir. Remember Sally Field in *The Flying Nun* and Debbie Reynolds in *The Singing Nun*? Here, Helen Reddy is the flying *and* singing nun, in an airplane that may crash. At least that'll shut her up. ★

Airport '77 (1977). Jerry Jameson, dir. George Kennedy (from the first two films), this time tries to save the sinking plane of a millionaire (James Stewart). Better-than-average cast also includes Jack Lemmon. Worth a look. ★★★

Avalanche (1978). Corey Allen, dir. Trimmed down genre entry. Rock Hudson impersonates a tough guy, opens a huge ski lodge, argues with wife Mia Farrow, as the title event shapes up. Slow, uninvolving until the final event.   ★★

Beyond the Poseidon Adventure (1979). Irwin Allen, dir. Belated sequel to the film that started it all for the seventies. Michael Caine is a looter who steals from the sinking ship, until Sally Field reforms him. Worthless.   ★

City on Fire (1979). Alvin Rakoff, dir. Canada's entry in the disaster sweepstakes. An oil refinery ignites, sending an entire urban area up in flames. Henry Fonda and Ava Gardner look tired and in need of work. So-so special effects.   ★★

Concorde—Airport '79 (1979). David Lowell Rich, dir. One year before *Airplane!* came this, the final *Airport* movie with the title plane in peril, and it's even funnier than the parody. John Davidson, Charo, and Martha Ray star. I'm not kidding.   ★

Daylight (1996). Rob Cohen, dir. An assortment of people find themselves trapped in a tunnel beneath the Hudson River. Sly Stallone must get them out. One more example of today's disaster epics being a cut above earlier incarnations.   ★★★

Deep Impact (1998). Mimi Leder, dir. Journalist Tea Leoni discovers a comet hurtling toward Earth and informs President Morgan Freeman. Can top gun Robert Duvall explode the thing? Recent revival of the genre is far better than many of the orignals.   ★★★★

Earthquake (1974). Mark Robson, dir. Los Angeles rips apart; Charlton Heston tries to rescue the love of his life (Ava Gardner), surrounded by all-star cast. Oscar-winning special effects heighten all-time great "guilty pleasure."   ★★★★

Gray Lady Down (1978). David Green, dir. No, it's not about the sex lives of senior citizens. A nuclear sub sinks, with Charlton Heston, David Carradine, and Stacy Keach among the endangered men. Small-scale, but better than most.   ★★★

High and the Mighty, The (1954). William A. Wellman, dir. The predecessor of all *Airport* films and a huge hit in its time. Hero John Wayne and coward Robert Stack attempt to land a damaged plane. Overlong (147 min.), tepid suds.   ★★

Hindenberg, The (1978). Robert Wise, dir. What's obviously missing here is suspense: We know before it starts how this one is going to end. George C. Scott heads up solid cast playing dull characters. Final F/X are disappointing.   ★★

Charlton Heston attempts to save Ava Gardner in the final action sequence of *Earthquake.*

Hurricane (1979). Jan Troell, dir. Easily the worst film of its genre, an elaborate though unconvincing remake of the John Ford classic with Dorothy Lamour, her part here played by Mia Farrow (!?). Hawaii blows away, but you won't care. ★

Juggernaut (1974). Richard Lester, dir. Omar Sharif realizes his luxury liner is about to explode owing to a terrorist-planted bomb. Richard Harris is a demolitions expert hoping to defuse it. Little-known thriller among the best of its type. ★★★★★

Krakatoa, East of Java (1969). Bernard Kowalski, dir. Forget about the ridiculous "human drama" (played by an embarrassed-looking Maximian Schell, among others), but don't miss the best F/X sequences ever assembled for a volcano flick.   ★★★

Meteor (1979). Ronald Neame, dir. Sean Connery and Natalie Wood among those stuck in one of the genre's worst. As in the recent but far superior *Comet,* the earth is about to be struck. The F/X are even worse than the clichéd script.   ★★

Perfect Storm, The (2000). See "George Clooney" in chapter 3.   ★★★

Poseidon Adventure, The (1972). Ronald Neame, dir. Luxury liner goes belly-up, Gene Hackman leads survivors to safety. Great suspense and special effects redeem superficial drama. Early and good example of the era's disaster epics.   ★★★★

Rollercoaster (1977). James Goldstone, dir. A crazy kid (Timothy Bottoms) plans to blow up an amusement park as Richard Widmark and George Segal set out to stop him. A cut above the average, thanks to convincing characters.   ★★★★

Skyjacked (1972). John Guillerman, dir. Charlton Heston takes over the *Airport* films as a pilot whose craft is hijacked in mid-air. *Hollywood Squares*–type cast includes Roosevelt Grier, Walter Pidgeon, and Leslie Uggams. Fair.   ★★★

Swarm, The (1978). Irwin Allen, dir. "What am I doing here?" best describes the look on Richard Widmark's face, valiantly trying to make something of his role fighting killer bees. Almost as funny as John Belushi's *Saturday Night Live* skit.   ★

Tentacles (1977). Ovidio Assonitis, dir. The disaster-epic equivalent of the spaghetti western, with Henry Fonda and John Huston menaced by a huge squid. Watch Disney's *20,000 Leagues Under the Sea* for a far better rendering.   ★

Titanic (1997). James Cameron, dir. The Oscar-winning smash is indeed brilliant when depicting, in documentary fashion, the ship going down. But the Leonardo DiCaprio/Kate Winslet love story is strictly for women and wussies.   ★★★★

Towering Inferno, The (1974). John Guillerman, dir. One of the best of a bad genre. All-star cast (Steve McQueen, Paul Newman, and William Holden) deals with burning skyscraper. Of course, you have to enjoy watching people *burn* . . .   ★★★★

Steve McQueen successfully saves people from a burning building in *The Towering Inferno*.

Twister (1996). Jon De Bont, dir. Who says they don't make 'em like they used to? Modern F/X allow for a far more convincing depiction of natural disasters. Helen Hunt and Bill Paxton are in the path of an oncoming tornado. Well done.   ★★★★

Vertical Limit (2000). Martin Campbell, dir. Chris O'Donnell must climb the legendary K-2 if he's to save a loved one, though avalanches threaten to stop him. If the plotting isn't always convincing, the action is first-rate.   ★★★

When Time Ran Out . . . (1980). James Goldstone, dir. It's *The Poseidon Adventure* again, only this time Paul Newman and William Holden deal with an exploding volcano. Even diehard fans of disaster epics will want to skip this one. ★

White Squall (1996). Ridley Scott, dir. A motley group of boys find themselves at sea with dictatorial teacher/captain (Jeff Bridges) as a perfect storm hits. Strong drama and superb F/X, neatly delivered by a first-rate director. ★★★★

14

SECOND STRING: THE RUNNER-UP TIER OF ACTION STARS

When you took me, who did you *really* want?

—Sterling Hayden, to his producer at the
conclusion of shooting each film

These are the stars who never quite made it to the top of the action heap. Though a level of success did come, something went wrong, often poor timing—being in the right film at the wrong time or the wrong film at the right time. Consider this a salute to tier two of action heroes, undeniably stars if, just as certainly, not quite superstars.

Tom Berenger (Thomas Michael Moore)

Born May 31, 1949, in Chicago, Illinois. Attended University of Missouri, majoring in journalism. As a lark, he tried out for and won role of "Nick" in production of *Who's Afraid of Virginia Woolf?* Hooked, Tom sought out stage work and did a soap opera (*One Life to Live*). First appeared on screen (along with Richard Gere) as one of Diane Keaton's casual flings in *Looking for Mr. Goodbar* (1977). Dared do then-shocking nude scenes for romantic romp, *In Praise of Older Women*. Impressive appearance in Lawrence Kasdan's *The Big Chill* (1983), yet that film's huge success failed to ignite Berenger's career. Still, he turned down

Tom Berenger in *The Dogs of War*.

155

numerous Tom Selleck/Lee Horsley–type TV action shows to continue pursuing "serious" film ventures. A history buff (Tom collects Civil War memorabilia), he enjoyed playing General Longstreet in *Gettysburg*. Such love of the past explains his desire to executive produce TNT's *Rough Riders* in 1997, playing General Teddy Roosevelt for director John Milius. Disdains the L.A. lifestyle, calling Hollywood a "dog and pony show." When not working, lives quietly in South Carolina with third wife, Patricia Alvaran.

ACTION FILMOGRAPHY

Butch and Sundance: The Early Days (1979); *The Dogs of War* (1980); *Fear City* (1984); *Platoon* (1986); *Last Rites* (1988); *Shoot to Kill* (1988); *Born on the Fourth of July* (1989); *Major League* (1989); *The Field* (1990); *At Play in the Fields of the Lord* (1991); *Sniper* (1993); *Gettysburg* (1993); *Major League II* (1994); *Chasers* (1994); *Last of the Dogmen* (1995); *The Substitute* (1996); *An Occasional Hell* (1996); *The Gingerbread Man* (1998); *One Man's Hero* (1990); *Diplomatic Siege* (1999); *In the Company of Spies* (1999); *Takedown* (2000); *Fear of Flying* (2000); *Cutaway* (2000); *Training Day* (2001); *True Blue* (2001); *Watchtower* (2001); *D-Tox* (2002); *Sea Devils* (2002).

MUST-SEE

Platoon: See chapter 19.

Born on the Fourth of July: See chapter 19.

Sniper (Luis Losa, dir.). Ordinary actioner (a surprise box-office hit in its time) with Tom as a hired gun out to eliminate drug dealer. Never dull, but to call it routine is to be kind.

Gettysburg (Ronald Maxwell, dir.). Originally made for TV, then released theatrically, highly accurate depiction of famed three-day 1863 battle, employing Civil War "re-enactors" for epic scope, with Berenger as Longstreet and Richard Jordan (in final role) as Armistead. From Michael Shaara's *The Killer Angels*, Pulitzer-prize winner.

One Man's Hero (Lance Hool, dir.). Highly personal project for the producer-star. Irish Americans choose to fight against their own country in Mexican American war. Based on an actual incident John Wayne had long hoped to bring to the screen. More than worth a look, but far from the important film Berenger hoped to make.

Michael Biehn

Born July 31, 1956, raised in Lincoln, Nebraska. Sensed early on that acting was what he wanted to do, appearing in local theater productions. Biehn won a drama scholarship to the University of Arizona, though he left before graduation and headed for Hollywood. What seemed "the big break"—a showy part as a crazed killer in *The Fan* (1981), opposite Lauren Bacall—proved instead a possible ticket to oblivion when the film bombed. Came back, though, in little-seen flicks like *Lords of Discipline* (1983). Then, a heroic role in *The Terminator* changed everything. Also appeared in non-action films (including *The Seventh Sign*, opposite Demi Moore, 1988). But action had become his metier, in big movies like *Aliens* and *The Abyss*. *Tombstone* was hit, though after that he was mostly typecast as badguys in ever less prestigious pictures. A TV version of *The Magnificent Seven* was supposed to revive his career. When the series plummeted in ratings, so did any final hopes for true star status. A solid and sometimes exceptional actor, he continues to work, more often than not in B-budget projects that fail to provide the roles his talent deserves.

ACTION FILMOGRAPHY

The Terminator (1984); *Aliens* (1986); *Rampage* (1988); *The Abyss* (1989); *Navy SEALs* (1990); *Timebomb* (1991); *A Taste for Killing* (1992); *K-2* (1992); *Deadfall* (1993); *American Dragons* (1997); *Chain of Command* (2000); *The Art of War* (2000).

MUST-SEE

The Terminator: See chapter 9.

Aliens: See chapter 9.

The Abyss (James Cameron, dir.). Undersea combination of Spielberg's *E.T.* and Cameron's own *Aliens*. Biehn (as the villain) opposes good guys Ed Harris and Mary Elizabeth Mastrantonio as they rescue a sunken sub by their oil rig. Terrific underwater action special effects rightly won an Oscar.

Navy SEALs (Lewis Teague, dir). Biehn, Charlie Sheen, and Rick Rossovich as members of title group, fighting terrorists. Pays off big-time for action fans, though don't expect the script to make sense.

Tombstone: See chapter 6.

Pierce Brosnan

Born in Navan, County Meath, Ireland, May 16, 1953. His father deserted the family and Mom moved to England to study nursing, Pierce then raised by grandparents. When they died, the boy was passed about to various relatives until finally reunited with mother in London, age 10. Her second husband was a fine father figure who took the lad to see his first film, *Goldfinger*. Pierce fantasized about someday playing that part. Dropped out of school, age 15, tried various jobs including fire eater, commercial illustrator, and, at long last, acting. Studied at the Drama Center of London, soon earned rep-

**Pierce Brosnan in
GoldenEye.**

utation as acclaimed stage actor in the West End. Picked to star on *Remington Steele*, as a Bond-like spy, opposite Stephanie Zimbalist. Believability in that role led to his casting as 007 when his TV series came to an end. Ironically, upon this announcement, *Steele* producers decided to extend the show and forced him to honor his contract, Bond going to Timothy Dalton. Several years later, Pierce was finally free and the role went to him. Cassandra, beloved wife of ten years, died of ovarian cancer in 1991. Currently living with Keely Shaye Smith.

ACTION FILMOGRAPHY

The Long Good Friday (1980); *Nomads* (1986); *The Fourth Protocol* (1987); *Taffin* (1989); *Mister Johnson* (1990); *Live Wire* (1992); *GoldenEye* (1995); *Robinson Crusoe* (1996); *Tomorrow Never Dies* (1997); *Dante's Peak* (1997); *Grey Owl* (1999); *The World Is Not Enough* (1999); *Die Another Day* (2002).

MUST-SEE

GoldenEye (Martin Campbell, dir.). Brosnan (finally!) gets to play the part he was born for, making an impressive debut as 007 in a large-scale spy-thriller about devastating events inside Russia. Bond breaks the Cold War climate to investigate. Famke Janssen is the best Bond "bad girl" in a generation, literally crushing her lovers to death between her legs.

    Tomorrow Never Dies (Roger Spottiswoode, dir.). Good, if not great, 007 outing, with Brosnan in fine form, joined by Asian martial arts star Michelle Yeoh as his new partner. Her remarkable ability to perform a variety of action stunts raises this above the ordinary.

    The World Is Not Enough (Michael Apted, dir.). About as good as the contemporary Bond films get, with Sophie Marceau a deliciously duplicitous leading lady, Denise Richards equally sexy as a teenage nuclear physicist babe (!?). Inventive stunts, gags, and gadgets.

James Caan

Born March 26, 1939, in the Bronx, to Arthur and Sophie Caan. Played football while student at Michigan State, then studied at Sanford Meisner's Neighborhood Playhouse in NYC. Old-timer Howard Hawks cast Caan in several films. Then, The New Hollywood's Francis Coppola handed Jimmy several offbeat, demanding parts, most notably a brain-damaged youth in *The Rain People* (1969). ABC's *Brian's Song* (1971) created first major public recognition. Always on deck for Coppola's *The Godfather,* originally set to play the "Michael" role. Film's success put Jimmy on A-list. His own worst enemy, passed up *M*A*S*H* (1970), *One Flew Over the Cuckoo's Nest* (1975), *Apocalypse Now!* (1979) to do minor movies. Married four times, resulting in four sons, one daughter. During 1970s, enjoyed a long-time relationship with *Playboy* centerfold Connie Kreskie. Personal problems and a serious drug habit took their toll. After completing his most personal project, *Hide in Plain Sight* (director as well as star), Jimmy dropped out of films for more than five years, finally returning with notably aged appearance.

ACTION FILMOGRAPHY

The Glory Guys (1965); *Red Line 7000* (1965); *El Dorado* (1967); *Journey to Shiloh* (1968); *Submarine X-1* (1968); *The Godfather* (1972); *Freebie and the Bean* (1974); *Rollerball* (1975); *The Killer Elite* (1975); *A Bridge Too Far* (1977); *Comes a Horseman* (1978); *Gardens of Stone* (1987); *Alien Nation* (1988); *The Program* (1993); *Tashunga* (1995); *Eraser* (1996); *Bulletproof* (1996); *The Way of the Gun* (2000); *The Yards* (2000); *In the Shadows* (2001); *City of Ghosts* (2002).

MUST-SEE

El Dorado (Howard Hawks, dir.). As Mississippi, with a ridiculous hat and oversized shotgun, Caan steals every scene he's in from big boys John Wayne and Robert Mitchum. Hawks's unofficial remake of his own earlier *Rio Bravo* is a hoot all the way, with much engaging action, often played with surprising comic tone. Caan's Chinese bit is hilarious.

The Godfather: See chapter 11.

Rollerball (Norman Jewison, dir.). Caan's most famous action role. He plays the violent star of a futuristic sport. Incredibly prophetic vision and strong stunt work hardly compensate for numbing effect of "hit audience over the head with the theme" approach top an all-star cast in an ambitious but failed attempt to create an allegorical sci-fi epic.

James Coburn

Born August 31, 1928, in Laurel, Nebraska. Following service discharge, Coburn headed for NYC, pursuing a TV acting career. Lanky physique and laconic grin caused him to be compared with both Lee Marvin and Steve

NO ITALICS

McQueen. Film debut in Randolph Scott western, *Ride Lonesome* (1959). Two TV action shows, *Klondike* and *Acapulco*, both flopped. Then, the big break—*The Magnificent Seven* for John Sturges. Coburn proved his versatility with a menacing Texan in high-style thriller *Charade* (1963) and a charming goldbrick in the WWII comedy *The Americanization of Emily* (1964). Then, back to supporting roles in actioners for Sturges and Sam Peckinpah. Finally achieved stardom playing Derek Flint, negligible if undeniably popular riff on the post-Bond superspy genre. Like sometimes co-star McQueen, became interested early on in martial arts and helped to set the pace for its eventual mainstream acceptance. He and Bruce Lee collaborated on a script, *The Silent Flute* (see chapter 15). Eventually won Best Supporting Oscar for "serious" film *Affliction* (1997). Died November 19, 2002.

James Coburn in *The Magnificent Seven.*

ACTION FILMOGRAPHY

Ride Lonesome (1959); *Face of a Fugitive* (1959); *The Magnificent Seven* (1960); *Hell Is for Heroes* (1962); *The Great Escape* (1963); *Major Dundee* (1965); *Our Man Flint* (1965); *In Like Flint* (1967); *Waterhole #3* (1967); *Hard Contract* (1969); *Duck, You Sucker* (1971); *The Honkers* (1972); *Massacre at Fort Holman* (aka *A Reason to Live, a Reason to Die*, 1973); *Pat Garrett and Billy the Kid* (1973); *Internecine Project* (1974); *Hard Times* (1975); *Bite the Bullet* (1975); *Sky Riders* (1976); *The Last Hard Men* (1976); *Midway* (1976); *Cross of Iron* (1977); *Firepower* (1979); *High Risk* (1981); *Young Guns II* (1990); *Deadfall* (1993); *Eraser* (1996); *Keys to Tulsa* (1997).

MUST-SEE

The Magnificent Seven: See chapter 18.
    Hell Is for Heroes: See chapter 27.
    The Great Escape: See chapter 18.
    Duck, You Sucker (aka *A Fistful of Dynamite*, Sergio Leone, dir.). Having

unwisely turned down Leone's offer to play *The Man With No Name*, Coburn collaborated with the legendary director on this Mexican revolution tale. He's the explosions expert, Rod Steiger a populist hero turned bandit. Brilliant from start to finish, with rousing action.

Pat Garrett and Billy the Kid (Sam Peckinpah, dir.). High-rating applies *only* to prints that run 122 min. or longer ("European cut"), *not* the aborted U.S. release version rightly disowned by Peckinpah. Vivid and atmospheric retelling of the Lincoln, New Mexico, range war, with Coburn perfect as tight-lipped Pat Garrett, Kris Kristofferson miscast as New Yorker Billy Bonney.

Bite the Bullet: See chapter 15.

Sky Riders: See chapter 21.

Timothy Dalton

Born March 21, 1946, in Colwyn Bay, Wales. His mixed background includes Italian, English, and others. Was raised (with four younger siblings) in Derbyshire, an upscale neighborhood near Manchester. Saw stage production of *Macbeth* at age 16, immediately set previous interests in sports and science aside to pursue acting. Tim studied at the Royal Academy of Dramatic Art, which he despised, leaving to join Birmingham Repertory Theatre. Film break came with role of young Philip of France in *The Lion in Winter* (1968), after being recommended to producers by Peter O'Toole. *Cromwell* (1970) and *Mary, Queen of Scots* (1971) helped established his reputation as modern swashbuckler. Involved in a long personal and professional relationship with actress Vanessa Redgrave, often co-starring together onstage. Green-eyed, 6-foot-2, Dalton made a dashing Bond, perhaps more like the character as originally conceived by Ian Fleming than any other actor to play the part. For complex reasons, his duo of spy capers didn't click with audiences on the hoped-for level. Producers decided to go with Pierce Brosnan after that.

ACTION FILMOGRAPHY

Permission to Kill (1975); *El Hombre* (1978); *Flash Gordon* (1980); *The Living Daylights* (1987); *License to Kill* (1989); *Brenda Starr* (1989); *Hawks* (1989); *The King's Whore* (1990); *The Rocketeer* (1991); *The Informant* (1997); *The Reef* (1997); *Made Men* (1999); *American Outlaws* (2001).

MUST-SEE

The Living Daylights (John Glen, dir.). Dalton debuts as Bond in first-rate series entry, minus the low-camp antics that had dragged the franchise down. Some of the best stunts and action sequences ever put on film; Maryam d'Abo makes a classy Bond babe.

License to Kill (John Glen, dir.). Worthy follow-up to Dalton's first go-round, marred only by less-than-scintillating pair of leading ladies (Cary Lowell and Talisa Soto). Other than that, non-stop action, all of it convincing (if quite violent for this series).

Richard (St. John) Harris

Born October 1, 1930, in Limerick, Ireland, one of nine children born to a dirt farmer and his wife. Early on, Richard drew the attention of locals for his considerable talent as a rugby player, particularly his powerful tackles. A natural gift for acting earned him a spot at the London Academy of Music and Dramatic Art, where he concentrated on the classics. Prestigious director Lindsay Anderson typecast Harris as a rugby star in the searingly realistic *This Sporting Life* (1963). The role won the near-unknown an Oscar nomination, catapulting him into the big leagues of Brit performers (Richard Burton, Peter O'Toole, etc.). Harris also appeared as a mod-pop performer, his recording of Jimmy Webb's "MacArthur Park" a top ten hit. Played roles in all sorts of films, from spy caper opposite Doris Day in *Caprice* (1966) to musical with Vanessa Redgrave in *Camelot* (1967). Gradually slipped into action-hero

Richard Harris in *Gladiator*.

mold, often in negligible projects. During marriage to Ann Turkel (1974–1981), Richard accepted leads in junk movies so long as she could co-star. Admittedly a heavy drinker, he enjoyed a major comeback as a character actor thanks to *Unforgiven* and *Gladiator*. Died October 25, 2002.

ACTION FILMOGRAPHY

Shake Hands With the Devil (1959); *The Wreck of the Mary Deare* (1959); *A Terrible Beauty* (aka *Night Fighters*, 1960); *The Long and the Short and the Tall* (1960); *The Guns of Navarone* (1961); *Mutiny on the Bounty* (1962); *Major Dundee* (1965); *The Heroes of Telemark* (1965); *The Molly Maguires* (1970); *A Man Called Horse* (1970); *The Deadly Trackers* (1973); *Juggernaut* (1974); *99 and 44/100% Dead* (1974); *Ransom* (1975); *Return of a Man Called Horse* (1976); *The Cassandra Crossing* (1976); *Robin and Marian* (1976); *Orca, the Killer Whale* (1977); *The Wild Geese* (1978); *The Ravagers* (1979); *A Game for Vultures* (1979); *Tarzan, the Ape Man* (1981); *Triumphs of a Man Called Horse* (1982); *Strike Commando 2* (1989); *The Field* (1990); *Patriot Games* (1992); *Unforgiven* (1992); *Gladiator* (2000); *The Count of Monte Christo* (2002).

MUST-SEE

Return of a Man Called Horse: See chapter 15.

The Wild Geese (Andrew V. McLaglen, dir.). Mercenaries (Harris, Richard Burton, and Roger Moore) on a deadly mission in Africa. Action galore, yet desperately in need of a stylish action-director—preferably Peckinpah or Aldrich—to make the material come vividly to life, which never quite happens here. Still, one of Harris's most memorable action vehicles.

Patriot Games: See "Harrison Ford" in chapter 10.

Unforgiven: See "Clint Eastwood" in chapter 10.

Gladiator: See chapter 2.

The Count of Monte Cristo (Kevin Reynolds, dir.). Fine redux of the adventure classic, with Guy Pearce terrific in title role, Richard Harris lending strong swashbuckling support.

Sterling (Relyea Walter) Hayden

Born in 1916, precise date unknown. Following poverty-stricken youth in rural New Hampshire, attended a posh Maine prep school. Chucking it all, Sterling ran off to sea, first as a ship's boy, then commanding his own vessel by age 19. An action hero in real life, Hayden served as a commando for the O.S.S. before Pearl Harbor, the marines during the war, eventually running guns to Yugoslave freedom fighters after. Silver Star awarded for parachute mission into Croatia. A rough-hewn intellectual, he flirted with communism but quickly turned aganst it. Called before the House Committee on Un-American Activities, desperately admitting his one-time radicalism to avoid the blacklist, hating himself in the morning and, in truth, forever after. His career has no consistency—he might appear as the lead in an A-film, then turn around and do a B-movie villain. Perceived acting as a necessary evil, something he did to finance beloved sailing trips. Greatest performance as Jack D. Ripper in Stanley Kubrick's black comedy *Dr. Strangelove* (1964), finally made a comeback one decade later as an Irish cop in *The Godfather*. Spielberg wanted Hayden for "Quint" in *Jaws*, but legal entanglements with IRS kept him from the part. Tarantino envisioned Sterling as the old mastermind in *Reservoir Dogs*, but he'd passed away (cancer) in 1986.

ACTION FILMOGRAPHY

The Asphalt Jungle (1950); *Denver and the Rio Grande* (1951); *Flaming Feather* (1951); *Flat Top* (1952); *Hellgate* (1952); *Kansas Pacific* (1953); *The Golden Hawk* (1952); *Johnny Guitar* (1954); *Prince Valiant* (1954); *Naked Alibi* (1954); *Arrow in the Dust* (1954); *Suddenly* (1954); *Crime Wave* (1954); *The Last Command* (1955); *Top Gun* (1955); *Shotgun* (1955); *Timberjack* (1955); *The Eternal Sea* (1955); *The Killing* (1956); *Battle Taxi* (1956); *Crime of Passion* (1957); *Five Steps to Danger* (1957); *The Iron Sheriff* (1957); *Terror in a Texas Town* (1958); *Ten Days to Tulara* (1958); *Hard Contract* (1970); *The Godfather* (1972); *Last Days of Man on Earth* (1973).

MUST-SEE

The Asphalt Jungle (John Huston, dir.). One of the two film noirs that inspired Tarantino to write *Reservoir Dogs,* arguably the greatest "dark" film of all, as an odd assortment of petty criminals bicker among themselves while planning to take a bank. Gentle giant Hayden reveals quiet dignity. Marilyn Monroe in a showy early role. Taut, tense, terrific.

Johnny Guitar (Nicholas Ray, dir.). Perhaps the most bizarre, Freudian (and prefeminist) western ever made, with Joan Crawford and Mercedes McCambridge shooting it out at the end while "real men" Hayden and Scott Brady stand by and watch. The key inspiration for Sergio Leone's remarkable *Once Upon a Time in the West.*

The Last Command (Frank Lloyd, dir.). Originally planned by Republic for John Wayne (who later did his own Alamo movie). Hayden is James

Bowie in a big-budget (if overly talky) tale of early Texas, with a first-rate staging of the legendary last stand and an equally fine mid-movie fight with Mexican cavalry on the Guadalupe River.

The Killing (Stanley Kubrick, dir.). This is the *other* film that inspired Tarantino's *Reservoir Dogs*, similar to *Asphalt Jungle* but edgier and more off-beat in orientation. A caper flick (this time involving a race track) in which Hayden's sympathetic crook goes up against unfeeling bureaucratic "good guys." You'll never forget the final shot.

Terror in a Texas Town (Joseph H. Lewis, dir.). Finally playing the role he was born for, Hayden is cast as a Swedish sea captain who shows up in the old west. Final fight, with Hayden's harpoon going up against the villain's six-gun, is innovative to say the least.

The Godfather: See chapter 11.

Tommy Lee Jones

Born September 15, 1946, in San Saba, Texas. Jones worked at various visceral jobs—underwater construction, oil rig—yet attended posh St. Mark's prep school in Dallas, admitted on scholarship. Then, Harvard as an English Major. Roommates with Al Gore, Tommy Lee excelled at sports, particularly football, a key player in famed Harvard/Yale '68 tie game. Made Broadway debut in *A Patriot for Me*, 1969. Did a soap opera, *One Life to Live*. A move to L.A. led to first big role as Howard Hughes on a TV mini-series, also bad movies like *The Betsy* and *Eyes of Laura Mars* (both 1978). Finally, found worthwhile work in *Coal Miner's Daughter* (1980) as husband of Loretta Lynn (Sissy Spacek). Pock-marked face and cryptic eyes made him too diffi-cult to cast. An uncertain period followed, Jones finally settling in as an action star, thanks to first-rate TV mini-series *Lonesome Dove* (1989). More recently, began directing, including TNT's acclaimed *The Good Old Boys* (1995), also co-authored the teleplay.

ACTION FILMOGRAPHY

Jackson County Jail (1976); *Rolling Thunder* (1977); *Nate and Hayes* (1983); *Black Moon Rising* (1986); *The Big Town* (1986); *The Package* (1989); *Fire Birds* (1990); *Under Siege* (1992); *The Fugitive* (1993); *Natural Born Killers* (1994); *The Client* (1994); *Blown Away* (1994); *Batman Forever* (1995); *Men in Black* (1997); *Volcano* (1997); *U.S. Marshals* (1998); *Rules of Engagement* (2000); *Space Cowboys* (2000); *The Hunted* (2002); *Men in Black 2* (2002).

MUST-SEE

Under Siege: See "Steven Seagal" in chapter 20.

The Fugitive (Andrew Davis, dir.). Glorious redux of the popular 1960s' TV show, here played more for action than suspense, either way a great "ride" from the first shot to the last. Harrison Ford is fine as the beleaguered Dr. Kimble, though this time around, his obsessive pursuer (Jones, in an Oscar-winning performance) steals the show.

Natural Born Killers (Oliver Stone, dir.). Love it or hate it, you can't ignore this in-your-face update of *Bonnie and Clyde*, from a story by Tarantino. Woody Harrelson and Juliette Lewis terrorize the country, become media celebs. Endless action during which Jones steals every scene he's in.

The Client (Joel Schumacher, dir.). Solid vehicle for Jones as a federal agent attempting to protect a child who has overheard mob plans and was then targeted for elimination. Susan Sarandon likewise tops as a dedicated lawyer. Not that much action, but stick with it.

Men in Black: See "Will Smith" in chapter 3.

U.S. Marshals (Stuart Baird, dir.). Reviving his character from *The Fugitive*, Jones is matched with Wesley Snipes for a suspenseful story. An action chase ensues after an outlaw plane crash-lands, with Robert Downey, Jr. providing effective comic relief.

Space Cowboys (Clint Eastwood, dir.). Charming if geriatric actioner with Eastwood, Jones, James Garner, and Donald Sutherland playing a lovable quartet of aged astronauts who head into space for one last grand mission. Despite such heady competition, Jones owns this movie.

Tommy Lee Jones in *U.S. Marshals*.

Victor Mature

Born June 29, 1913. More than any other actor from Hollywood's golden age, a precursor to today's pumped-up stars (Stallone, Schwarzenegger). In that very different pop-culture climate, Mature never achieved their level of celebrity. Chosen owing to his body-beautiful for the male lead—opposite Carole Landis—in Hal Roach's dinosaur epic, *One Million B.C.* Led to studio contract at 20th Century Fox, cast in everything from the film noir *I Wake Up Screaming* (1941) to the gaudy musical *Footlight Serenade* (1942). Then back to period musclemen, first for Cecil B. DeMille in *Samson and Delilah*, followed by the mighty swordsman in *Demetrius and the Gladiators*, an Indian warrior in *Chief Crazy Horse*, a desert chieftan in *Zarak,* finally that elephant-riding conqueror in *Hannibal*. With advent of the sixties, studio program-pictures disappeared. Like other nominal stars, Vic drifted to Europe, worked in ever-less-prestigious action epics. When such production dried up, so did

Victor Mature (with Carole Landis) in *One Million B.C.*

his source of income. Mature played Samson's father in a 1984 TV version of his famous role. All but forgotten, Vic passed away at age 86.

ACTION FILMOGRAPHY

One Million B.C. (1940); *Captain Caution* (1940); *My Darling Clementine* (1946); *Kiss of Death* (1947); *Cry of the City* (1948); *Samson and Delilah* (1949); *Las Vegas Story* (1952); *The Glory Brigade* (1953); *The Robe* (1953); *Demetrius and the Gladiators* (1954); *The Egyptian* (1954); *Dangerous Mission* (1954); *Chief Crazy Horse* (1955); *Violent Saturday* (1955); *The Last Frontier* (aka *Savage Wilderness*, 1956); *The Sharkfighters* (1956); *Safari* (1956); *Zarak* (1957); *Tank Force* (1958); *The Big Circus* (1959); *Hannibal* (1960); *The Tartars* (1961).

MUST-SEE

One Million B.C. (Hal Roach, dir.). D.W. Griffith—who created the movie myth of cavemen battling dinosaurs early in the silent era—purportedly directed portions of this silly but irresistible mini-epic featuring Mature in loincloth, battling back-projection komodo dragons to save luscious Carole Landis. A wondrous hoot.

My Darling Clementine (John Ford, dir.). Not really an action western, per se, though the O.K. Corral finale is rough stuff. A true American classic, one of the first postwar psychological westerns. Mature (as Doc Holiday) delivers his best performance ever.

Kiss of Death (Henry Hathaway, dir.). One of the all-time great crime/action films tells the tale of a robber (Mature) who, for the love of a girl (Coleen Gray), turns in his former cohorts, with violent and ultimately tragic results. Mature more than adequate, though in truth this terrific film belongs to scene stealers Brian Donlevy and Richard Widmark.

Demetrius and the Gladiators (Delmer Daves, dir.). Follow-up to *The Robe* avoids the talky religiosity of its predecessor, focusing instead on bloody bouts, as well as Mature's forbidden romance with evil Messalina (Susan Hayward).

Violent Saturday: See chapter 15.

The Last Frontier (Anthony Mann, dir.). Offbeat and overlooked western about mountain men Mature and James Whitmore taking jobs as scouts for army, in time realizing they have far more in common with the Indians they're tracking than Anglo society. Catch this one!

Roger (George) Moore

Born October 14, 1927, in Stockwell, London, to a policeman father. He excelled at art and drawing. Roger's first professional job was at an animation company. Out of work in the summer of 1940 when a friend suggested he earn a few dollars by working as an extra on *Caesar and Cleopatra*. Intrigued by the experience, Moore studied at the Royal Academy of Dramatic Arts. Classmate Lois Maxwell would in time play "Miss Moneypenny" to his Bond. During the war, served in Bond-like capacity with Military Intelligence division. After, back to acting. In 1954, Roger was offered contracts with Royal Shakespeare Company and MGM. Noel Coward said, "Go for the money!" Several roles followed, though Moore hit it big on TV: (*Ivanhoe, The Alaskans, Maverick, The Saint*, and *The Persuaders*). Considered for James Bond several times, though always under some contract that kept him from the part until 1975. Played the role seven times before growing too long in the tooth to continue. Married, divorced four times. Semi-retired, Moore is active in UNICEF drives to collect money for impoverished Third World children.

ACTION FILMOGRAPHY

Gold of the Seven Saints (1961); *Rape of the Sabine Women* (1961); *No Man's Land* (1962); *Crossplot* (1969); *Live and Let Die* (1973); *Gold* (1974); *The Man With the Golden Gun* (1974); *Street People* (1976); *Shout at the Devil* (1976); *The Spy Who Loved Me* (1977); *The Wild Geese* (1978); *Escape to Athena* (1979); *Moonraker* (1979); *ffolkes* (1980); *The Sea Wolves* (1980); *For Your Eyes Only* (1981); *The Cannonball Run* (1981); *Octopussy* (1983); *A View to a Kill* (1985); *Fire, Ice, and Dynamite* (1990); *Bullseye!* (1990); *The Quest* (1996); *The Enemy* (2001).

MUST-SEE

Live and Let Die (Guy Hamilton, dir.). Moore's first outing as Bond. The script seems more tailored for Connery's meaner, leaner 007. Jane Seymour plays the heroine, Geoffrey Holder a voodoo practitioner in Caribbean. The theme song, by Paul McCartney and Wings, more memorable than the movie itself. Numerous stunt sequences worth catching.

The Man With the Golden Gun (Guy Hamilton, dir.). Moore continues to make the Bond part his own, with Britt Ekland, Maud Adams the babes. Some good gimmicks, great villain portrayal by Christopher Lee.

The Spy Who Loved Me: See chapter 12.

ffolkes (Andrew McLaglen, dir.). Terrific suspense-action film, a surprise considering the ordinarily mundane director. Moore is in fine form as a specialist in counterterrorism, out to stop destruction of isolated oil rig.

Octopussy (John Glen, dir.). Pretty much everything clicks in this above-par 007 outing, with Maud Adams as the title character. It was the first time that the female lead from a previous Bond film (*Man With the Golden Gun*) came back in a new role, as well as a single woman replacing the old dichotomized good girl/bad girl gambit.

Nick (Nicholas King) Nolte

Born February 8, 1941, in Omaha, Nebraska. A football scholarship to Arizona State University fizzled owing to flunked classes. Nick then sentenced to a five-year probationary period for selling fake draft cards in 1962. Soon appeared in regional theater, studied at famed Pasadena Playhouse. His first lead was as an overgrown adolescent in *Return to Macon County*. The following year, he achieved stardom—and won an Emmy nomination—for the acclaimed mini-series *Rich Man, Poor Man* (1976). Runner-up for career-making role of Han Solo in *Star Wars* (1977), then turned down an offer to play Indiana Jones. An alcoholic, Nick was publicly upbraided by Kate Hepburn after falling down drunk while shooting *Grace Quigley* (1984). Best acting job was in *Q & A* (1990), sadly little-seen police film. Nolte became a latter-day Sterling Hayden, whom he physically resembles, taking roles that more bankable actors turn down, and railing at others in his profession at the Cannes Film Festival, 2000. Married, divorced three times since 1966. Nick has a son (Brawley) with his third wife.

Nick Nolte on the set of *Cannery Row.*

A paradoxical personality, Nick consumes huge doses of vitamins for his health but also smokes.

ACTION FILMOGRAPHY

Dirty Little Billy (1972); *Return to Macon County* (1975); *The Deep* (1977); *Who'll Stop the Rain* (1978); *North Dallas Forty* (1979); *48 Hrs.* (1982); *Under Fire* (1983); *Extreme Prejudice* (1987); *Farewell to the King* (1989); *Everybody Wins* (1990); *Another 48 Hrs.* (1990); *Q & A* (1990); *Cape Fear* (1991); *Blue Chips* (1994); *Mulholland Falls* (1996); *The Thin Red Line* (1998); *The Hulk* (2003).

MUST-SEE

The Deep: See "Robert Shaw" in chapter 14.

North Dallas Forty (Ted Kotcheff, dir.). Nolte excels as maverick member of the title team, running into trouble on and off the gridiron. To call this the best film ever made about football is to drastically underappreciate the impact of the film's rebel versus Establishment theme.

48 Hrs.: See "Eddie Murphy" in chapter 7.

Extreme Prejudice (Walter Hill, dir.). Virtual redux of the kind B-picture that Rod Cameron once starred in for Republic. Nolte's the tight-lipped contemporary Texas Ranger out to stop drug dealer Powers Boothe. Irresistibly straight-faced rendering of beloved clichés.

Farewell to the King: See chapter 15.

George Peppard

Born October 1, 1928, in Detroit, Michigan. Dad a blue-collar building constructor, Mom an opera singer. George dropped out of school to join the marines, afterward worked as a bank clerk and disc jockey, setting sights on civil engineering. Studied at Purdue, graduated Carnegie Mellon. Following Mom's interests, attended classes at Actor's Studio, won Broadway role in *The Strange One*, repeating his part in the 1957 film. Shot to stardom opposite Audrey Hepburn in *Breakfast at Tiffany's* (1961). Elizabeth Ashley, his *Carpetbaggers* co-star, became Peppard's second wife. The couple briefly hoped to share love, family, and careers like Newman/Woodward. Tumultuous breakup ended all such dreams. After, Peppard drifted away from serious acting, pursuing career as an action star. He played lead in *The A-Team*, arguably the most popular TV action series ever. In 1978, the still boyishly rugged six-footer (married to third wife, Sherry Boucher) mortgaged their house to finance *Five Days From Home*, a highly personal project which he directed. When the film failed, so too did his marriage. Heavy drinking and smoking problems led to death from pneumonia on May 9, 1994.

ACTION FILMOGRAPHY

Pork Chop Hill (1959); *How the West Was Won* (1962); *The Victors* (1963); *Operation Crossbow* (1965); *The Blue Max* (1966); *Tobruk* (1967); *Rough Night in Jericho* (1967); *P.J.* (1968); *The Executioner* (1970); *Cannon for Cordoba* (1970); *One More Train to Rob* (1971); *The Groundstar Conspiracy* (1972); *Newman's Law* (1974); *Damnation Alley* (1977); *From Hell to Victory* (1979); *Battle Beyond the Stars* (1980); *Race for the Yankee Zephyr* (1981); *Target Eagle* (1982); *Ultra Warrior* (1990); *Tigress* (1992).

MUST-SEE

The Victors: See chapter 27.

    Operation Crossbow (Michael Anderson, dir.). Shamefully overlooked WWII film in the *Guns of Navarone* tradition (including Anthony Quayle from that film) features Peppard as the team leader on an impossible mission. The battle-sequence finale has never been topped. Best appreciated when viewed in the original widescreen format.

    The Blue Max (John Guillermin, dir.). Terrific WWI aerial stunt sequences, recreating the early use of planes in combat. Ever-watchable James Mason and the natural beauties of of semi-nude Ursula Andress almost compensate for uninvolving central character.

    Damnation Alley: See chapter 21.

    Battle Beyond the Stars: See chapter 21.

Kurt Russell

Born March 17, 1951, in Springfield, Massachusetts. Shortly, Kurt moved to California where father, a former ballplayer, became regular on *Bonanza*. Kurt hoped to follow in dad's original athletic path, though a starring role in 1963 series *The Travels of Jamie McPheeters* led to a ten-year contract with Walt Disney. Kurt appeared in *The One and Only Original Family Band* (1968) opposite Goldie Hawn, who became his life partner fifteen years later when

Kurt Russell in *Escape From New York*.

they met again on *Swing Shift* (1964). Unlike most child stars who feel betrayed after reaching maturity, Kurt viewed it as a blessing. At last, he could play pro-ball, if only second base for the minor league California Angels. But a torn shoulder put him out of the game, so he reluctantly returned to acting. Title role in the acclaimed TV Elvis bio-pic made him a star, Kurt next appearing in *Escape From New York*, comedy *Used Cars* (1980). Occasionally, Russell attempted to break out of the action mold, appearing opposite real-life partner in *Overboard* (1987), which wasn't a hit. Hard to believe, but he won coveted role opposite Stallone in *Tango & Cash* only when first choice Patrick Swayze backed out.

ACTION FILMOGRAPHY

Mosby's Marauders (1966); *Escape From New York* (1981); *The Thing* (1982); *Mean Season* (1985); *Big Trouble in Little China* (1986); *Tango & Cash* (1989); *Backdraft* (1991); *Tombstone* (1993); *Stargate* (1994); *Escape From L.A.* (1996); *Executive Decision* (1996); *Breakdown* (1997); *Soldier* (1998).

MUST-SEE

Escape From New York (John Carpenter, dir.). Near-classic blend of sci-fi and action, with Kurt achieving Eastwood/Stallone status as loner "Snake" Pliskin, on a mission in the devastated New York City of the near future. Great support from Harry Dean Stanton, Lee Van Cleef, and others. One of Carpenter's best before his career fell apart.

The Thing (John Carpenter, dir.). Much-maligned sci-fi action epic is less a remake of Howard Hawks's 1951 suspense classic than a far more faithful adaptation of J. W. Campbell's original short story "Who Goes There?" Every bit as good (and similar to) John Cameron's *Aliens*, which appeared a few years later.

Big Trouble in Little China (John Carpenter, dir.). Highly enjoyable action epic, with tongue firmly placed in cheek, this film recalls the golden age of movie serials. An Asian princess is abducted, so fearless macho soldier of fortune Russell embarks on a rescue mission. Kim Cattrall is on board for glamour.

Tango & Cash (Andrei Konchalovsky, dir.). Clichéd action film clicks owing to strong chemistry between Russell and Sylvester Stallone, independently taking on such supervillains as Jack Palance and James Hong. Well mounted if awfully familiar.

Tombstone: See chapter 6.

Tom Selleck

Born January 29, 1945, in Detroit, Michigan. Attended University of Southern California on a basketball scholarship. Tom planned to study architecture. Those classes were filled, but acting courses listed right above them in the booklet, so he signed up. Interest in machismo activities always evident; as a member of the National Guard, Tom was called up for active duty during Watts riots. Taking theater more seriously, he studied at Beverly Hills Playhouse, leading to small role as Mae West's lover in *Myra Breckinridge* (1970). Following six failed pilots, finally made it in *Magnum, P.I.*, enjoying a great boy's toy, the show's bright red Ferarri. In 1984, won an Emmy for series

**Tom Selleck in
*A High Road to
China*.**

work. Ingenious playing of boyish tough guy caused Steven Spielberg to consider him for Indiana Jones, though rigors of TV contract kept him from doing it. Proved his comic ability in *Three Men and a Baby* (1987). Wisely passed up mediocre movie parts to star in high-quality made-for-TV westerns: *The Sacketts* (1979), *Concrete Cowboys* (1979), *The Shadow Riders* (1982), *Last Stand at Sabre River* (1997), and *Crossfire Trail* (2001). Unapologetic conservative, member of NRA, once engaged in angry TV debate over gun control with Rosie O'Donnell.

ACTION FILMOGRAPHY

Daughters of Satan (1972); *Terminal Island* (1973); *Midway* (1976); *The Gypsy Warriors* (1978); *High Ride to China* (1983); *Lassiter* (1984); *Runaway* (1984); *An Innocent Man* (1989); *Quigley Down Under* (1990); *Christopher Columbus: The Discovery* (1992).

MUST-SEE

High Road to China (Brian G. Hutton, dir.). Tom's belated compensation for not getting to do *Raiders of the Lost Ark* is this similarly old-fashioned if not nearly so great attempt at big-scale flyboy adventure that never quite clicks. Bess Armstrong makes for an uninspired romantic interest, though Selleck is fabulous as the soldier/flyer of fortune. Good stunts

Quigley Down Under (Simon Wincer, dir.). Fine Australian western. Selleck stars as a cowboy down under, protecting damsel (Laura San Giacomo) in distress, fighting wicked land baron (Alan Rickman). A winner all the way, and the only theatrical film so far to properly project Selleck's potential as an old-time western star.

Robert Shaw

Born August 9, 1927, in Westhoughton (Lancashire), England. Father, a doctor, was prone to outbursts of violence owing to his alcohol dependency. Eager to escape, young Robert applied to Royal Academy of Dramatic Art. Soon performed Shakespearean roles at London's Old Vic, appeared in the classic Boulting Brothers comedy *The Lavender Hill Mob* (1951). Picked for the lead in an American action show, *The Buccaneers*, which failed after single season. Shaw then turned to more serious stuff, earning lofty reputation as a novelist (*The Hiding Place*) and playwrite (*Man in the Glass Booth*). Acting roles were mostly as flinty, cynical, dangerously edgy characters in indie pictures, notably Canadian-lensed charmer *The Luck of Ginger Coffey* (1964) opposite wife Mary Ure. Action roles balanced with "serious" parts (i.e., "Henry VIII" in *A Man For All Seasons*, 1966). Early 1970s, when careers of other Brits—Richard Burton, Peter O'Toole, etc.—were fast fading, Shaw became a major staple at Universal, notably as "the mark" in *The Sting*. Heavy-drinking star died of a sudden heart attack on August 28, 1978, while driving in Tourmakeady, Ireland.

ACTION FILMOGRAPHY

The Dam Busters (1954); *A Hill in Korea* (1956); *From Russia With Love* (1963); *Battle of the Bulge* (1965); *Custer of the West* (1967); *The Battle of Britain* (1969); *Royal Hunt of the Sun* (1969); *A Town Called Hell* (1971); *The Taking of Pelham, One, Two, Three* (1974); *Jaws* (1975); *Diamonds* (1975); *Swashbuckler* (1976); *Robin and Marian* (1976); *Black Sunday* (1977); *The Deep* (1977); *Force 10 From Navarone* (1978); *Avalanche Express* (1979).

MUST-SEE

From Russia With Love: See chapter 17.

The Taking of Pelham, One, Two, Three (Joseph Sargent, dir.). Perhaps the best combo thriller/action movie turned out during entire 1970s. Shaw plays the leader of a terrorist operation that takes over a NYC subway train. Walter Matthau the cagey cop who must outsmart his adversary in one hour. Marvelous edge-of-your-seat suspense, followed by an exciting action finale.

Jaws: See chapter 12.

The Deep (Peter Yates, dir.). Irresistible undersea action film with Shaw—in a role written for him by Peter Benchley, author of *Jaws*—the tough old mariner who helps an attractive couple (Nick Nolte and Jacqueline Bisset) search for hidden treasure. The trio is menaced by modern pirates (Lou Gossett and Eli Wallach). Fabulous diving sequences, some strong undersea action.

Black Sunday (John Frankenheimer, dir.). Thomas Harris's popular novel, brought to the screen as a slow-moving suspenser about agent Shaw versus beautiful terrorist Marthe Keller. Main attraction here is her attempt to use Goodyear Blimp to blow up the Super Bowl, leading to exciting finale, though the film meanders while getting there.

Rod(ney Stuart) **Taylor**

Born January 11, 1930, in New South Wales, Australia. Taylor was torn between his creative mother, who wanted Rod to be an artist, and construction-worker father, who hoped he would become a pro boxer. He opted for acting after attending Sydney's Technical and Fine Arts College. Early jobs included performances on Australian radio, then a small role as a pirate in the Aussie-lensed *Return of Long John Silver*. First onscreen lead was in *The Time Machine*. Soon starred in lavish soap operas (*The V.I.P.s*, 1963; *Hotel*, 1967) and Doris Day comedies (*Do Not Disturb*, 1965; *The Glass Bottom Boat*, 1966). Excelled at action roles, including *Hong Kong, The Bearcats, Oregon Trail, Masquerade* all on TV, each lasting only a single season. Unaccountably, Taylor never played James Bond, despite being perfect for the part as conceived by Ian Fleming in a way none of the actors who played 007 were. Best performance ever was as playwrite Sean O'Casey in John Ford's *Young Cassidy* (1964). Settled into character roles, and his performance as a TV exec in 1996's *Open Season* was worthy of (but didn't receive) a Best Supporting Actor Oscar. Happy marriage to third wife, Carol, whom he met in youth but didn't wed until years later.

ACTION FILMOGRAPHY

Return of Long John Silver (1954); *The Virgin Queen* (1955); *Hell on Frisco Bay* (1955); *World Without End* (1956); *King of the Coral Sea* (1956); *The Time Machine* (1960); *Seven Seas to Calais* (1962); *The Birds* (1963); *A Gathering of Eagles* (1963); *The Liquidator* (1965); *Chuka* (1967); *Dark of the Sun* (1968); *The Hell With Heroes* (1968); *Darker Than Amber* (1970); *The Heroes* (1972); *Trader Horn* (1973); *The Deadly Trackers* (1973); *The Train Robbers*

(1973); *Hell River* (1974); *Jamaican Gold* (1979); *Hellinger's Law* (1981); *A Time to Die* (1982); *Open Season* (1996); *Warlord* (1998).

MUST SEE

The Time Machine: See chapter 8.

The Birds (Alfred Hitchcock). Only film by the master of suspense that can be considered an action flick, featuring dazzling F/X sequences of Taylor fighting title invaders in Armageddon-like duel for survival. Hitch always insisted Taylor was the logical heir to Cary Grant's roles, and this stirling performance in a classic work proves him right.

Dark of the Sun (Jack Cardiff, dir.). Mercenaries (Taylor and Jim Brown, making a terrific team) in Africa, involved with rampaging terrorists while searching for a fortune. A huge hit in its time, this serves as a significant predecessor to many modern actions films. Why isn't it better known and more highly regarded among action fans?

Billy Dee (December) Williams

Born April 6, 1937, in New York City. His father was a janitor, his mother an elevator operator. Obvious talent led to Billy Dee's acceptance at the legendary Performing Arts high school, Diahann Carroll a classmate. Enjoyed great success as a painter before and after becoming an actor. Film debut was in *The Last Angry Man* (1959), final film of Paul Muni. In the eartly seventies, when civil rights issues exploded on screen, he avoided then-palpable black-exploitation flick trap by starring in big-scale, middlebrow romances—*Lady Sings the Blues* (1972), *Mahogany* (1975), both opposite Diana Ross—aimed at mixed audience. Appeared ready to assume high-status position as African Amercan star for mainstream viewers. The big (potential) break came with the potent *Star Wars* franchise as Lando Calrissian. Somehow, though, the casting coup didn't pay off. Before long, Williams was playing supporting roles in big movies like *Batman*, leads in direct-to-video features. Downward slump in the late 1990s, particularly after live-in girlfriend Patricia Von Heitman charged him with battery.

ACTION FILMOGRAPHY

Final Countdown (1972); *Hit!* (1973); *The Take* (1974); *Bingo Long Traveling All-Stars & Motor Kings* (1976); *The Empire Strikes Back* (1980); *Nighthawks*

Billy Dee Williams in
Return of the Jedi.

(1981); *Return of the Jedi* (1983); *Fear City* (1984); *Time Bomb* (1984); *Courage* (1986); *Deadly Illusion* (1987); *Number One With a Bullet* (1987); *Batman* (1989); *Secret Agent 00-Soul* (1990); *Marked for Murder* (1992); *Alien Intruder* (1993); *Message From Nam* (1993); *Steel Sharks* (1996); *Moving Target* (1996); *Mask of Death* (1996); *The Contract* (1998); *The Last Place on Earth* (2000); *Good Neighbor* (2001).

MUST-SEE

Hit! (Sidney J. Furie, dir.). Long overlooked but excellent actioner, with Billy Dee and Richard Pryor teamed in tale of government agent out to get the drug dealers he holds responsible for killing his daughter. Taut, intelligent, quite violent but never exploitive.

The Empire Strikes Back (Irvin Kershner, dir.). By far the best of the trilogy, Billy Dee earning his nickname "The Black Gable" as charming rogue who tries to win Princess Leia away from Han Solo. Battle on the ice, drawn from Sergei Eisenstein's Soviet classic *Alexander Nevsky* (1938), sets the pace for the action-laden, appealing second entry.

Nighthawks (Bruce Malmuth, dir.). One more tough cop buddy-buddy team, given an incredible jolt of new energy thanks to the palpable chemistry of Williams and Sylvester Stallone, as they pursue evil Rutger Hauer. Not one weak or dull moment in the film.

Return of the Jedi: See chapter 8.

Batman (Tim Burton, dir.). Fabulous revival of The Dark Knight, with Michael Keaton fine in title role, though Jack Nicholson the whole show as The Joker. B.D.W., introduced as the D.A., didn't get to continue the role (as Two Face) in 1995's *Batman Forever* (the part went to Tommy Lee Jones), but that one wasn't any good anyway.

15

RIPE FOR REVIVAL: FORGOTTEN ACTION FILMS TO REMEMBER

Some of the following were huge hits in their time, then virtually forgotten, while others were unaccountably overlooked on initial release. Each is an excellent example of the genre, many worthy of inclusion in ESSENTIALS. Each of the following is highly recommended for fans of action at its best.

Adventures of Robinson Crusoe (1952). Luis Bunuel, dir. Dan O'Herlihy, Jaime Fernandez. Daniel Defoe's great story—a combination of action adventure and allegory about mankind's propensity for survival—reaches the screen in fine form. This film marks the only time Bunuel (*Viridiana, Belle De Jour*) ventured away from kinky arthouse classics and lent his talents to a macho tale involving a stranded sailor, his "man" Friday, as well as the pirates and wild beasts that threaten them.

Behold a Pale Horse (1964). Fred Zinnemann, dir. Gregory Peck, Anthony Quinn, Omar Sharif. This Hemingway-esque yarn combines macho action, edgy suspense, and keen intellect in a gripping moral fable about Spanish Civil War vets. Peck is the liberal hero who's never forgotten the atrocities committed by a fascist military leader (Quinn). As each grows older, painful memories increase until the only solution is a final man-to-man confrontation between the two.

Billy Jack (1971). Tom Laughlin (aka "T.C. Frank"), dir. Tom Laughlin, Delores Taylor, Kenneth Tobey. Once potent cult film from the late-hippie era now curiously forgotten by almost everyone, and in some respects, with reason—the dialogue and acting are atrocious. Yet there was something to Laughlin's personal vision of a half-Indian Vietnam vet who uses his martial arts skills to protect a southwestern commune of love and peace types from local rednecks. The character earlier appeared in a biker flick, *The Born Losers* (see chapter 21) and (unfortunately) two terrible sequels.

Bite the Bullet (1975). Richard Brooks, dir. Gene Hackman, James Coburn, Candice Bergen, Ben Johnson, Jan-Michael Vincent. Marvelous if largely unheralded western. The stars are among participants in a rugged race across the American west, which, in 1899, is fast fading. The writer-director who gave us *The Professionals* a decade earlier delivers the goods again. Bergen's liberated-female long rider adds a feminist touch to the proceedings, in tune with the advent of women's liberation into the mainstream during the early seventies.

Big Wednesday (1978). John Milius, dir. Gary Busey, William Katt, Jan-Michael Vincent. One of Milius's best as a writer-director, also his least known. The three young actors (all ripe for superstardom) play surfers, traveling the world in search of a perfect wave. Each departs on his own journey toward self-knowledge, coming together at the end in hopes of realizing together the dream they failed to consummate as individuals. Surfing has never before (not even in the documentary *Endless Summer*) appeared more a Zen-like endeavor. Beware shorter prints!

Blue Thunder (1983). John Badham, dir. Roy Scheider, Daniel Stern, Malcolm McDowell, Warren Oates. Huge success on initial release, inspiring TV series takeoff and numerous imitations, *Airwolf* included. A police team (Scheider and Stern) works with helicopters to try and stop one more of those supervillains (McDowell, chewing the scenery) with plans to destroy Los Angeles. Silly melodrama can't put a dent in this film's effectiveness for stunts and action, convincingly staged.

Capricorn One (1978). Peter Hyams, dir. James Brolin, O. J. Simpson, Telly Savalas. The second worst filmmaker to ever labor in this genre (Michael Winner is still champ) came up with a near-classic example of post-Watergate paranoia cinema. The actual moon landing (changed to Mars for the movie), it turns out, was not a triumph for mankind but a disaster that didn't work. To give the country something to cheer for, the government stages and tapes a faux "successful" landing. Shortly, the surviving astronauts realize that, because they know the truth, they must be eliminated.

Circle of Iron (1979). Richard Moore, dir. David Carradine, Roddy McDowall, Eli Wallach. During his tenure as an L.A. kung fu instructor, Bruce Lee became close friends with student James Coburn. They co-scripted *The Silent Flute*, a martial arts project they hoped to co-produce and star in. The project did not jell, so each let it go and moved on. Eventually, the film was made in Israel with a change of title. Esteemed writer Sterling Silliphant provided the script's final draft. Carradine plays the roles originally intended for *both* Coburn *and* Lee, in a work that dramatizes kung fu's more philosophc side.

Dillinger (1973). John Milius, dir. Warren Oates, Michelle Phillips, Richard Dreyfuss, Ben Johnson, Harry Dean Santon. Screenwriter and first-time director Milius transforms the Depression-era rural outlaw myth into something far closer to an elegiac western of the John Ford variety than the usual gangster-crime drama. As Dillinger, Oates recalls Bogie in early films like *The Petrified Forest*. Shoot-outs and robberies staged with a post-Peckinpah approach to the violence. Interesting casting includes Johnson as G-man Mel Purvis and Cloris Leachman as the famed lady in red.

Excalibur (1981). John Boorman, dir. Nigel Terry, Nicol Williamson, Helen Mirren. The best film ever made about Arthurian legend, breathtakingly rendered by a great director. Intriguingly, this is as "informed" by *Star Wars*—Williamson's Merlin is obviously influenced by Alec Guinness as Obi-Wan Kenobi—even as the Lucas films were in large part drawn from Arthurian myth. Epic retelling of Arthur from boyhood to his death, enhanced by a gloriously dark sensibility that perfectly translates Malory's famed book on the subject to the screen. Does a copy of the four hour director's cut exist anywhere?

Nigel Terry (as "King Arthur") in *Excalibur*.

Farewell to the King (1989). John Milius, dir. Nick Nolte, James Fox. Ten years after he penned the screenplay for *Apocalypse Now!*, Milius wrote and directed this more modest action epic that tells the same story from the Brando character's point of view. The setting is Borneo during the closing days of World War II. Nolte plays a Kurtz-like soldier who goes A.W.O.L. in the jungle, hoping to convert tribesmen to the Allied cause. Finding his loyalties tested as he "goes over" to their way of life, he becomes a white warrior legend among the tribesman.

Golden Voyage of Sinbad, The (1974). Gordon Hessler, dir. John Phillip Law, Caroline Munro. Second entry in special-effects artist Ray Harryhausen's *Sinbad* trilogy never quite captures the near-miraculous charm of the original, but that's a minor criticism considering the abundance of riches. The action sequences, facilitated by the charming table top models that Harryhausen employed to create a convincing world of myth and magic, are first rate, particularly a duel between the seafaring hero and a statue with six arms (and six swords) that attacks him.

Harder They Come, The (1973). Perry Henzell, dir. Jimmy Cliff, Janet Barkley. "Diamond in the rough" crime caper, with Cliff supporting himself as gangster while trying for a music career, eventually succeeding as a recording star only to have his earlier evil ways haunt him. Film impressively integrates reggae into the film's sensibility, helping to make this one of the most popular Jamaican productions ever in the United States. "Many Rivers to Cross" is the title of an irresistible song Cliff performs on one of those rare occasions when he's not busy killing people in Kingston.

Hidden Fortress, The (1958). Akira Kurosawa, dir. Toshiro Mifune, Misa Uehara, Takashi Shimura. Surprisingly little-known samurai epic from the master of the form, Kurosawa, featuring his most famous star. The plot will strike you as strangely familiar; this is the movie that inspired *Star Wars*. Strip away the space-fantasy elements and it's all here, as Princess Leia— make that Princess Uhara—and a dedicated warrior (Mifune) escape evil forces and head for her homeland in the company of two lovable peasants who look like R2D2 and C-3P0.

High Wind in Jamaica, A (1965). Alexander Mackenderick, dir. Anthony Quinn, James Coburn. Two pirates capture several small children and become enamored of their seeming "innocence." But this anti-romantic fable reveals that children can be even more deadly than their elders. Imagine a cross between *Treasure Island* and *Lord of the Flies* and you're there. In particular, watch Coburn's cagey acting in his last great character role before taking the lead in the terrible *Flint* spy series.

Last Voyage, The (1960). Andrew L. Stone, dir. Robert Stack, Dorothy Malone, Woody Strode. This forerunner to the disaster epics of the 1970s is better than most. A massive ocean liner sinks, causing passengers and crew members to reveal their true personalities. Stack is in top form as an ordinary guy who's wife (Malone) is trapped in a room that's filling with water. Strode plays the decent crew member willing to risk his life to help. The suspense mounts with the water; action-filled final shot a knockout!

Lighthorsemen, The (1987). Simon Wincer, dir. Jon Blake, Bill Kerr.

Forget about that *Crocodile Dundee* garbage and catch this, a *real* Australian action film. Based on fact, it tells the story of a crack cavalry regiment that, during the first World War, is ordered to take a seemingly impregnable enemy position during the desert campaign. If at all possible, try and catch the original Aussie letterboxed print which, at 128 min., tells the story more completely than the abridged American version.

Lusty Men, The (1952). Nicholas Ray, dir. Robert Mitchum, Susan Hayward, Arthur Kennedy. The best movie ever made about rodeo, particularly what it means to the modern-day cowboys who participate—and I'm *not* forgetting Sam Peckinpah's *Junior Bonner*. In addition to on-location footage, including a death-defying ride on a Brahma bull, what makes this absorbing is a close attention to the addictive aspect of the sport. Mitchum's character, though relatively young, is over the hill owing to an incapacitating lung injury. Kennedy's the newcomer who begs him to be a manager, Hayward the woman they both love.

Man Who Loved Cat Dancing, The (1973). Richard Sarafian, dir. Burt Reynolds, Sarah Miles, George Hamilton. Proof positive that Reynolds could have been a great cowboy star, if only the genre hadn't then been fast fading from sight. He's a rugged outlaw who kidnaps the wife (Miles) of a rich man (Hamilton). At first, she resists, then gradually questions her old values and finally fights alongside her bandit-lover. Talk about a bizarre coincidence—this film was released at the same time that kidnapee Patty Hearst announced she'd seen the light and joined the Simbionese Liberation Army.

Naked Jungle, The (1954). Byron Haskin, dir. Charlton Heston, Eleanor Parker, William Conrad. Forget about the first half of producer George Pal's jungle epic, merely a romantic contrivance about Heston rejecting his mail-order bride because she's a widow (i.e., not a virgin). Cut to the chase, based the famed short story, "Leningen vs. The Ants," to watch the breathtaking assault on a South American plantation by an army of man-eating ants as they cut across a continent, devastating everything.

Naked Prey, The (1966). Cornel Wilde, dir. Cornel Wilde, Ken Gampu. Of the independent action films Wilde directed and starred in once his Hollywood studio contract expired, this is the most interesting. The story is not unlike that of America's John Colter, a mountain man forced to flee on foot from an Indian band that relentlessly tracked him. Here, the story is switched to twentieth-century Africa. The concept of making the chase (and violent combat along the way) a subject unto itself, rather than the climax to a conventional story, helped pave the way for many future films.

Return of a Man Called Horse (1976). Irvin Kershner, dir. Richard Harris, Jorge Luke, Geoffrey Lewis. Dorothy Johnson's eloquent short story "A Man Called Horse" provided a perfect scenario for a pro-Indian action epic, yet the original 1970 film missed the mark. It was, however, a hit, leading to this far superior sequel. This time around, they get the Lakota Sun Dance ceremony right, and tell a worthy tale of a white renegade who fights Anglo invaders alongside his red brothers. The final assault on a fur trader's fort is not to be missed.

RoboCop (1987). Paul Verhoeven, dir. Peter Weller, Nancy Allen, Daniel O'Herlihy. Less "forgotten" than most of the films included here. Still, this huge hit is (surprisingly) rarely discussed when fans talk about *Blade Runner* and other classic combinations of sci-fi and action from that era. Weller is a post-apocalyptic cop in semi-destroyed Detroit, dying in the line of duty only to be brought back as a heroic cyborg. Before long, he takes the vengeance trail. Two awful sequels followed.

Peter Weller in
RoboCop.

Rocketeer, The (1991). Joe Johnston, dir. Bill Campbell, Jennifer Connelly, Timothy Dalton. Certain that they had a superhero hit, Disney hyped this handsome screen adaptation of Dave Stevens's graphic novel from a decade earlier. A smart, funny revival of late 1930s' cliffhangers, featuring a rocket backpack that looks suspiciously like the one in Republic's *King of the Rocketmen* serial. The young hero goes up against Nazi enclaves in and around Hollywood. Dalton is an Errol Flynn–like star with a darker side, Connelly a spunky heroine modeled on Bettie Page. The highlight is a final fight on top of a Zeppelin.

Shaft (1971). Gordon Parks, dir. Richard Roundtree, Moses Gunn. The recent remake was disappointing, but it did have one positive effect—getting people back in touch with the original, one of the very few black exploitation flicks that crossed over and became a mainstream hit. John Shaft is a big city detective hired to find a missing girl, her total innocence never quite allowing him to forget that the man who signs John's paychecks is a drug dealer. Memorable score by Isaac Hayes, an urban-action star himself. Can ya dig it?

Richard Roundtree in *Shaft*.

Sodom and Gomorrah (1963). Robert Aldrich and Sergio Leone, dirs. Stewart Granger, Pier Angeli. The only collaboration between two of the world's great action directors was dismissed by critics as a comic book posing as a biblical spectacle. Shouldn't that be a compliment? Combining techniques from Hollywood's historical films with approaches then used in Italian sword-and-sandals mini-epics, this contains one of the best (and longest) large-scale fights ever filmed—as Lot (Granger) and Hebrew warriors decimate an invading cavalry force by wittily destroying their dam to drown their enemies.

Stunt Man, The (1980). Richard Rush, dir. Peter O'Toole, Steve Railsback, Barbara Hershey. A truly one-of-a-kind movie, part mystery and part action flick, this rates as a film classic, though almost no one's ever seen it. Railsback, at the time hyped for action movie stardom, is a criminal on the lam who inadvertantly appears on the isolated site where a movie is being shot and, in a bizarre accident, causes the stunt man to be killed. To compensate and stay hidden, he volunteers to take the dead man's place, gradually realizing that the director (O'Toole) has a hidden agenda.

Tarzan's Greatest Adventure (1959). John Guillermin, dir. Gordon Scott, Anthony Quayle, Sean Connery. All the usual baggage (Jane, Boy, etc.) are dropped to concentrate on an intense, violent jungle action tale. A believable (and surprisingly sophisticated) jungle king—James Bond in a loincloth—takes on sharply drawn villains, including one played by the future 007. The women (particularly Sara Shane) are also Bond-like in their sophisticated sexuality. A terrific action yarn.

Too Late the Hero (1970). Robert Aldrich, dir. Cliff Robertson, Henry Fonda, Michael Caine. Two years after his great success with *The Dirty Dozen*, Aldrich returned with a similar tale, this time concerning English and Canadian volunteers on a mission impossible in the South Pacific. A box-office dud when initially released, this is in every respect the equal of its more famous predecessor, with longer, more involved, and (truth be told) more involving combat sequences.

Violent Saturday (1955). Richard Fleischer, dir. Victor Mature, Ernest Borgnine, Lee Marvin. In the mid-fifties, Hollywood tried something new: Color noir. This may have been the best, a knockout combination of *The Killers* and *Peyton Place*. Three professional robbers (including Marvin) case a small town, planning to rob the bank. In a parallel story, a mild-mannered husband/father (Mature) goes about his everyday life, unaware he will suddenly clash with killers, as civilized values disappear in a moment of violent truth. An unknown gem.

Wind and the Lion, The (1975). John Milius, dir. Sean Connery, Candice Bergen, Brian Keith. Underappreciated on initial release, this offers a wonderful blend of old-fashioned Hollywood exotic romance (on the order of *The Shiek*) with Peckinpah style violence (a la *The Wild Bunch*). Connery is a charismatic desert chieftan who carries Anglo woman (Bergen) off to his tent. Keith plays President Teddy Roosevelt, who sends in the marines to get her back. Inspired by actual events, this film achieves a happy medium between past and present styles for high adventure and modern action.

Yakuza, The (1975). Sydney Pollack, dir. Robert Mitchum, Takakura Ken, Brian Keith, Richard Jordan. Shortly after the massive importation of Asian action flicks into America, this arty film (written by Paul Schrader and Robert Towne) marked Hollywood's first big budget attempt at portraying Japan's "Mafia." Mitchum (magnificent) is the world-weary soldier of fortune who returns to the East to recover a kidnapped girl, stepping into a hotbed of intrigue and martial arts combat.

Zulu (1964). Cy Endfield, dir. Stanley Baker, Michael Caine, Jack Hawkins. This film paved the way for many of the action films that followed. *Zulu* depicts an actual battle not in compressed form, as the finale to a romantic drama, but as the very subject of the film. Baker plays the commander of 105 South Wales Borderers who, on January 22, 1879, are surrounded and attacked by more than 4,000 Zulu warriors. The unique manner in which Zulus approach combat—literally terrifying their enemies with war chants—and the Brit response is detailed with remarkable accuracy.

16

ACTION BABES: THE WOMEN OF MODERN ACTION

More often than not, early cliffhangers focused on women. Linda Sterling and Kay Aldridge forged entire careers playing such parts—each took a turn as "Nyoka," the jungle goddess. As the modern action movie forged its distinct identity during the seventies and eighties, once-radical feminist ideas made their way into mainstream thinking and popular culture. Modern action babes relied on everything from kickboxing to castration when eliminating their enemies. In the nineties, such women gradually came to equally share the action scene, in movies and on TV, as the celebrity status of Lucy Lawless (*Xena: Warrior Princess*) and Jessica Alba (*Dark Angel*) make clear. Without key precursors, *Lara Croft, Tomb Raider* could not exist as a big-budget franchise. Here are the most notable women of postwar action films—despite its masculine title, this volume wouldn't be complete without them.

PAMELA ANDERSON, veteran of *Playboy* pictorials, the *Baywatch* TV series, and an on-again, off-again tabloid marriage to rocker Tommy Lee, did the bad-ass babe thing in *Barb Wire* (1996), based on a popular comic book about a black-leather blonde.

Pam Anderson in *Barb Wire*.

URSULA ANDRESS. The first Bond babe, in *Dr. No* (1962), her "Honeychile Rider" was anything but helpless. When Bond discovers her rising out of the ocean like Venus on the halfshell, the bikini-beauty pulls a knife in self-defense and knows how to use it.

JEANNE BELL, one of *Playboy*'s earliest African American centerfolds, muscled in on Pam Grier's territory, playing a topless karate expert up against the Chinese Mafia in *T.N.T. Jackson* (1974) for director Cirio Santiago and martial arts fight choreographer Ken Metcalf. Then, she joined Jim Brown, Fred Williamson, and Jim Kelly for their L.A. action flick, *Three the Hard Way* (1974). Jeanne played a modern pirate girl who employs martial arts to free her sister (Trina Parks) from an evil plantation owner (Jayne Kennedy) in *The Muthers* (1976). If you'd like to see her in a more prestigious film, check out the African American woman working in David Proval's bar in *Mean Streets* (1973).

SANDAHL BERGMAN. An offbeat beauty with a perfect body and a strange but appealing face, made her debut as "Valeria," the warrior woman who fights alongside Arnold Schwarzenegger in *Conan the Barbarian* (1982). She slipped into cheap movies, more often than not playing the bad girl, as in *Programmed to Kill* (1986). Another character in that film refers to Sandahl's character as "a Barbie/Rambo killing machine."

HALLE BERRY. The first African American ever to win the Oscar for Best Actress will continue to balance her serious work with status as an action babe, playing "Storm," the heroine who can control the weather, in the *X-Men* films. Latest Bond babe in *Die Another Day* (2002).

SANDRA BULLOCK. One of the many big-league stars who excels at both comedy and drama but also chooses to play action babes, as she's done in *Speed* (1994), *Speed II* (1997), and *Miss Congeniality* (2000).

AHNA CAPRI. One of the first glamour-girls to pump up, flexing her muscles in everything from *Darker Than Amber* (1970) with Rod Taylor to *Enter the Dragon* (1973) with Bruce Lee. She took center stage as an action-heroine as an early incarnation of seductive cinematic hit women in *The Specialist* (1975) for B-budget movie maven Hikmet Avedis.

CARITA. Played a Bodaccia-like warrior woman of ancient England in Hammer's *The Viking Queen* (1967).

HOPE MARIE CARLTON. A *Playboy* alum, played a female James Bond in *Hard Ticket to Hawaii* (1987), made by Andy Sidaris and family—famed for their combination of well-mounted action sequences and softcore porn. She followed that up with *Picasso Trigger* (1988) and *Savage Beach* (1989) for the same team. She left their stable of centerfold stars to appear as the kickboxing babe in Albert Pyun's *Bloodmatch* (1990).

LYNDA CARTER. Played one of television's best remembered bad-ass babes, *Wonder Woman* in the mid-seventies. Before that, she appeared as a (sometimes topless) modern equivalent to Bonnie Parker in *Bobbie Jo and the Outlaw* (1976), a Drive-In item from director/producer Mark L. Lester.

CHERI CAFFARO. Won a Brigitte Bardot look-alike contest sponsored by *Life* magazine. She parlayed her fifteen minutes of celebrity status into cult movie stardom as the first major action-babe of the seventies. Cherry starred as "Ginger," a government-sponsored agent who, like Bond, was licensed to kill. Ginger appeared in three films for her husband, director/ screenwriter Don Schain: *Ginger* (1970), *The Abductors* (1971), and *Girls Are For Loving* (1973). Her last lead, for Schain again, was in *Too Hot to Handle* (1975), playing a hit woman who seduces her marks before doing them in.

MARILYN CHAMBERS. Will always enjoy a footnote in film history as the first truly beautiful X-rated star, thanks to *Beyond the Green Door* (1974). She later attempted to break into mainstream movies, playing a seductive vampire for cult horror director David Cronenberg in *Rabid* (1977) and—in her only bid for action-babe stardom—as a female James Bond in *Angel of H.E.A.T.* (1981).

MAGGIE CHEUNG. Showed her stuff in *Twin Dragons* (1991) with Jackie Chan. She became such a Hong Kong attraction that she actually got to play herself in *Irma Vep* (1996), a French arthouse item about the making of modern action movies.

LANA CLARKSON. A striking 6-footer, appeared as a topless warrior woman in *Deathstalker* (1983). Roger Corman's Cocorde productions then tailor-made *Barbarian Queen* (1985) specifically for Lana. She played "Amethea," an obvious variation on her *Deathstalker* character, this time the lead. Lana showed up in a similar role, but in a more prestigious project, as one of the title characters in John Landis's spoof of beloved junk movies, *Amazon Women on the Moon* (1985), then in *Wizards of the Lost Kingdom II* (1988), making mincemeat out of any male who gets in her way. Her best known character returned (with her name unaccountably changed to "Athelia") in *Barbarian Queen II: The Empress Strikes Back* (1989).

CINDY CRAWFORD. Attempted to make the difficult leap from supermodel to action babe with the box-office disaster *Fair Game* (1995), as a Miami lawyer tracking down a former KGB agent while looking ultra-cool in designer T-shirts.

RAVEN DE LA CROIX. First achieved fame as a notably big-breasted erotic dancer, parlaying this into a role for Russ Meyer in *Up* (1976). She became an action babe for B-budget filmmaker Jim Wynorski in *The Lost Empire* (1983), as a gladiator woman who takes on ninjas and samurai.

JAMIE LEE CURTIS. Having survived the masked menace of John Carpenter's *Halloween,* pumped herself up and became one of the first mainstream stars to reveal muscle tone in the otherwise abominable *Perfect* (1985) opposite John Travolta. This at least led to some tough babe parts, including the role of a Manhattan cop who terminates upscale-criminal Ron Silver in Kathryn Bigelow's stylish neo-noir *Blue Steel* (1990). She joined Arnold Schwarzenegger in James Cameron's *True Lies* (1994) as a spy's spouse who helps her hubbie fight the baddies.

SYBIL DANNING (aka Sybelle Denniger). Appeared on-screen after a brief run as a glamour model. She played "Kriemhild" in *Maiden Quest* (1970), a West German sexploitation remake of the classic silent mythological film *Die Nibelungen* (1924), and was one of Richard Burton's glamorous victims in *Bluebeard* (1972). In search of an image, she was a spy villainess in the inexpensive James Bond copycat film, *Salamander* (1980), opposite Franco Nero. Her first superwoman role was as the Valkyrie in *Battle Beyond the Stars* (1980), a Roger Corman–produced variation on *The Magnificent Seven* by way of *Stars Wars*. This opened a floodgate. She played the gorgeous witch "Circe" opposite Lou Ferrigno in *Hercules* (1983) and, later that same year, the equally evil Angel, a coke-dealing criminal in *Jungle Warriors*. The following year, she reteamed with Ferrigno for another Golan/Globus mini epic, *The Seven Magnificent Gladiators*. Then Sybil cinched her image as B-budget bad girl as a cruel countess in Andy Sidaris's *Malibu Express* (1984). Perhaps her standout role is as the title character in *Warrior Queen* (1985), one of the many proto-*Xena* films, for action/quickie expert Chuck Vincent. As younger action babes began to win the prime roles in exploitation flicks, she attempted to produce her own pictures. This began with *Panther Squad* (1984), a weak all-female *Dirty Dozen* variation, then spoofed her own galaxy girl image in a spaced-out sex comedy, *The Phantom Empire* (1986).

CAMERON DIAZ. Proved the action-babe model has finally become respectable. One of today's most sought-after stars, she comfortably moved from such serious stuff as *Being John Malkovich* (1999) to the karate kicking babe in *Charlie's Angels* (2000).

LUCINDA DICKEY. First revealed her perfectly pumped-up body in *Breakin'* (1984) and *Electric Bugaloo* (1984), break-dancing exploitation flicks. Next, her magnificent muscle tone was on view in *Ninja III: The Domination* (1984), playing an Arizona teenager who suddenly kills an incredible number of people with martial arts skills, including a hot tub full of beautiful hookers. She convincingly holds her own in a fight against good (for a change) ninja Sho Kosugi.

TAMARA DOBSON. One of the first black supermodels, at 6-foot-2⅛, was made to order for the urban-oriented action flicks of the early seventies. She moved directly into a starring role with *Cleopatra Jones* (1973) as a CIA agent who employs martial arts in the crusade against drug dealers. In the bigger-budgeted but less successful follow-up, *Cleopatra Jones and the Casino of Gold* (1975), Tamara took her act to Hong Kong, where she faught it out with villainess Stella Stevens.

ANITA EKBERG. Typecast, owing to her abundant décolletage, as a lush lady of leisure in such films as *War and Peace* (1956) and *La Dolce Vita* (1960). Lest we forget, she was the original choice to play "Sheena" on TV. Her most memorable action role was as "Hulina," the warrior woman who rides with Genghis Khan's army, in *The Mongols* (1960).

CORY EVERSON. A pumped-up Glamazon who attempted to make the transition from body builder to movie star. Her biggest role was as a villainess who matches wits (and fists) with Jean-Claude Van Damme in *Double Impact* (1991).

BRIDGET FONDA. Niece of Jane who interrupted her "serious" career to play an action heroine in *Point of No Return* (1993), the American remake of *La Femme Nikita*, about a street criminal transformed by the government into a beautiful killing machine.

Jane Fonda in
Barbarella.

JANE FONDA. The first major star/actress to dare try an action-babe role, in her then-husband Roger Vadim's elaborate sci-fi sex fantasy, *Barbarella* (1968).

LAURA GEMSER. Famous as Sylvia Kristel's Asian alter-ego in the *Black Emanuelle* movies. She also appeared as an action babe, kicking the butt of bad-ass guys, in *Emanuelle and the White Slave Trade* (1977) and *Trap Them and Kill Them* (1977) for director Aristide Massaccesi.

PAM GRIER. First flexed her muscles as the villainous warden in *Women in Cages* (1971), one of the first Philippine-lensed prison pictures to hit the Drive-In circuit. Next came her original heroine in *The Big Bird Cage* (1972, sometimes circulated as *Women's Penitentiary II*). Pam played "Blossom," the toughest babe in a bamboo prison, leading the eventual jail break. The following year, she starred in *Coffy*, as a dedicated nurse who moonlights as a sexy vigilante ("Miss Tique"). *Foxy Brown* (1974) again cast Pam as a nurse taking on drug dealers. *Friday Foster* (1975), a comic book–based adventure in which she played a danger-seeking photographer, was another of her urban-action epics, disappointing fans owing to a lack of scenes showing off Grier either nude or in combat. Only a few years later, she popped up in small roles, most notably the excellent police-action film *Fort Apache—The Bronx* (1981) with Paul Newman. Her career was revived when Quentin Tarantino devised the big-budget *Jackie Brown* (1997) specifically for Grier.

LINDA HAMILTON. Mostly ran around screaming in fear in the first *Terminator* film (for then-husband James Cameron), but got to pump up and fight back in the sequel, *Terminator 2* (1991).

DARRYL HANNAH. A perfect choice to portray the cave-woman heroine when Jean Auel's *Clan of the Cave Bear* became a film in 1986, but this was one Neanderthal epic that didn't score the way Raquel Welch's had back in the mid-sixties.

GLORIA HENDRY. Appeared in gritty urban dramas such as *Black Caesar* (1973), but they failed to establish her as a serious rival to Pam Grier. So Hendry teamed with Jim Kelly to fight organized crime in his best-known mini-epic, *Black Belt Jones* (1974), matching him kick for kick against the heavies in that film's famed car wash fight finale. That same year, she played one of the bad girls running a Philippines prison for women in *Savage Sisters*. Her final action role was in *Bare Knuckles* (1977), for director/ screenwriter/producer Don Edmonds, who previously created the *Ilsa* series.

NATASHA HENSTRIDGE. Played the gorgeous female creature in *Species* (1995), a clever combination of sci-fi, horror, and action from director Roger Donaldson. She also appears in the sequel, *Species II* (1998), an awful follow-up from pretentious filmmaker Peter Medak.

FAMKE JANSSEN. Had the lead in *Model By Day* (1993), as a Manhattan mannequin who moonlights as a crime-fighting heroine known as "Lady X." She reached top action-babe status as the bad-girl who takes on Pierce Brosnan's James Bond in *GoldenEye* (1995).

CLAUDIA JENNINGS. The most fascinating of the women who leaped from the pages of *Playboy* to B-movie stardom. She appeared in a slew of low-budget films, beginning with *Group Marriage* (1972), following that supporting part with the lead in *The Unholy Rollers* (1972), as a derby winner. Jennings' oeuvre includes three exploitation classics. In *Gator Bait* (1973), she's an abused swamp girl who methodically tracks down and kills her male tormentors. In *Truck Stop Women* (1974), Claudia's a redneck babe who won't take any guff from rugged males. And in *The Great Dixie Dynamite Chase* (1977), she appears in an action-comedy precursor to *Thelma and Louise*, also starring Jocelyn Jones. Hoping to go mainstream, she was reportedly despondent when the role of a *Charlie's Angels* replacement went instead to Shelley Hack. Shortly thereafter, Claudia was killed in a freak highway accident in Los Angeles.

Angelina Jolie in *Lara Croft, Tomb Raider*.

ANGELINA JOLIE. Beautiful and talented daughter of Oscar-winner Jon Voight, herself won an Academy Award for *Girl Interrupted* (1999). Action flicks are clearly in her blood. Early on, she played the martial arts robot in *Cyborg II* (1993), then returned to the genre (if on a notably higher level of project) in *Lara Croft, Tomb Raider* (2001).

GRACE JONES. Musical performance artist, played action babes in *Conan the Destroyer* (1984) with Arnold, the James Bond film A *View to a Kill* (1985) opposite Roger Moore, and was the leader of a vampire-stripper cult in *Vamp* (1986).

JILLIAN KESSNER. Claims to have been the winer of the 1981 North American Black Belt Olympics, though her title has been questioned. She played the karate fighter and kickboxer in search of her younger sister's killers in Ciro H. Santiago's Philippines-lensed *Firecracker* (1981), a remake of the same director's *T.N.T. Jackson*.

SUSAN LYNN KIGER. A lush blond *Playboy* centerfold, is probably best remembered for her good-natured sex comedy, *H.O.T.S.* (1975). She played in several action flicks, including *Angels Brigade* (1978), an all-female variation on *The Magnificent Seven*. Just such a team was fully integrated with both men and women in *Seven* (1979), an early Andy Sidaris flick.

TAWNY KITAEN. Best known as a one-time girlfriend of O. J. Simpson and the female lead in Tom Hanks's first hit, *Bachelor Party* (1984). Once, though, she played an action babe—the title character in a film which, like *Barbarella*, was inspired by an adults-only comic book: *The Perils of Gwendoline (in the Land of Yik Yak)* (1983).

LAURENE LANDON. Revealed her pumped-up sex appeal in . . . *All The Marbles* (1981), portraying half of a female wrestling team (with Vicki Frederick) in Robert Aldrich's film that predicted the eventual success of women in the world of wrestling. She went to work for Matt Cimber, who guided both Jayne Mansfield and Pia Zadora through some of their sleaziest vehicles. Their collaborations included *Hundra* (1983), featuring Landon as a sword-swinging Viking woman, and *Yellow Hair and the Fortress of Gold* (1984) as a female version of Indian Jones, complete with whip; both were shot in Spain.

BRIGITTE LIN (aka CHING HSAI). The female sword-master who protects royal children of the Ming dynasty from assassins in the Hong Kong–lensed *Dragon Inn* (1992).

LUCY LIU. Graduated from a supporting role in TV's *Ally McBeal* to action-babe stardom (alongside Drew Barrymore and Cameron Diaz) in the modernized version of *Charlie's Angels* (2000), which Barrymore produced.

KATHY LONG. A well-regarded kickboxer, did the body-double work for Michelle Pfeiffer (as Catwoman) in *Batman Returns* (1992). The following year, she had the lead in Albert Pyun's considerably less prestigious *Knights*, playing a female version of the Harrison Ford character from *Blade Runner*—a futuristic cyborg tracker.

ANGELA MAO. A top martial arts expert, portrays a Chinese detective who helps former "James Bond" star George Lazenby fight the drug dealers in the Hong Kong/Australian co-production *Stoner* (1976).

MARGARET MARKOV. A tall blond Glamazon, became the cult queen of Philippines-lensed action-exploitation following the box-office success (on the Drive-In circuit) of *The Hot Box* (1972), a women-in-prison flick co-scripted by future Oscar winner Jonathan Demme (*Silence of the Lambs*). Then, she was matched with black beauty Pam Grier in *Black*

Mama, White Mama (1973, also written by Demme), an action-oriented unofficial remake of *The Defiant Ones* (1958). The two women clicked with audiences and became something of a team, next appearing in *The Arena* (1973) for producer Roger Corman.

IRISH McCALLA. A Mamie Van Doren look-alike, put on a leopard-skin outfit and became TV's first female action hero in the mid-fifties' *Sheena* series. She later played a tough cowgirl as one of the title characters in *Five Bold Women* (1959).

REBA McENTIRE. Legendary country-western singer, played a pistol-packin' mama in the cult classic *Tremors* (1987).

RACHEL McLISH. A popular female bodybuilder, was featured in *Pumping Iron II: The Women* (1985) hoping to become a female Schwarzenegger. That never happened, but she did appear in several movies, including *Aces: Iron Eagle III* (1991) with Lou Gosset Jr., and played the lead in *Raven Hawk* (1995) as a Native American action babe.

DEMI MOORE. Pumped up for her part in *G.I. Jane* (1997) about the first woman to pass through the vigorous Navy SEALS program.

JULIE NEWMAR (real name, Julie Newmeyer). So tall and statuesque that Hollywood had trouble figuring out what to do with her. Finally, she became an action babe as Catwoman on TV's *Batman,* then as an evil Native American Amazon in the otherwise abominable *McKenna's Gold* (1969).

BRIGITTE NIELSEN. Played the wife of Sylvester Stallone's Russian boxing opponent (Dolph Lundgren) in *Rocky IV* (1985), then married Sly (briefly) in real life. She appeared opposite his action superstar rival Arnold Schwarzenegger (Nielsen receiving top billing!) in *Red Sonja* (1988), based on yet another book by Robert E. Howard. This character, unofficially the inspiration for TV's *Xena: Warrior Princess,* allowed Nielsen to show off her strong-but-beautiful body in fight sequences.

YUKARI OSHIMA. Portrayed the most memorable villainess to appear in any martial arts movie as "Madame Yeoung," a kickboxing drug lord in *Iron Angels* (1986) for Teresa Woo, one of the few women to write and direct action flicks in Hong Kong.

ANNE PARILLAUD. Played the lead in Luc Besson's *La Femme Nikita* (1989), an arty film that took the hitwoman action genre (previously restricted to Drive-In theaters and direct-to-video release) and made it respectable.

LORI PETTY. Supposed to become a big mainstream star (but didn't) following the success of the girls' baseball film *A League of Their Own* (1992). She switched over to female action flicks for the lead in *Tank Girl* (1995) as the futuristic kick-ass babe created in the comic books by Alan Martin and Jamie Hewlett.

MICHELLE PFEIFFER. Played an action babe only once, but once was enough: Her performance as "Catwoman" in *Batman Returns* (1992) was almost enough to make one forget Julie Newmar in that role.

LINNEA QUIGLEY. Unchallenged queen of B movies throughout the 1980s, was a kick-ass biker-babe "Spider" in *Sorority Babes in the Slimeball Bowl-O-Rama* (1987).

ANNE RANDALL. The first *Playboy* centerfold to star for Andy Sidaris as one of his proto-feminist James Bond variations in *Stacey* (1973). The film that set the pace for all other Sidaris flicks to follow, as its invincible heroine handles an onslaught of badguys.

TANYA ROBERTS. The last cast member to join the TV series *Charlie's Angels*, dared in 1984 to take on *Sheena*, the role of a jungle goddess/action babe once played by Irish McCalla on 1950s' TV.

CYNTHIA ROTHROCK. Earned a lofty reputation as a martial arts expert and starred in numerous B-budget action flicks, originally in Hong Kong productions, including *No Retreat, No Surrender II* (1987). Her first American-made feature was *Eye of the Dragon* (1988), for kung fu actor-turned-director Leo Fong. She played yet another of those righteous female avengers so basic to the action-babe subgenre. Rothrock shared top billing with Steve McQueen's son Chad in *Martial Law* (1990), in which they karate-kick their way through a crime syndicate run by David Carradine. She then accepted a supporting role as a kickboxer in *Fast Getaway* (1990) and its sequel, *Fast Getaway II* (1994). In between those assignments, she played a New York cop (teamed with Jalal Merhi) in *Tiger Claws* (1991) and a kickboxing FBI agent who protects America's atomic secrets in *Honor and Glory* (1992).

CATYA "CAT" SASSOON. The daughter of Vidal Sassoon and actress Beverly Adams, who played "Lovey Kravzit" in the Dean Martin/Matt Helm movies of the sixties. Far from the available sex object embodied by her mother, however, Cat played the modern incarnation of a beautiful-but-strong babe, most memorably as the topless kickboxer in *Angelfist* (1992), shot in the Philippines by action-expert Cirio H. Santiago. She then showed up in *Secret Games 3* (1994), an erotic thriller that cast her in a supporting role. She died suddenly, and under mysterious circumstances, in 2001.

TURA SATANA. Portrayed a groundbreaking prodecessor to what would become the modern cliché of a bad-ass hit woman in Russ Meyer's highly influential *Faster, Pussycat! Kill, Kill* (1966), considered by many to be that auteur's masterpiece.

ETUSKO "SUE" SHIOMI. Puts together a Magnificent Seven team of martial arts experts (including Sonny Chiba) to achieve vengeance in *Legend of the Eight Samurai* (1984); earlier, she had taken on street criminals in *Sister Streetfighter* (1975), also in Chiba's company.

KATHY SHOWER. Another *Playboy* centerfold who enjoyed a brief spurt of B-budget movie stardom, alternated between erotic thrillers, juvenile comedies, and action flicks. As to the latter, she first appeared as a gorgeous-but-deadly drug-enforcement agent who heads for Mexico when her male partner is captured by a cartel, in *Commando Squad* (1987). She co-produced and starred in *Roboc.h.i.c.* (1990) as a female variation on the popular *RoboCop* films.

SABRINA SIANI. A warrior woman in *Ator* (1983), one more *Conan* wannabe. She returned as the crazed queen of a post-Apocalyptic warrior society in *Conquest* (1984), wearing only a miniscule golden bikini and matching mask. She remained in the realm of negative-utopia action, in *Invincible Barbarian* (1985), filmed in Italy. Two years earlier, she had played beautiful princesses in two other Italian-made actioner, *Sword of the Barbarians* and *Throne of Fire*. Some fans claim that *2020 Texas Gladiators* (1982), in which she must survive in a Mad Max futureworld, offers her best work as an action babe.

HELEN SLATER. Had the bad fortune to make her screen debut in *Supergirl* (1984), a dreadfully dull attempt to extend the then-recently revived *Superman* franchise.

MARIA SOCAS. Joined David Carradine as half the title team in *The Warrior and the Sorceress* (1984), playing the entire film topless.

ELKE SOMMER. Typecast early-on as a wholesome Swedish (in fact, she was German) flower child in *The Prize* (1963) opposite Paul Newman and *A*

Shot in the Dark (1964) with Peter Sellers. She pumped herself up for an image-alteration, portraying a no-nonsense hit lady in *Deadlier Than the Male* (1966) with Richard Johnson (as "Bulldog Drummond") and *The Wrecking Crew* (1969) with Dean Martin (as Matt Helm).

RENEE SOUTENDIJK. Left European arthouse items behind to play a beautiful female robot off on a killing spree in *Eve of Destruction* (1991).

DONA SPIER. Among the many *Playboy* centerfold veterans who appeared as a pumped-up martial arts action babe for the husband-and-wife producer/director team of Arlene and Andy Sidaris. Speir originally teamed with Hope Marie Carlton in *Hard Ticket to Hawaii* (1987) and *Savage Beach* (1989), and with Carlton and Roberta Vasquez in *Picasso Trigger* (1988). When Carlton left the series, Spier teamed only with Vasquex in *Do Or Die* (1990), *Guns* (1990), *Hard Hunted* (1992), and *Fit to Kill* (1993).

REBECCA ROMJIN STAMOS. The shape-shifting action babe, "Mystique," in the ongoing *X-Men* franchise.

SHARON STONE. While waiting for superstardom to happen, appeared opposite Richard Chamberlain in both *King Solomon's Mines* (1985) and *Allan Quartermain and the Lost City of Gold* (1986), though less as an action babe than a screamer in need of constant rescuing. *Total Recall* (1990) reintroduced her as a cross between Grace Kelly and Rambo, able to take on Schwarzenegger himself in hand-to-hand combat. Following the success of *Basic Instinct* (1992), Sharon played several more action roles, including the vengeance-crazed blonde in *The Specialist* (1994) with Sylvester Stallone and Sam Raimi's laughably bad attempt to create a female equivalent to Clint Eastwood's "Man With No Name" in *The Quick and the Dead* (1995).

JULIE STRAIN. First played a villainess named "Jewel Panther" in *Enemy Gold* (1993) from the Sidaris family of filmmakers, though her character (killed off at the end) proved so popular that she was brought back in *Fit to Kill* (1993). More recently, she has moved from villainess to lead heroine in the ongoing franchise.

MERYL STREEP. Multi-Oscar-winning actress, put her varying dialects aside to play an action babe only once. In *The River Wild* (1994), she starred as a vacationer in the far west whose rapids-riding river trip is interrupted by a psycho killer (Kevin Bacon).

HILARY SWANK. Who would win an Oscar for the non-action flick *Boys Don't Cry* (1999), made her initial impact as Ralph Macchio's replacement in *The New Karate Kid* (1994).

ZOE TAMERLIS. Played a rape victim who becomes a somnumbulist until rage builds up and explodes, turning her into a female terminator in *Ms. 45* (1981) for edgy director Abel Ferrara.

TEAGAN. Yet another of the woman bodybuilders who hoped to emerge as the female Schwarzenegger. Her major contribution to the genre was as a Glamazon warrior wearing a bikini top fashioned from scrap metal in schlockmeister Fred Olen Ray's *Alienator* (1989).

UMA THURMAN. Picked up where Honor Blackman and Diana Rigg had left off, portraying the leather lady in a big-budget (but, other than her presence, disastrous) film version of English TV's beloved *The Avengers* (1998).

TINA TURNER. Aunt Entity, the bad-ass babe who dares to take on Mel Gibson, in *Mad Max Beyond Thunderdome* (1985), the third and final film in the series.

DEBORAH VAN VALKENBURG. The kung fu kicking female who helps Andrew Dice Clay (as a Portland bouncer) protect a supermodel (Teri Hatcher) from Asian villains in *Brainsmasher: A Love Story* (1993).

ROBERTA VASQUEZ. A striking brunette who could be called the Madeline Stowe of junk action movies, was one of the black leather biker babes who kick redneck male butt in *Women on Wheels* (1988). She also co-starred with Donna Speir in several of the Andy Sidaris action films.

VICTORIA VETRI. A *Playboy* centerfold under the pseudonym "Angela Dorian," using that name when she was introduced to films in the action western *Chuka* (1967) opposite Rod Taylor. She then, under her real name, headlined Hammer's production of *When Dinosaurs Ruled the Earth* (1970) and played the lead in *Invasion of the Bee Girls* (1973) as an alien amazon who loves men to death.

MONICA VITTI. Looks like a cross between Brigitte Bardot and Barbra Streisand, graduated from the existential ennui of Michelangelo Antonioni films to play a low-camp superheroine in *Modesty Blaise* (1966)—based on a popular comic strip (what Barbarella was to outer space, she was to spies), directed by Joseph Losey.

SIGNOURNEY WEAVER. Excels at everything from serious drama (*The Year of Living Dangerously*, 1983) to light comedy (*Working Girl*, 1988) and proves to be one of the most successful action babes of all time—first in Ridley Scott's suspenseful *Alien* (1979), then (in a more pumped-up manner) in James Cameron's in-your-face sequel, *Aliens* (1986), and several more lesser installments in the series.

RAQUEL WELCH. Often bemoaned that she was born an anachronistic glamour girl in an age of flower children, but her best bet would have been to stick with the action films that brought her fame. Posing as a cave girl in Hammer's *One Million Years, B.C.* (1966) led to pop-icon status, and her action sequences with Ray Harryhausen's dazzling dinosaurs are still engaging to watch. Her female James Bond in *Fathom* (1967) may have inspired the entire series of Andy and Arlene Sidaris movies that began a decade later. Raquel convincingly portrayed a kick-ass cowgirl in *100 Rifles* (1969), in which she held her own against Burt Reynolds and Jim Brown, and *Hannie Caulder* (1971), a *Nevada Smith*–type tale of vengeance but with a female in the lead. She also excelled as a rough-and-ready roller derby babe in *Kansas City Bomber* (1972).

Raquel Welch in *One Million Years, B.C.*

MICHELLE YEOH. Played the "Invisible Woman," one of a triad of warrior women in the Hong Kong–produced *Heroic Trio* (1992), her martial arts skills impressive enough to give her a second go-around in a sequel, *The Executioners* (1993). Swiftly, she became the First Lady of Asian action films. The American mainstream audience became of aware of Michelle when she teamed with Pierce Brosnan for the James Bond action thriller, *Tomorrow Never Dies* (1997). Her crowning achievement was, of course, *Crouching Tiger, Hidden Dragon* (2000), opposite Chow Yun-Fat for Ang Lee.

ZHANG ZIYI. Established herself as Asia's answer to Jessica Alba with her stunning performance of a raven-haired, extremely youthful action babe in *Crouching Tiger, Hidden Dragon* (2000).

17

MANO E MANO: THE GREAT FIGHT SCENES

It all began in 1914. Director Colin Campbell, working for the newly formed Selig company, shot a screen version of *The Spoilers*, Rex Beach's adventure novel about Alaska gold miners. In the final reel, a pair of brutes—Tom Santschi and William Farnum—went at it in a muddy street. There was no such thing as stunt doubles or camera trickery then, so the two stars beat the blazes out of each other in the silver screen's first mano e mano bout. Other filmmakers would, over the years, try to top the archetype that had set into motion one of the best loved elements in action films. What follows is a brief connoisseur's collection of the best of the best since 1945.

Any Which Way You Can (1980). Clint Eastwood goes mano e mano with William Smith at the conclusion of this rare comedy-action film for the usually taciturn star. Though a supporting actor in A-movies, Smith has headlined many B-films.

Bad Day at Black Rock (1955). The film that introduced martial arts to American audiences as one-armed Spencer Tracy employs karate to devastate town bully Ernest Borgine.

Barabbas (1961). Anthony Quinn (as the title character) takes on evil Jack Palance in gorey gladiator combat in an otherwise talky religious spectacle.

Big Country, The (1958). Gregory Peck and Charlton Heston (in their only co-starring project) battle through a long night, their brutal encounter viewed from a distance, in William Wyler's American epic about conflicting values of East and West.

Captive Girl (1950). Minor league program-picture in the *Jungle Jim* series of African adventures, rendered memorable by the lengthy fight between two former Tarzans, Buster Crabbe and Johnny Weissmuller.

Cool Hand Luke (1967). Newly admitted to a Southern chain gang, Paul Newman dukes it out with the reigning champion, Oscar-winner George Kennedy.

Darker Than Amber (1970). Rod Taylor, as detective Travis McGee, and perennial bad guy William Smith have at one another in a brutal fight aboard a yacht.

Emperor of the North Pole (1973). Ernest Borgnine as a train guard and Lee Marvin as a freeloading Depression-era hobo hack away at each other atop a roaring locomotive.

Enter the Dragon (1973). Bruce Lee versus Chuck Norris in one of the most memorable martial arts sequences ever filmed (see chapter 12).

From Here to Eternity (1953). In this Oscar-winning Best Picture about life on Pearl Harbor before the attack, catch *two* great fights: Frank Sinatra versus Ernest Borgnine duking it out in a bar, and Borgnine versus Monty Clift with switchblades in a Honolulu back alley.

From Russia With Love (1963). Sean Connery, in his second go-round as James Bond, takes on inhuman fighting machine Robert Shaw on the Orient Express.

High Noon (1952). Town marshal Gary Cooper and his own deputy (Lloyd Bridges) engage in a furious fistfight shortly before Coop must shoot it out with four gunslingers in this social-commentary anti-western.

Iron Mistress, The (1952). As "Jim Bowie," Alan Ladd engages in several well-staged duels, including a knife-to-knife competition with a New Orleans saloon owner, then (better still) a knife-versus-sword duel in the darkness of a small chamber, illuminated only by sudden bolts of lightning from a ceiling window.

Kentuckian, The (1955). Burt Lancaster, using only his fists, goes up against Walter Matthau, wielding a bullwhip. Later, Burt takes on an enemy armed with a rifle.

Lonely Are the Brave (1962). Contemporary cowboy Kirk Douglas takes on Bill Raisch (*The Fugitive*'s one-armed man) in an extended southwest bar-room brawl.

Manchurian Candidate, The (1962). Henry Silva employs martial arts to combat Frank Sinatra in this Cold War suspense classic about the birth of contemporary political paranoia.

Quiet Man, The (1952). As a boxer repulsed by violence after killing a man in the ring, John Wayne finally decides to take on Victor McLaglen in a 17-minute fight amid Ireland's lush greenery.

Rashomon (1950). Samurai warriors Toshiro Mifune and Masayuki Mori duel in "the bush" over Machiko Kyo. Uniquely, we see the fight twice, from differing points of view.

Corey Allen versus James Dean in ***Rebel Without a Cause.***

Rebel Without a Cause (1955). In the greatest juvenile delinquency movie ever, "Jimbo" (James Dean) and "Buzz" (Corey Allen) slash away at each other with switchblades and anything else handy only hours before entering a deadly "chickie race" on a cliff.

Red River (1948). John Wayne and Montgomery Clift go at one another with guns, then fists, in the classic if controversial conclusion (wait'll you see how the fight ends!) of Howard Hawks's first western.

Romeo and Juliet (1967). The fight between Romeo (Leonard Whiting) and the Capulets' kinsman Tybalt (Michael York) in Verona's mean streets, staged with swords and fists, will convince any doubter that Shakespeare was a proponent of the action tale.

Scaramouche (1952). The sword fight in a crowded theater between swashbucklers Stewart Granger and Mel Ferrer rates as the longest, most complex duel ever filmed.

Shane (1953). Gunfighter Alan Ladd takes on cowboy Ben Johnson in a classic barroom brawl, and later goes one on one with farmer Van Heflin.

Montgomery Clift versus John Wayne in *Red River*.

Spartacus (1960). Kirk Douglas combats Woody Strode as gladiators in the arena, each realizing the man he fights is not actually an enemy. (See also chapter 18.)

Stalking Moon, The (1969). As the foster father of a half-Indian child, frontier scout Gregory Peck must ultimately fight the lad's biological father in a duel that lasts more than 20 minutes.

Wild One, The (1954). Leather-biker "Johnny" (Marlon Brando) takes on his crazed counterpart (Lee Marvin) while life in a small town screeches to a halt.

18

ESSENTIALS: THE SIXTIES

"Ask not what your country can do for you," the new president announced, "but what you can do for your country." This promised to be a time to open new frontiers, something that could be accomplished only by swift disassociation with the rugged individualism that had characterized 1950s' thinking. Now required was a commitment to community, however makeshift and tenuous, explaining the emphasis on "the group" in most action movies turned out during the decade's early years, an optimistic belief that through subscription to a common cause, all dragons could be defeated. However, everything changed in November 1963. The assassination of John Kennedy plunged America into spiritual darkness, our country shortly ravaged by escalating civil rights activism and protests against the undeclared war in Vietnam. Our popular culture—everything from the music we listened to, to the clothes we wore, to the movies we watched—necessarily transformed. No wonder, then, that a decade which began with the studio system and its code for "proper" motion picture fare firmly in place ended with the studios in shambles and a new ratings system applied to an anything-goes attitude. Though group-endeavor movies continued to dominate, they grew first cynical, then pessimistic, and finally nihilistic in tone—reflecting our national mind-set at each step along the way.

The Magnificent Seven (1960)

CREDITS

> Director, John Sturges; screenplay, William Roberts and (uncredited) Walter Bernstein and Walter Newman, inspired by a script by Akira Kurosawa; producers, Sturges and Walter Mirisch; original music, Elmer Bernstein; cinematography, Charles Lang, Jr.; running time, 126 min.

CAST

Yul Brynner (*Chris Adams*); Eli Wallach (*Calvera*); Steve McQueen (*Vin*); Horst Buchholz (*Chico*); Charles Bronson (*Bernardo O'Reilly*); Robert Vaughn (*Lee*); Brad Dexter (*Harry Luck*); James Coburn (*Britt*); Vladimir Sokoloff (*Old Villager*).

THE FILM

The internationalization of the action film in general and the western in particular began with this seminal work. It's doubtful any of the great films to follow—notably the entire spaghetti-western genre—could have come into existence had Sergio Leone not seen Sturges's instant classic. *The Magnificent Seven* appeared (and was a huge hit) simultaneous with the release of John Wayne's personal project, *The Alamo*, one of the last of Hollywood's old-fashioned westerns, before the form darkened (*The Man Who Shot Liberty Valance*, 1962) or curdled into self-caricature (*How the West Was Won*, 1962). Lack of public enthusiasm for *The Alamo* indicated a sea change in tastes; likewise, the overwhelming acceptance of *The Magnificent Seven* set the pace for the future. Sturges based his movie on Akira Kurosawa's *Seven*

Robert Vaughn, Steve McQueen, Charles Bronson, Yul Brynner, Brad Dexter, Horst Bucholz, and James Coburn in *The Magnificent Seven*.

Samurai (1954), apparently unaware Kurosawa had drastically re-imagined the samurai figure from Japanese mythology and/or history, transforming him into an Eastern equivalent of the American gunfighter he'd become fascinated while watching films by Sturges and Ford. The result—a revision of a revision, and the cast added to this impact. Yul Brynner would become so identified as an icon of the gunfighter that he'd be called upon to caricature that role in *Westworld*, yet he had been chosen in a reversal of typecasting. At the time, it was considered bizarre that the Asian-looking star of *The King and I* (1956) could be cast as a cowboy. Likewise, Austrian Horst Bucholz played the youngest member of the team, the Mexican "Chico," without explanation for his European accent. Mexican settings had been employed before, in such films as Robert Aldrich's *Vera Cruz* (1954), though here they were further emphasized. A wisecracking mentality for the anti-heroes clicked with audiences, and would be continued in films to come.

Spartacus (1960)

CREDITS

Director, Stanley Kubrick; screenplay, Dalton Trumbo and (uncredited) Calder Willingham and Peter Ustinov, from the novel by Howard Fast; producers, Douglas and Edward Lewis; original music, Alex North; cinematography, Russell Metty and Clifford Stine; running time, 184 min.

CAST

Kirk Douglas (*Spartacus*); Laurence Olivier (*Marcus Licinius Crassus*); Jean Simmons (*Varinia*); Charles Laughton (*Sempronius Gracchus*); Peter Ustinov (*Lentulus Batiatus*); John Gavin (*Julius Caesar*); Tony Curtis (*Antoninus*); Nina Foch (*Helena*); John Ireland (*Crixus*); Herbert Lom (*Tigranes Levantus*); Charles McGraw (*Marcellus*); Harold J. Stone (*David*); Woody Strode (*Draba*).

THE FILM

During the late 1960s, the pioneers of modern action grew pensive and self-reflective, setting into motion a series of super-productions that summed up the screen work of their fading youth. If Wayne's *The Alamo* stands as the ultimate example of such a film being done in a conservative vein, then Douglas's *Spartacus* offered the liberal alternative, serving as a paeon to commu-

Kirk Douglas and Woody Strode in *Spartacus*.

nal values based on a novel of the same name that had employed an actual slave rebellion as an objective correlative for twentieth-century socialism. Cinching this was Douglas's hiring of blacklisted writer Dalton Trumbo (who'd been working under the name "Richard Rich"). Proof that a new age was upon us came when Douglas insisted Trumbo's name be listed in the credits. Though a few on the lunatic fringe protested, the blacklist was finally broken. Another sign of the changing times: An old hand at action films— Anthony Mann, who had begun directing—departed after arguments erupted on the set between himself and producer/star Douglas. Mann left to work with a stridently old-fashioned star, Charlton Heston, on the more conservatively inclined *El Cid*. Douglas brought in his still relatively young (31) protégée from *Paths of Glory*, Stanley Kubrick. Far more comfortable with Kirk's vision, Kubrick understood that, despite the one-name title, the man called Spartacus would not be the film's true subject. When every one of the slaves rises, claiming "I am Spartacus!", each is correct. Spartacus is an idea, embodied by any common man who dares rise to heroic proportions. There are no great men, only men who achieve greatness.

The Guns of Navarone (1961)

CREDITS

Director, J. Lee Thompson; screenplay, Carl Foreman, from the novel by Alistair MacLean; producer, Foreman; original music, Dimitri Tiomkin; cinematography, Oswald Morris; running time, 157 min.

CAST

Gregory Peck (*Capt. Keith Mallory*); David Niven (*Corporal Miller*); Anthony Quinn (*Andrea Stavros*); Stanley Baker (*Private "Butcher" Brown*); Anthony Quayle (*Major Roy Franklin*); James Darren (*Private Spyros Pappadimos*); Irene Papas (*Maria Pappadimos*); Gia Scala (*Anna*); James Robertson Justice (*Commodore Jensen*).

THE FILM

During the early 1960s, talents that had been blacklisted were finally able to mount their dream projects, Carl Foreman among them. The man had written *High Noon* (1952), then subsequently been driven out of Hollywood by those who felt the final image of a star in the dust was anti-American. For his comeback, Foreman wrote and produced this big-budget item, which transferred the group mentality of action to a WWII setting by way of an Alistair McLean novel. Foreman, however, had not abandoned his liberal values. *Guns of Navarone* may, like *High Noon,* work as a ticking clock suspense thriller that leads to an eye-filling series of grand explosions, yet Foreman managed to layer his action epic with a notable anti-war sensibility. He points out the absurdity of war, particularly in that sequence depicting the execution of a beautiful woman (Gia Scala), who is discovered to have betrayed the mission. Acknowledging civil rights and feminist themes, this magnificent seven team is of more diverse ethnic backgrounds and includes two females. The movie's success set the pace for future WWII films, be they successful (*Operation Crossbow*), mediocre (*Where Eagles Dare*), or misfires (*Tobruk*).

The Great Escape (1963)

CREDITS

Director, John Sturges; screenplay, James Clavell and W. R. Burnett, from the book by Paul Brickhill; producers, Sturges and (uncredited)

Clavell; original music, Elmer Bernstein; cinematography, Daniel L. Fapp; running time, 168 min.

CAST

Steve McQueen (*"Cooler King" Hilts*); James Garner (*"The Scrounger" Hendley*); Richard Attenborough (*"Big X" Bartlett*); Charles Bronson (*"Tunnel King" Danny*); James Donald (*Senior Officer Ramsey*); James Coburn (*"The Manufacturer" Sedwick*); Donald Pleasence (*"The Forger" Blythe*); David McCallum (*Ashley-Pitt*); Gordon Jackson (*MacDonald*); John Leyton (*Willie*).

THE FILM

John Sturges, a veteran of such excellent films as *Gunfight at the OK Corral* (1958) and *Last Train From Gun Hill* (1959), revealed his ability to change with the times. First, he re-imagined the western with *The Magnificent Seven*, then he took the old *Stalag 17* type of tale about a fascinating group of POWs and transformed it into an early example of the new action movie. The film offers an interesting hybrid of the yin/yang sides of the genre. Ordinarily, such movies deal either with a rugged individualist or a group of odd-balls who come together as a community. Here, we get the best of both worlds. Steve McQueen more or less exists in a film all his own, his character taking a unique path as he attempts to escape the Nazis; Richard Attenborough is the organizer of "the group," each team member's quirks adding to its power. McQueen also insisted that he be allowed to include a motor-cycle sequence, which became the film's highlight. Today, *The Great Escape* is unimaginable without this stunt's presence. McQueen did attempt the hair-raising 60-ft. jump but was unable to manage it; at that point, his close friend Bud Elkins, a biker expert who often rode with McQueen, performed it in Steve's place. This led to a new career for the bike-store manager, who became a stunt double for Steve.

Goldfinger (1964)

CREDITS

Director, Guy Hamilton; screenplay, Richard Maibaum and Paul Dehn, from the novel by Ian Fleming; producers, Albert R. Broccoli and Harry Saltzman; original music, John Barry and Monty Norman (James Bond theme); cinematography, Ted Moore; running time, 111 min.

Sean Connery and
Honor Blackman in
Goldfinger.

CAST

Sean Connery (*James Bond*); Honor Blackman (*Pussy Galore*); Gert
Fröbe (*Auric Goldfinger*); Shirley Eaton (*Jill Masterson*); Tania Mallet
(*Tilly Masterson*); Harold Sakata (*Oddjob*); Bernard Lee ("*M*"); Martin
Benson (*Martin Solo*); Cec Linder (*Felix Leiter*); Lois Maxwell (*Miss
Moneypenny*); Burt Kwouk (*Mr. Ling*); Desmond Llewelyn ("*Q*").

THE FILM

The suave, sexy spy had already become the key action hero of the 1960s
when *Goldfinger* was released. There had been two earlier Bond films, modestly successful, while the popular *Man From U.N.C.L.E.* was already riding
high on TV. This was the movie, however, that soldified the spy as *the*
modern anti-hero. Violence and sex—and, most important, sexy violence—
overnight became a "hip" (at the time) trend in films. Numerous elements
contributed to the pop-culture explosion, including a then-daring *Life* (the
country's most middlebrow magazine) cover featuring Shirley Eaton, semi-
nude and gilded. Also, the film rode the coattails of the Beatles' invasion in
music, as well as the sudden popularity stateside of the "mod" look from
Carnaby Street. It only stood to reason that, given such a climate, the time
was ripe for a British action hero. Such phrases as "the jet set," "the in crowd,"

"la dolce vita," and "the sexual revolution" had, with the advent of the early 1960s, become a part of the popular idiom. This big-scale entertainment (shot on a then-impressive $4 million budget) encapsulated all of the above into a movie that was then taken (mistaken?) for the ultimate in "sophistication." Bond's being "licensed to kill"—a bit ahead of its time when *Dr. No* opened in 1962—seemed far more appropriate following the death of Kennedy. Other touches that would strongly influence future films included the comic-bookish quality that pervades this mainstream item, as well as the introduction of a glib protagonist who could be as cruel as his enemies. Bond takes obvious pleasure in killing, whereas that had strictly been the case with villains in past action films. Also, his intense sexual interest in women but lack of desire for any kind of lasting relationship made him a great favorite with readers of *Playboy*, around since 1954 though the magazine failed to catch on big time until the early sixties. Group action movies would continue to dominate throughout the decade, yet the presence and success of 007, a man who works alone, implied that the return of the rugged individualist as a cultural icon was far from gone.

The Professionals (1966)

CREDITS

Director, Richard Brooks; screenplay, Brooks, from the novel *A Mule for the Marquesa* by Frank O'Rourke; producer, Brooks; original music, Maurice Jarre; cinematography, Conrad Hall; running time, 116 min.

CAST

Lee Marvin (*Henry Fardan*, aka *Rico*); Burt Lancaster (*Bill Dolworth*); Robert Ryan (*Hans Ehrengard*); Woody Strode (*Jack Sharp*); Claudia Cardinale (*Maria Grant*); Jack Palance (*Jesus Raza*); Ralph Bellamy (*Mr. Grant*).

THE FILM

The major link between *The Magnificent Seven* and *The Wild Bunch*, this blockbuster hit was the most significant mercenary-team action film (other than *The Dirty Dozen*, which also top-billed Lee Marvin) to appear in the mid-sixties. A rich old American (Ralph Bellamy) sends the deadly quartet on a mission to retrieve his beautiful young wife (Claudia Cardinale), who's been kidnapped by a ruthless bandido (Jack Palance). Loyal to the letter of the contract, as well as to one another, they have no respect for a man who has used them by concealing the fact that she willingly rode off with her lover. Along the way, there was plenty of opportunity for elements that were soon considered basic to the evolving action movie. Even the title proved significant, emphasizing the calculated aura with which the protagonists went about performing their mission-for-money—though they did prove surprisingly moral in the final sequence. This movie is also significant for making the group interracial, African American Woody Strode (as the archer) portrayed as a full-and-equal member. *The Professionals* also set the pace for future employment of a twentieth-century west, during the age of Villa and Zapata, any quaint codes of conduct from "the old days" fast fading. Brutal gunmen are, despite their violence, ironically viewed as the last men with values and integrity. Violent encounters are staged on a grand scale, numerous quips and one-liners undercut the situation's seriousness, and time is taken out for Socratic explorations of existential angst about the meaning of positive action in a world gone sour. Significant too is the tone, for this small coterie of aging adventurers would feel quite at home in the kind of cosmos once envisioned by Howard Hawks or, for that matter, Ernest Hemingway. But the world such directors and writers created no longer existed. Sensing that they now live in a world devoid of values, the professionals react by growing ever more loyal to one another, their sense of responsibility directed toward their self-contained group rather than society at large.

The Dirty Dozen (1967)

CREDITS

Directed by Robert Aldrich; screenplay, Nunnally Johnson and Lukas Heller, from the novel by E. M. Nathanson; producer, Kenneth Hyman; original music, Frank De Vol; cinematography, Edward Scaife; running time, 150 min.

CAST

Lee Marvin (*Major Reisman*); Charles Bronson (*Joseph Wladislaw*); Jim Brown (*Robert Jefferson*); John Cassavetes (*Victor Franko*); Richard Jaeckel (*Sgt. Bowren*); Trini Lopez (*Pedro Jiminez*); Clint Walker (*Samson Posey*); Telly Savalas (*Arthur Maggot*); Donald Sutherland (*Vernon Pinky*); Tom Busby (*Milo Vladek*); Ben Car-

Lee Marvin and company in *The Dirty Dozen*.

ruthers (*Glenn Gilpin*); Stuart Cooper (*Roscoe Lever*); Robert Phillips (*Carl Morgan*); Colin Maitland (*Seth Sawyer*); Al Mancini (*Tassos Bravos*); George Roubicek (*Arthur James Gardner*); Dora Reisser (*German Girl*); Ernest Borgnine (*Gen. Worden*); George Kennedy (*Maj. Armbruster*); Ralph Meeker (*Capt. Stuart*); Robert Ryan (*Col. Dasher-Breed*).

THE FILM

This film transformed the WWII movie from a simplistic homage to great guys getting a difficult job done with dignity to something far more in line with the cynicism that had come to pervade America as the Vietnam war raged out of control. Lee Marvin's hero is a rebel within the system, dealing with simple-minded bigoted officers similar to the caricatures in Joseph Heller's *Catch-22*. Here, such portrayals were absorbed into a mainstream project. Clearly, the heroes of *Guns of Navarone* are long gone. Indeed, these characters mark a sharp step down the social scale from those in *The Magnificent Seven* and *The Professionals*. This "group" comprises killers and rapists who display much difficulty in becoming loyal even to one another, as a cadre of fighting men, or to their mission, much less the army. America was moving into a dark period in its social and cultural history, compared with more idealistic hopes at decade's beginning. Such attitudes would be reflected in movies. *The Dirty Dozen* would be outdone in its caustic tone a mere two years later by Sam Peckinpah's *The Wild Bunch*.

The Good, the Bad, and the Ugly (1967)

CREDITS

Director, Sergio Leone; screenplay, Leone, Sergio Donati, Agenore Incrocci, Furio Scarpelli, and Luciano Vincenzoni; producer, Alberto Grimaldi; original music, Ennio Morricone; cinematography, Tonino Delli Colli; running time, 161 mins.

CAST

Clint Eastwood (*The Man With No Name/ Blondie/The Good*); Lee Van Cleef (*Angel Eyes/Sentenza/The Bad*); Eli Wallach (*Tuco Benedito Pacifico Juan Maria Ramirez/ The Ugly*).

THE FILM

The most famous of all "spaghetti westerns," this film was shot entirely in Spain, though numerous Italian craftsmen worked on it. No matter, though, for the term had long come to mean any film set in the American west but shot somewhere in southern Europe.

Clint Eastwood in *The Good, the Bad, and the Ugly*.

With the notable exception of *The Magnificent Seven* and *The Professionals*, the westerns still being produced by Hollywood were largely out of touch with swiftly changing tastes, while their formulaic studio fabrications featured fading stars. Shortly, Eastwood would return home, bringing the new sensibility with him. Clint would star in violent, cynical, semi-surreal movies directed by Don Siegel, and learn from that American action expert as he had from his earlier European mentor, Sergio Leone, eventually going on to direct his own action westerns. Leone had, like Sturges, already absorbed elements of samurai fable into the western, as *Fistful of Dollars* (see chapter 21)—a remake of *Yojimbo*—made clear. With his third such film, he moved into epic territory, exaggerating the genre's enduring cliches into ritualized archetypes. In the process, Leone endowed them with new life, every image so self-conscious in its references to earlier films that this gradually transforms into a movie about movies. Politically, too, the film is important. Released in Europe in 1966, then in America more than a year later, this film caught the darkening world view that followed the first Kennedy assassination and preceded the second one. Gone from Leone's vision was the once-potent sense of group activity and communal commitment. In its place, we see rugged individualism, as three self-serving characters search for hidden gold even as an "idealistic" war wages around them. In comparison to such mass carnage, the callous killing by the three heroes and villains (another irony is that "the good" and "the bad" are virtual doppelgongers for one another rather than the contrasting foils of earlier films) seems dwarfed. Eastwood sums up Sergio's attitude, one informed by an anti-Vietnam attitude: "I've never seen so many good men been wasted so badly."

Planet of the Apes (DATE?) 1968

CREDITS

Director, Franklin J. Schaffner; screenplay, Michael Wilson and Rod Serling, from the novel by Pierre Boulle; producer, Arthur P. Jacobs; original music, Jerry Goldsmith; cinematography, Leon Shamroy; running time, 112 min.; rating, G.

CAST

Charlton Heston (*Col. George Taylor*); Roddy McDowall (*Dr. Cornelius*); Kim Hunter (*Dr. Zira*); Maurice Evans (*Dr. Zaius*); James Whitmore (*President, Ape Assembly*); James Daly (*Dr. Honorious*); Linda Harrison (*Nova*).

THE FILM

However lofty a form of entertainment the science fiction action film may have been at the advent of film history—Fritz Lang's *Metropolis* (1926) comes to mind—the form had degenerated into junk movies by the early 1960s, and most "serious" actors would have nothing to do with them. Fortunately, Charlton Heston did not feel that way. By agreeing to participate in this large-scale undertaking, he helped re-establish the fantasy film as a legitimate form of popular entertainment while extending his own career at that moment when many of his collegues—fellow pioneers of the contemporary action movie—were slipping from the limelight. Thanks to this film and Stanley Kubrick's *2001: A Space Odyssey*—released more or less simultaneously—the sci-fi genre was reborn and rendered "respectable" again. In the case of Kubrick's film, the emphasis was on cerebral and metaphysical elements. Here, audiences experienced a more obvious message-movie combined with futuristic action on a grand scale. The makeup (which won an Academy Award for John Chambers) offered a major breakthrough. Actors played apes not by wearing head masks but by having fur carefully contoured to their faces, so the personality of each could be perceived. The cautionary-fable theme, as revealed in the rightfully famous final scene, took all our collective fears of nuclear holocaust, which had haunted less prestigious films for two decades, and solidified them into a single image that would

Charlton Heston in *Planet of the Apes*.

become an enduring pop-culture icon. The movie touched on environmentalist themes, including our blase treatment of animals. Here mankind experiences a reversal of roles and, perhaps, learns something from the experience. Others took the relationship between humans and apes as an allegory for the civil rights struggle then raging. Such ideas had often been expressed in the legendary *Twilight Zone* TV series of the late fifties and early 1960s, so it seemed only natural that the show's creator, Rod Serling, was brought on board as one of the writers.

The Wild Bunch (1969)

CREDITS

Director, Sam Peckinpah; screenplay, Peckinaph, Walon Green, and Roy N. Sickner; producers, Sickner and Phil Feldman; original music, Jerry Fielding; cinematography, Lucien Ballard; running time, 134 min.; rating, R.

CAST

William Holden (*Pike Bishop*); Ernest Borgnine (*Dutch Engstrom*); Robert Ryan (*Deke Thornton*); Edmond O'Brien (*Freddie Sykes*); Warren Oates (*Lyle Gorch*); Ben Johnson (*Tector Gorch*); Jaime Sánchez (*Angel*); Emilio Fernández (*Gen. Mapache*); Strother Martin (*Coffer*); L. Q. Jones (*T.C.*); Bo Hopkins (*Crazy Lee*).

THE FILM

Sam Peckinpah's career, however awkward and uncertain, provided clear evidence that a genius was at work. He became to the mean-spirited contemporary action western what John Ford had been to the form in a more sentimental era of values and films. But no sooner had the smoke cleared from this, his masterpiece, than such problems would haunt him again, films taken out of his creative control and—as had been the case with *Major Dundee* (1964), occuring again with *Pat Garrett and Billy the Kid* (1973)—edited into something other than what he intended. If *The Wild Bunch* is the only movie to fully convey this artist's personal vision, that is enough. It rates as one of the towering films, so important that entire books have been written about its aesthetics and social import. This was an ultraviolent western, designed specifically for an audience that had been treated to daily doses of blood and guts on early evening news reports from Vietnam. By way of a seemingly realistic—yet stylized, balletic, even choreographed, in slow motion—portrayal of violence, Peckinpah hoped to shock his jaded viewer into a realization of the absolute horror, as well as the undeniable beauty, of bloodletting. In this sense, *The Wild Bunch* can be considered the last of the great group action movies, a bookend to an era that began with *The Magnificent Seven*. That existential western had presented initially cynical loners who gradually grow commited to a cause and achieve some final good by self-sacrifice. The group-action form, at regular stop-gaps, grew ever more pessimistic until it reaches the outright nihilism we encounter here: The betrayer of the title outfit (Robert Ryan) is left alive at the end, along with a semi-mad old timer (Edmund O'Brien), whose crazed laughter at senseless slaughter expresses an absurdist view of the universe. The quartet of non-heroes did come together to do the right thing, trying to save their captured comrade Angel. Still, their combat with the Mexican army takes place *after* he is dead, so their ecstatic laughter at their own oncoming ends—which they will into being—serves as a postmortem on a bygone value system that no longer seemed tenable. As they go down, the 1960s' group-action movie dies with them.

19

THE NAM: THE VIETNAM WAR ON FILM

In the mid-sixties, people allowed themselves to believe that this unwinnable war was all Lyndon Johnson's fault. In fact, our involvement could be traced back through Kennedy to Eisenhower, even—if one considers America's first forays into southeast Asia—to Truman's final years in the White House. The war divided America as Korea had not, but likely would have were that police action allowed to drag on for what threatened to become an indefinite length. At first, few filmmakers dared deal with the touchy issue of Vietnam. Five years after it was over, several did begin, with varying degrees of artistry, to at last answer the abiding question—"Why were we in Vietnam?"—via serious movies on the subject. Only films focusing on combat will be covered here, each rated between one (low marks) and five (high score) stars in terms of quality and action.

Anderson Platoon, The (1967). Pierre Schoendorffer, dir. Fifteen years before Oliver Stone mounted his legendary *Platoon*, this excellent (and Oscar-winning) documentary (financed by a French filmmaking company) told pretty much the same story, only in this case, without actors. Life on the front-lines, related with unsparing honesty. ★★★★★

Apocalypse Now! See chapter 12. ★★★★★

Bat*21 (1988) Peter Markle, dir. Gene Hackman, Danny Glover, Jerry Reed, Clayton Rohmer. An actual rescue attempt served as the basis for this strong if curiously unmemorable film. Danny Glover has only a limited amount of time to rescue Hackman from behind enemy lines before his own troops attack. Exciting. ★★★★

Born on the Fourth of July (1989). Oliver Stone, dir. Tom Cruise, Tom Berenger, Willem Dafoe. Stone's follow-up to *Platoon* is even more impressive on the level of human drama, balancing a vivid combat center-section with before and after incidents in the life of wheelchair-bound vet Ron Kovic. Authentic battle scenes. ★★★★★

Boys in Company C, The (1978). Sidney J. Furie, dir. Andrew Stevens, Stan Shaw, Lee Ermey. Attempt to do *A Walk in the Sun* for the Vietnam war comes close enough to rate as worthwhile. Made the same year as *The Deer Hunter* though considerably less known, this actually comes closer to the truth. ★★★★

Casualties of War (1989). Brian De Palma, dir. Sean Penn, Michael J. Fox, Thuy Thu Lee, Ving Rhames. Earnest but at moments overplayed account of decent soldier Fox who feels compelled to report the brutal massacre of Asian civilians by crazed officer Penn. Would've been far more intriguing if the lead roles were reversed! ★★★

China Gate (1957). Samuel Fuller, dir. Nat "King" Cole, Angie Dickenson, Lee Van Cleef. The first Hollywood film to deal with combat in Indonesia, written and directed by ever-edgy WWII combat vet who dared rush in where others feared to tred. During French occupation, an international force fights commies in fierce combat. ★★★★

Dead Presidents (1995). The Hughes Brothers, dirs. Larenz Tate, Keith David, Chris Tucker, N'Bushe Wright. Effective film is one of few to relate the Nam experience from a young black soldier's viewpoint. He survives brutal combat (powerfully staged) only to find his beloved Bronx streets have become a combat zone upon returning home. ★★★★

Deer Hunter, The (1978). Michael Cimino, dir. Robert De Niro, John Cazale, Meryl Streep, Christopher Walken, John Savage. Blue collar boys' lives are uprooted when they are drafted, become prisoners of war. More a symbolic statement than a realistic depiction of actual combat. Quite remarkable—Oscar winning Best Picture of the Year. ★★★★★

84 Charlie Mopic (1989). Patrick Duncan, dir. Jonathan Emerson, Nicholas Cascone, Jason Tomlins, Richard Brooks. Yet another bloody tale of a squad in Southeast Asia is bolstered by a unique and fresh approach—the entire episode is related *You Are There* style, as a documentary camera-man might have captured it on the fly. Unique. ★★★★

Flight of the Intruder, The (1991). John Milius, dir. Danny Glover, Willem Dafoe. From the contemporary writer-director most associated with macho subjects comes this rare rah!rah! Vietnam combat film about the efforts of flyboys to provide ground troops with cover. Some exciting action scenes, though the drama is awfully clichéd. ★★★

Full Metal Jacket (1987). Stanley Kubrick, dir. Lee Ermey, Dorian Harewood, Matthew Modine, Adam Baldwin, Vincent D'Onofrio. Towering director's personal epic about young men training on Paris Island that prepares them for the inevitable combat in Vietnam. Visually stunning, intellectually overwhelming, emotionally hazy. ★★★★

Adam Baldwin (standing) leads marines into battle in *Full Metal Jacket*.

Go Tell the Spartans (1978). Ted Post, dir. Burt Lancaster, Marc Singer, Dolph Sweet, James Hong. The novel *Incident at Mac Wa* by Daniel Ford served as the basis for this superior Nam flick with lots of action and an anti-war bias. Overshadowed in its time by *The Deer Hunter*, but almost as rewarding. Gritty combat action.   ★★★★

Green Berets, The (1968). John Wayne, dir. John Wayne, Raymond St. Jacques, Aldo Ray, David Janssen. Hollywood's last loyal warrior, the Duke himself, dared mount the only major movie made during the war's height, a hackneyed collection of old combat movie clichés reset in Southeast Asia. Today, a kitschy time capsule.   ★★★

Hamburger Hill (1987). John Irvin, dir. Don Cheadle, Steven Weber, Dylan McDermott, Patrick Boatman, Don James. Expert action bolsters this factual story about the 101st Airborne Division and the deadly consequences incurred by all-out attempt to take Hamburger Hill in Nam, 1969. Only weakness—underdeveloped characterizations.   ★★★★

Hanoi Hilton, The (1987). Lionel Chetwynd, dir. Michael Moriarty, David Soul, Paul LeMat, Lary Pressman. G.I.s captured by the enemy find themselves torn between deep depression and a hopeful belief that perhaps escape is possible. Overlong (130 min.) and unrewarding, despite the obvious fine-intentions of bringing their story to life.   ★★

Iron Triangle (1989). Eric Weston, dir. Haing S. Ngor, Johnny Hallyday, James Ishida, Beau Bridges, Liem Whatley. Respectable if uninspired attempt to reduce the Vietnam War to a more human (and humane) scope, as a single American officer and a young Vietcong volunteer find themselves matched against one another in the jungle.   ★★★

Jump Into Hell (1955). David Butler, dir. Jacques Sernas, Kurt Kaznar, Peter Van Eyck, Pat Blake. Interesting, offbeat international cast in a solid B-picture, made shortly after the Korean Conflict had come to an end. The focus is on paratroopers heading for the next line of battle against spreading communism: Southeast Asia.   ★★★

Lost Command (1966). Mark Robson, dir. Anthony Quinn, Alain Delon, Claudia Cardinale, George Segal, Maurice Ronet. First major Hollywood film to deal with the conflict in Southeast Asia. Quinn is well cast as the commander of Dien Bien Phu, whose scant French troops are overcome. Well-intentioned, but unfocused point of view.   ★★★

Platoon (1986). Oliver Stone, dir. Tom Berenger, Willem Dafoe, Charlie Sheen, Forest Whitaker. The Oliver Stone morality play, as good (Dafoe) and bad (Berenger) soldiers vie for soul of recently arrived replacement (Sheen). Such dramatic simplification doesn't detract from the raw power of that rare Vietnam film actually made by a veteran.   ★★★★★

Platoon Leader (1988). Aaron Norris, dir. Michael Dudikoff, Robert F. Lyons. Chuck Norris's brother, who often helms that star's projects, took charge of this superficial actioner. Marginal star Dudikoff (of *American Ninja* mini-fame) leads his boys into fierce combat, staged so routinely even diehard action buffs will be bored.   ★

Quiet American, The (1958). Joseph Mankiewicz, dir. Audie Murphy, Michael Redgrave. Ambitious if muddled attempt to film Graham Greene's superb novel. A seemingly innocent youth is in fact the first C.I.A. agent to slip into post–WWII Southeast Asia as an agent provocateur. Murph cannot convey his character's moral complexity.   ★★

Tigerland (2000). Joel Schumacher, dir. Colin Farrell, Matthew Davis, Shea Whigham. Yet another story about soldiers training for combat, but bolstered by a unique plot twist—the boys are assigned to attack a "virtual" enemy, constructed to look like the real thing, right here in America, with ironic results. Strong, innovative actioner. ★★★★

Uncommon Valor (1983). Ted Kotcheff, dir. Gene Hackman, Fred Ward, Robert Stack, Reb Brown, Michael Dudikoff. Extremely watchable film combines the realism of *Platoon* with the rah!rah! heroics of *Rambo* and somehow makes it work. This is a *Magnificent Seven* variation about combat vets who return to rescue "lost" MIAs. ★★★★

We Were Soldiers (2002). Randall Wallace, dir. Mel Gibson. True story of soldiers fighting in Ia Drang Valley, jungle area that saw some of the most brutal combat of the war. The most blatantly patriotic take on Vietnam since John Wayne's *The Green Berets*, though all similarity ends there, for this is authentic and convincing. ★★★★★

Yank in Viet-nam, A (1964). Marshall Thompson, dir. Marshall Thompson, Enrique Magalona, Mario Barri. Most people had not yet heard of Vietnam (they soon would!) when Thompson, the road company John Wayne, made this B-movie about America's early entry into Southeast Asia. So-so staging of action scenes diminishes potential. ★★★

Mel Gibson as the combat team leader in *We Were Soldiers*.

20

THE B-MOVIE BOYS

In the beginning there were Buster Crabbe and Johnny Weissmuller, Olympic greats whose athletic abilities made them appropriate for a limited range of screen stardom. Over the decades, others came to Hollywood from far-flung fields, likewise proving that a minimalist approach to acting, coupled with an emphasis on stunt work, would allow for a killer career as action hero. Here are the best.

Jim (Nathaniel) Brown

Born February 17, 1936, on St. Simons Island, Georgia, achieved fame as a sports hero long before becoming a movie star. While a student at Syracuse University, Brown proved his mettle not only as a gridiron great but also on the lacrosse field. Football, though, remained his great love—after graduation, Jim played fullback for the Cleveland Browns from 1957–1965, becoming a Hall of Famer in 1971. Only man included in Halls of Fame for three sports: pro, college football, lacrosse. When Brown retired at age 29, he held a record career total of 12,312 yards gained. Rugged (6-foot-2) good looks had Hollywood beckoning even while still a pro-athlete, mostly for action roles. He did appear in several dramatic movies, most notably opposite Jacqueline Bisset in *The Grasshopper* (1970). Smart enough to realize he'd never threaten Brando, Brown glanced at Clint Eastwood in spaghetti westerns, quipped: "Hell, I can do *that!*" Following a stint as supporting actor in big-budget action movies, notably *The Dirty Dozen*, he swiftly embraced stardom in B-budget black exploitation flicks, all the rage during the early to mid-1970s.

ACTION FILMOGRAPHY

Rio Conchos (1964); *The Dirty Dozen* (1967); *Dark of the Sun* (1968); *Ice Station Zebra* (1968); *The Split* (1968); *100 Rifles* (1969); *Riot* (1969); *Kenner* (1969); *tick . . . tick . . . tick* (1970); *El Condor* (1970); *Slaughter* (1972); *Black Gunn* (1972); *Slaughter's Big Rip-Off* (1973); *The Slams* (1973); *I Escaped*

From Devil's Island (1973); *Three the Hard Way* (1974); *Take a Hard Ride* (1975); *Kid Vengeance* (1977); *Pacific Inferno* (1979); *One Down, Two to Go* (1982); *The Running Man* (1987); *I'm Gonna Git You Sucka* (1988); *Crack House* (1989); *L.A. Heat* (1989); *Twisted Justice* (1990); *Killing American Style* (1998); *Divine Enforcer* (aka *Deadly Avenger*, 1991); *Original Gangstas* (1996); *Mars Attacks!* (1996); *He Got Game* (1998); *Small Soldiers* (voice only, 1998); *Any Given Sunday* (1999).

MUST-SEE

Rio Conchos (Gordon Douglas, dir.). Fine, unheralded action western with Richard Boone, Stuart Whitman, Tony Franciosca (as a Mexican!) feuding over cache of high-powered rifles. Brown, in debut, is appealing as a strong, softspoken soldier.

The Dirty Dozen: See chapter 18.

Dark of the Sun: See "Rod Taylor" in chapter 14.

Slaughter (Jack Starett, dir.). Famous black-exploitation flick with Brown as former Green Beret, back home, taking on white crime lords exploiting ghetto residents by selling them drugs. Jim, of course, wastes 'em all. A huge hit in its time, still potent and exciting.

Three the Hard Way (Gordon Parks, Jr.). Brown, Fred Williamson, and Jim Kelly as the three black musketeers, modern-day avengers taking on bigoted madman (Jay Robinson) who threatens African American community. Among the very best of its genre.

Bruce Campbell

Born June 22, 1958, in Royal Oak, Michigan. Bruce and his older brother, huge fans of TV action shows, persuaded neighborhood kids to "live out" episodes of *Lost In Space*. Officially announced intention to be an actor at age 8, after seeing his dad in local theatre—Bruce's earliest role was as the young prince in *The King and I*. Thereafter, became fascinated with making movies, directing super-8 action flicks. To finance such projects, he took baby-sitting jobs, one for Ted Raimi, linking Bruce with the child's older brother, Sam. The following summer, Bruce landed a job as apprentice at Traverse City's Cherry County Playhouse—then, on to Western Michigan University, where he took drama classes. Worked in Detroit, making TV commercials, in 1979 joining Sam for Indie film, raising $350,000 to make *Evil Dead*. On to L.A., where Bruce starred in the short lived *Brisco County, Jr.* series. Directed episodes of *Hercules* and portrayed a continuing character. Philosophic attitude toward ups and downs of show business revealed in 2001 autobiography, *If Chins Could Kill: Confessions of a "B" Movie Actor.*

ACTION FILMOGRAPHY

Within the Woods (1978); *Evil Dead* (1982); *Going Back* (1983); *Crimewave* (1985); *Evil Dead II* (1987); *Maniac Cop* (1988); *The Dead Next Door* (aka *Intruder,* 1988); *Moontrap* (1989); *Sundown: The Vampire in Retreat* (1989); *Maniac Cop 2* (1990); *Darkman* (1990); *Mindwarp* (1990); *Lost In Time* (1992); *Army of Darkness* (1993); *Congo* (1995); *Demolitionist* (1996); *Escape From L.A.* (1996); *Power.com* (1996); *Chase Moran* (1996); *Running Time* (1997); *Pitfall 3-D* (1997); *Gold Rush!* (1998); *Ice Rink* (2000); *From Dusk Till Dawn 2: Texas Blood Money* (1999); *Icebreaker* (1999); *Evil Dead: Hail to the King* (2000); *Tachyon: The Fringe* (2000); *Nobody Knows* (2000); *Hubert's Brain* (2001); *The Majestic* (2001); *Spider Man* (2002); *Phantasm's End* (2002); *Bubba Ho-Tep* (2002).

Bruce Campbell in *Army of Darkness*.

MUST-SEE

Evil Dead (Sam Raimi, dir.). Shot on miniscule budget, it's not difficult to see why this innovative indy was picked up by New Line and became video sensation. More horror than action. Young quintet engage in violent antics while hanging in isolated mountain cabin.

Crimewave (Sam Raimi, dir.). Absolutely unmissable movie for Campbell/Raimi fans, particularly as this Detroit-lensed gangster flick was co-written by Joel and Ethan Coen. Think *Natural Born Killers* played as an easygoing comedy—you've got the picture!

Evil Dead II (Sam Raimi, dir.). With nearly twenty times the budget of first film, Raimi and Campbell improve on their original. Less sequel than redux, this time around being sure to stuff in all the antics they couldn't afford before, particularly in terms of F/X.

Army of Darkness: See chapter 21.

David (John Arthur) Carradine

Born December 8, 1936, in Hollywood, son of legendary character actor John C. First taste of stardom came in 1966 when David played the role Alan Ladd had created in *Shane* (1952) on TV. Broadcast opposite Jackie Gleason on Saturday evenings, the high-quality series lasted thirteen weeks. Critics took note, though, one calling him "a cross between John Barrymore and Mick Jagger." Character roles (mostly bad guys) followed, then *Kung Fu*. A true iconoclast, David's quiet charisma and existential aura landed him leads in major movies, including Woody Guthrie in Hal Ashby's *Bound for Glory* (1976) and Ingmar Bergman's fascinating misfire *The Serpent's Egg* (1978). When both failed at the box office, David drifted into B-budget movies, playing leads in karate-oriented projects. After taking the villain's role in *Lone Wolf McQuade*, in which he is soundly defeated by Chuck Norris, David's once-invincible image shattered. Then, a gradual descent into ever less interesting programmers, often in supporting roles. Occasionally, he attempted something special with indie filmmaking, including the offbeat *Americana* (1981), which Carradine wrote, directed, and composed the music for.

ACTION FILMOGRAPHY

Taggart (1964); *The Violent Ones* (1967); *Young Billy Young* (1969); *Macho Callahan* (1970); *Boxcar Bertha* (1972); *Death Race 2000* (1975); *Cannonball* (1976); *Thunder and Lightning* (1977); *Gray Lady Down* (1978); *Deathsport* (1978); *Circle of Iron* (aka, *The Silent Flute*, 1979); *Fast Charlie, The Moonbeam Rider* (1979); *The Long Riders* (1980); *Q* (aka, *The Winged Serpent*,

1982); *Safari 3000* (1982) *Lone Wolf McQuade* (1983); *Rio Abajo* (1984); *The Warrior and the Sorceress* (1984); *Behind Enemy Lines* (1986); *Armed Response* (1986); *The Misfit Brigade* (aka, *Wheels of Terror*, 1987); *Wizards of the Lost Kingdom II* (1988); *Warlords* (1988); *Open Fire* (1988); *Crime Zone* (1988); *Nowhere to Run* (1989); *Bird on a Wire* (1990); *Martial Law* (1990); *Future Zone* (1990); *Future Force* (1990); *Dune Warriors* (1990); *Project Eliminator* (1991); *Karate Cop* (1991); *Field of Fire* (1991); *Distant Justice* (1992); *Kill Zone* (1993); *Code Death* (1993); *Macon County Jail* (1997); *Full Blast* (1997); *Light Speed* (1998); *The Defectors* (1998); *Stray Bullet II* (1998); *Natural Selection* (1999); *Down 'n Dirty* (2000); *Wheatfield With Crows* (2002).

MUST-SEE

Boxcar Bertha (Martin Scorsese, dir.). One of many post–*Bonnie and Clyde* cheapies about rural outlaws, this was the best, thanks to brilliant young director Scorsese's sense of style. David's dad appears in small part; co-star is Barbara Hershey in title role.

   Death Race 2000: See chapter 21.

   Circle of Iron: See chapter 15.

   The Long Riders (Walter Hill, dir.). Rare A-budget action movie for Carradine, cast as Cole Younger, his brothers playing on-screen siblings. James and Stacey Keach as Jesse and Frank James. Wonderful sense of post–Civil War period, fine shoot-outs.

   The Warrior and the Sorceress (John Broderick, dir.). *Yojimbo* transplanted to a post-apocalyptic future. D.C. is the anti-hero, Maria Socas his action babe.

   Lone Wolf McQuade: See "Chuck Norris," this chapter.

Sho(ichi) Kosugi

Born June 17, 1948, in a Tokyo suburb, Sho began studying martial arts at age 5 when his sisters urged the weakly youth (a hole existed in Sho's lung since birth) to find some way to defend himself against street gangs. *Shindo-Jinen Ryu* was the karate form that most intrigued him, Master Konishi becoming his instructor. A reclusive neighbor, Mr. Yamamoto, introduced the eager youth to the forbidden art of *Ninjitsu*. Hooked, Sho learned *Kendo* and *Judo* in grade school, *Iaido* and *Kobudo* in high school, became all-Japan karate champion at age 18. Such practice drew time away from other studies.

Near-suicidal after rejection by a Japanese college, Sho flew to the United States, studied at Pasadena City College, then California State University, graduating with bachelor's degree in economics. To pay tuition, taught karate. This became a lucrative business, allowing him to open his own *dojo*. Engaged in international competitions, won record 633 awards for martial arts expertise, including L.A. open in 1972, 1973, and 1974. As a result, Cannon films cast him in lucrative low-budget action movies. Co-starred on TV's *The Master* with Lee Van Cleef; Sho created a popular ninja game, *Tenchu: Stealth Assassins*, for SONY Playstation.

ACTION FILMOGRAPHY

Flash Challenger (1969); *Dance of Death* (aka, *Enter the Ninja*, 1981); *Revenge of the Ninja* (1983); *Ninja III—The Domination* (1964); *Master Ninja I* (1984); *Pray For Death* (1985); *Nine Deaths of the Ninja* (1985); *Rage of Honor* (1987); *Black Eagle* (1988); *Blind Fury* (1989); *Kabuto* (1990); *Journey of Honor* (aka, *Shogun Warrior*, 1992); *Kyokuto koku shakai* (1993).

MUST-SEE

Revenge of the Ninja (Sam Firstenberg, dir.). Follow-up to wildly successful first film is better, if far from great. At least Sho plays the lead this time, shows off his amazing skills.

Ninja III—The Domination (Sam Firstenberg, dir.). Beautiful babe (Lucinda Dickey) is possessed by ghostly spirit of an evil Ninja, kills off his old enemies. The bloodbath in a hot tub, involving bevy of bikini-clad hookers, is sure somethin' to see!

Black Eagle (Eric Karson, dir.). Change of pace for Sho, semi-successful at playing a James Bond–type supersuave hero, fighting against evil Russian (Jean-Claude Van Damme) in Cold War throwback. Their climactic fight scene is not to be missed.

Christopher (Guy Denis) Lambert

Born March 29, 1957, in Great Neck, Long Island. Father was a UN diplomat, so young Lambert attended posh boarding schools on the continent. In Geneva, he appeared in school plays, later attending Paris Conservatoire. Won small roles in Gallic movies, beginning with *Le Bar du Telephone* (1980). Some observers predicted myopia, an eye disease he'd contracted as a child,

Christopher Lambert in *Highlander.*

would rule him out as movie star owing to a perennial glazed-over expression. Others believed this would become his trademark. An international search was then held to find the new Tarzan and Lambert won over all contenders. This film and *Highlander* seemed likely to establish him as an A-list action star, though that never happened. Lambert married Diane Lane and, for a decade, they appeared together whenever possible—i.e., *Priceless Beauty* (1988)—though the marriage eventually ended (they share a daughter). Like other B-action stars, Lambert began producing. Also, he employed TV to bolster action hero image, appearing on a *WWF Smackdown!* broadcast, November 8, 2000.

ACTION FILMOGRAPHY

Greystoke: The Legend of Tarzan, Lord of the Apes (1984); *Highlander* (1986); *The Sicilian* (1987); *To Kill a Priest* (1988); *Highlander II: The Quickening* (1991); *Knight Moves* (1992); *Loaded Weapon I* (uncredited guest, 1993); *Fortress* (1993); *Gunmen* (1994); *The Road Killers* (1994); *Highlander III: The Sorcerer* (1994); *The Hunted* (1995); *Mortal Kombat* (1995); *North Star*

(1996); *Adrenalin* (1996); *Mean Guns* (1997); *Beowulf* (1999); *Gideon* (1999); *Fortress 2* (1999); *Highlander: Endgame* (2000); *Druids* (2001); *Point Men* (2001); *Absolon* (2002).

MUST-SEE

Greystoke: The Legend of Tarzan, Lord of the Apes (Hugh Hudson, dir.). Intelligent, upscale rendering of the Edgar Rice Burroughs classic, with Lambert impressive as the title character and wonderful ape makeup by Rick Baker. Great while in jungle, though second half, set in England, falters.

Highlander (Russel Mulcahy, dir.). Wonderful blend of period-piece action in ancient Scotland with postmodernist thriller set in modern America. Sean Connery adds great charm as Lambert's mentor, and the hero fights evil in two time periods.

Fortress (Stuart Gordon, dir.). One of Lambert's few solid hits after *Greystoke* and *Highlander*. The script pits a futuristic hero against ugly enemies who detain him in a high-tech prison. Nothing new, but very well done for what it is.

Dolph (Hans) Lundgren

Born November 3, 1959, in Stockholm, Sweden. Like Sonny Chiba, Dolph has come to represent incoherent brute strength on-screen, though nothing could be further from reality. As a child, it was apparent early on that he possessed an amazing intellect. Attended Royal Institute of Technology in Stockholm, then received a master's degree in engineering at University of Sydney, New South Wales. A Fullbright scholarship brought him to the United States, where he excelled at

Dolph Lundgren in *Red Scorpion*.

prestigious M.I.T. A chance meeting with drama coach Warren Robertson at NYC's then-trendy Limelight Disco convinced Dolph he had a shot at movie stardom. One of 5000 hopefuls who tried out for part of Russian boxer in pre-perestroka *Rocky IV*. Winning the part, he proceeded to star in series of inexpensive action flicks, often producing them through his own company, Thor Pictures/Red Orm. Holds a second degree black belt in the unique form of karate known, among *cognescenti,* as Kyokunshinkai. Dolph served as Team Leader of 1996 U.S. Olympic Penthalon Team.

ACTION FILMOGRAPHY

A View to a Kill (1985); *Rocky IV* (1985); *Masters of the Universe* (1987); *Red Scorpion* (1989); *The Punisher* (1989); *I Come in Peace* (1990); *Cover-Up* (1990); *Showdown in Little Tokyo* (1991); *The Universal Soldier* (1992); *Pentathlon* (1994); *Men of War* (1994); *The Shooter* (1995); *Silent Trigger* (1996); *The Peacekeeper* (1997); *John Woo's Blackjack* (1998); *The Minion* (aka *Fallen Knight,* 1998); *Sweepers* (1999); *Bridge of Dragons* (1999); *Storm Catcher* (1999); *Bone Ripper* (2000); *Last Patrol* (aka *Last Warrior,* 2000); *Agent Red* (2000); *Hidden Agenda* (2001); *Legion* (2001).

MUST-SEE

Rocky IV: See chapter 22.

　　Masters of the Universe (Gary Goddard, dir.). Lavishly mounted screen version of then-faddish comic book and line of action toys. He-Man (Lundgren) opposes evil Skeletor (Frank Langella) for a key that holds control of the cosmos.

　　The Punisher (Mark Goldblatt, dir.). From the pages of Marvel Comics—and the mind of Gerry Conway—comes this tale of a vengeance-driven cop, out to eliminate street slime.

　　The Universal Soldier (Roland Emmerich, dir.). Solid vehicle for both Lundgren and Jean-Claude Van Damme, as cyborgs locked in a bitter vendetta that's been festering since the Vietnam War. Constant duels between leads gives this action-movie its momentum.

Audie (Leon) Murphy

Born near Kingston, Texas June 20, 1924, into a poor farming family. When World War II broke out, diminutive (5-foot-5) 18-year-old Audie was rejected by the marines and navy before finally being accepted into the army.

Went on to serve in seven campaigns in Italy and France, winning thirty-three citations, including the Congressional Medal of Honor. Murphy played himself in *To Hell and Back*, a rare A-feature for the nominal star. Most of Murphy's movies were B-westerns, more often than not with Audie typecast as a shy, charming hero. He seemed precisely right to star in one of era's TV westerns, yet *Whispering Smith* (which he also produced) was a flop. As the sixties began, slipped into cheaper action films, accepted out of necessity owing to an addiction to gambling that had swallowed up his considerable earnings. Too old to play a brash youth any longer, he left films and became a spokesman for various business concerns. While flying to a speaking engagement, the small plane he traveled in crashed, on May 28, 1971. Buried in Arlington National Cemetery.

ACTION FILMOGRAPHY

The Kid From Texas (1950); *Sierra* (1950); *Kansas Raiders* (1950); *The Red Badge of Courage* (1951); *The Cimarron Kid* (1951); *Duel at Silver Creek* (1952); *Gunsmoke* (1953); *Column South* (1953); *Tumbleweed* (1953); *Ride Clear of Diablo* (1954); *Drums Across the River* (1954); *To Hell and Back* (1955); *Destry* (1955); *Walk the Proud Land* (1956); *Guns of Fort Petticoat* (1957); *Night Passage* (1957); *Ride a Crooked Trail* (1958); *The Gun Runners* (1958); *No Name on the Bullet* (1959); *The Wild and the Innocent* (1959); *Cast a Long Shadow* (1959); *Hell Bent for Leather* (1960); *Seven Ways From Sundown* (1960); *Posse From Hell* (1960); *Unforgiven* (1960); *Battle at Bloody Beach* (1961); *Six Black Horses* (1962); *Showdown* (1963); *Gunfight at Comanche Creek* (1964); *The Quick Gun* (1964); *Bullet for a Badman* (1964); *Apache Rifles* (1964); *Arizona Raiders* (1965); *Gunpoint* (1966); *The Texican* (1966); *40 Guns to Apache Pass* (1966); *A Time For Dying* (1967).

MUST-SEE

The Red Badge of Courage (John Huston, dir.). Reverse typecasting has Murphy playing a coward who deserts northern army during Civil War, later redeeming himself. Huston's vivid, historically accurate film version of Stephen Crane's novel was cut drastically by its studio and flopped financially. Despite that, it remains a true classic.

To Hell and Back: See chapter 27.

Night Passage (James Nielsen, dir.). The esteemed Anthony Mann was at one point supposed to direct this interesting hybrid of Universal's A-westerns, starring James Stewart, and that studio's B-pictures with Murphy.

They play brothers, one working for railroad, the other (Audie) attempting to rob a payroll train. Sturdy, atmospheric, winning.

No Name on the Bullet (Jack Arnold, dir.). Most highly regarded among Audie's B-westerns, thanks to clever reverse typecasting. Baby-faced gun for hire arrives in "respectable" town to kill an unnamed citizen who is actually a former criminal. Everyone in town turns out to have "a past" and each believes he is the target.

The Unforgiven (John Huston, dir.). Audie's only A-budget western, based on book by Alan Le May (*The Searchers*), casts him as member of a Texas ranching family. He and big brother (Burt Lancaster) gradually realize their "sister" (Audrey Hepburn) was actually stolen away from the hated Apache tribe. The siege of their sodhouse, with terrified cattle up on top, is incredible.

Chuck (Carlos Ray) Norris

Born March 10, 1940, in Ryan, Oklahoma. After graduation from high school (Torrance, California, where the family had moved), he enlisted in the air force. In Korea, first introduced to martial arts by instructor Bruce Lee, specifically *Tang Soo Do*, soon becoming a black belt. Back home, went to work for an aviation company, moonlighting as a karate instructor. One pupil, Steve McQueen, told Chuck: "When you can't do anything else, there's always acting." Norris concentrated on competitions, played small role in a Matt Helm spy flick. First won Professional World Middleweight Karate Champion in 1968, a title he maintained until retiring (undefeated) in 1974, then named Fighter of the Year by *Black Belt* magazine, 1969. Appeared

Chuck Norris in *Missing in Action*.

(as villain) opposite friend Bruce Lee in a Hong Kong flick. Didn't seriously consider a film career until the sudden popularity of *Kung Fu* TV series and simultaneous importation of martial arts movies. In a notable departure from the violence-oriented work of many others, Norris—a truly gentle person—insisted that his films depict combat only as a last resort, employed for self-defense, compared with the brutal flamboyance of, say, Sonny Chiba. Chuck's TV series, *Walker, Texas Ranger,* became a long run hit.

ACTION FILMOGRAPHY

The Wrecking Crew (1969); *Way of* (aka *Return of*) *the Dragon* (1972), *Enter the Dragon* (1973), *Slaughter in San Francisco* (1973); *Breaker! Breaker!* (1977); *Good Guys Wear Black* (1978); *A Froce of One* (1979); *The Octagon* (1980); *An Eye for an Eye* (1981); *Silent Rage* (1982); *Forced Vengeance* (1982); *Lone Wolf McQuade* (1983); *Missing in Action* (1984); *Code of Silence* (1985); *Invasion U.S.A.* (1985); *Missing in Action 2: The Beginning* (1985); *Delta Force* (1986); *Firewalker* (1986); *Braddock: Missing in Action III* (1988); *Hero and the Terror* (1988); *Delta Force II: Operation Stranglehold* (1990); *The Hitman* (1991); *Sidekicks* (1992); *Hellbound* (1993); *Top Dog* (1995); *Forest Warrior* (1996).

MUST-SEE

Enter the Dragon: See chapter 12.

Good Guys Wear Black (Ted Post, dir.). By far the best of the early Norris mini-epics, here playing a government agent out to stop anti-American forces. Several strong stunt sequences include unforgettable feet-first leap through a glass windshield.

Force of One (Paul Aaron, dir.). Good supporting cast (including Ron O'Neal, of *Superfly*) and James Whitmore, plus a convincing romance with gorgeous Jennifer O'Neill, makes this actionful opus a perennial winner with the star's solid cult following.

Lone Wolf McQuade (Steve Carver, dir.). One of Chuck's best, an imaginative precursor to the *Walker, Texas Ranger* series, filmed in a style recalling Sergio Leone spaghetti westerns. David Carradine makes a fine villain and their climactic duel is stupendous.

Code of Silence (Andy Davis, dir.). Effective, thanks to a strong script originally intended for Clint Eastwood, an excellent villain (Henry Silva), three well-staged matches (added to script specifically for Norris), and Chuck's best performance to date.

Firewalker (J. Lee Thompson). A real winner among Chuck's later films, thanks to terrific buddy-buddy casting with Oscar-winner Lou Gossett, Jr. They play mercenaries in search of hidden treasure. Constant action effectively played with an agreeable lcomic edge.

Sidekicks: See chapter 8.

Steve Reeves

Born January 21, 1926, in Glasgow, Montana. After Steve's father died in a farming accident, his mother moved with her 2-year-old son to Oakland, California. Steve delivered newspapers to help pay bills, finding time to exercise on route. Shortly, he was known as a tremendous wrist wrestler. When another lad, who regularly worked out, defeated Steve, he entered a bodybuilding regimen at Catlemont High. Served in the Philippines during World War II, afterwards winning the Mr. Pacific Coast title (1946), Mr. America (1947), and Mr. Universe (1950). Suffered a career setback, losing out on upcoming role of "Samson" in a Cecil B. DeMille film to Vic Mature. Only film work he could find at the time was for the ubiquitous Ed Wood, Jr. in his sleaze sensation *Jail Bait* (1954). Then came the big break, more or less playing himself in MGM's Debbie Reynolds musical, *Athena* (1954), about the sudden popularity of health foods. Dino de Laurentiis spotted him in it, invited Reeves to star in the early sand-and-sandal mini-epics. Personal life, which Reeves kept private, included marriage to a Polish countess, Aline Czarzawicz. Following his retirement from films, he helped initiate the concept of "power-walking"—that is, carrying weights while engaging in strenuous strolls.

Steve Reeves in *Hercules Unchained*.

ACTION FILMOGRAPHY

Hercules (1959); *Hercules Unchained* (1960); *Goliath and the Barbarians* (1960); *Last Days of Pompeii* (1960); *Duel of the Titans* (1961); *The White Warrior* (1961); *Morgan the Pirate* (1961); *The Thief of Baghdad* (1961); *The Trojan Horse* (1962); *The Slave* (1963).

MUST-SEE

Hercules (Pietro Francisci, dir.). Legendary strong man's key role in Jason's quest for the Golden Fleece (with young Ulysses thrown in for good measure) provides the basis for colorful action-filled adventure, more lavish than the numerous sword-and-sandal mini-epics to follow. Look for Lucianna Paluzzi and Gianna Maria Canale as Amazons.

    Hercules Unchained (Pietro Francisci, dir.). Hercules and wife Iole (Sylvia Koscina) head for Thebes and become involved in a civil war following the banishment of Oedipus. High points include Reeves's lengthy duel with former champion heavyweight Primo Carnera, amnesiac hero's torrid affair with beautiful siren Omphale (Sylvia Lopez).

    Goliath and the Barbarians (Carlo Campogalianni, dir.). Reeves's least-known feature is his best. He plays a good giant (no, not *that* Goliath!) whose exploits precede those of *Conan the Barbarian*. With Bruce Cabot (of *King Kong* fame) as the villain, and the incomparable Chelo Alonso as an erotic dancing princess.

    Morgan the Pirate (Andre de Toth, dir.). Nice change of pace for Reeves, this time as a seagoing adventurer, and for once blessed with a respected American action director. Try and catch the uncut (105-min.) print. Valerie Legrange and Chelo Alonso are the babes.

    The Thief of Baghad (Arthur Lubin, dir.). Imaginative redux of beloved fable can't live up to 1924 (Doug Fairbanks) or 1940 (Sabu) versions, though highly entertaining if taken for its own merits. Production values above par for such international fantasy fare.

Steven Seagal

Born April 10, 1951, in Lansing, Michigan. Whether he served as a secret agent for the CIA, as he's often suggested, remains questionable. Seagal did—as "Master ake Shigemichi"—perform as the chief instructor at Aikido Tenshin Donjo in Osaka, the first American to do so. Returned to United States,

teaching upscale residents in Beverly Hills. His key instructee was Mike Ovitz, super-agent, who once bragged that he could turn *anyone* into a star. There followed a deal allowing Steven to co-write and help produce as well as "act" in *Above the Law*. Steven's career took off when more lavish vehicle, *Under Siege*, loomed large at box office. Attempted to play down violence and make a "big statement" in *On Deadly Ground,* though the vast audience and his loyal fans deserted him in droves. Ever since, Seagal's been struggling to find a place in the rapidly shifting world of action movies. Married to actress-model Kelly LeBrock between 1987 and 1996, appeared opposite her in *Hard to Kill*. Only martial arts expert to be as associated with a single hand weapon as Dirty Harry Callahan and his oversized Magnum, S.S. carries an intimidating Colt M1911 automatic in each film.

Steven Seagal in *Under Siege.*

ACTION FILMOGRAPHY

Above the Law (1988); *Hard to Kill* (1990); *Marked for Death* (1990); *Out for Justice* (1991); *Under Siege* (1992); *On Deadly Ground* (1994); *Under Siege 2:*

Dark Territory (1995); *Executive Decision* (1996); *The Glimmer Man* (1996); *Fire Down Below* (1997); *The Patriot* (1998); *Get Bruce!* (1999); *Exit Wounds* (2001); *Ticker* (2001); *Half Past Dead* (2002).

MUST-SEE

Above the Law (Andrew Davis, dir.). Impressive premiere film for Seagal, playing "edgy" Chicago cop with martial arts skills who goes after a drug cartel as well as corrupt fellow officers, only to be attacked by both. Pam Grier and Sharon Stone are around for female companionship, and Henry Silva is always welcome as a slimey villain.

Hard to Kill (Bruce Malmuth, dir.). His second time around, Seagal once again plays a Dirty Harry clone only with aikido skills, uncovering corruption in police force. This man knows martial arts, and the film displays them well.

Under Siege (Andrew Davis, dir.). Terrific *Die Hard* variation, set on a battleship, where cook (?!) Seagal jumps into action as terrorists board, led by Tommy Lee Jones and Gary Busey, both excellent. Fine showcase for Seagal's martial arts skills, handsome production values, plus Erika Eleniak hops out of a cake topless.

Under Siege 2: Dark Territory (Geoff Murphy, dir.). This time around, *Die Hard* on a speeding train, with requisite number of terrorists out to steal nuclear weapons, though not reckoning on one-man army Seagal. Fine actor Eric Bogosian makes an over-the-top villain seem almost believable, and the stunts are spectacular.

Jean-Claude Van Damme (Camille Francois)

Born October 18, 1960, in Sint-Agatha Berchem, Belgium. Nicknamed "the Muscles from Brussels," J.C. self-consciously set out to achieve martial arts stardom like his hero Bruce Lee. Was named European Professional Karate Association middleweight champion, and learned to speak English by watching *The Flintstones*. Showed up on set of *Predator* to play the monster, left after a single day, uncomfortable with anonymity. Tried to mainstream his career with disastrous results via an appearance as self on *Friends*. When asked why his films aren't shot in Hollywood, J.C. insists it's because his stunts are so violent that he fears lawsuits. In fact, he *was* sued for "willfully" gouging an extra's eye during a scene for *Cyborg*. Yet another court case

Jean-Claude Van Damme in *Legionnaire*.

involved Frank Dux, a martial arts expert, who claimed to have collaborated on *The Quest* but received none of profits. Jean-Claude won owing to lack of evidence; later, he played a character named "Dux" in *Bloodsport*. Personal life has been notably turbulent—J.C. entered a substance abuse clinic in December 1996, then checked out a week later. Charged with DUI in September 1999.

ACTION FILMOGRAPHY

No Retreat, No Surrender (1988); *Bloodsport* (1988); *Black Eagle* (1988); *Cyborg* (1989); *Kickboxer* (1989); *Lionheart* (1990): *Death Warrant* (1990); *Double Impact* (1991); *Universal Soldier* (1992); *Nowhere to Run* (1993); *The Last Action Hero* (cameo, 1993); *Hard Target* (1993); *Timecop* (1994); *Street Fighter* (1994); *Sudden Death* (1995); *The Quest* (1996); *Maximum Risk* (1996); *Double Team* (aka *Colony*, 1997); *Legionnaire* (1998); *Universal Soldier: The Return* (1999); *Coyote Moon* (1999); *Replicant* (2001); *The Order* (2001); *The Monk* (2001); *Derailed* (2001); *Abominable* (2002).

MUST-SEE

Lionheart (Sheldon Lettich, dir.). Forget the title of an earlier film, as *this* is the one in which JCVD really does get to play a street fighter, with plenty of matches, well staged.

Black Eagle: See "Sho Kosugi" in chapter 20.

Double Impact (Sheldon Lettich, dir.). Impressive and imaginative opus with Van Damme as twins, one a hero and the other the villain. Good looking movie has some terrific fight sequences, notably those involving bodybuilder babe Cory Everson as the villainess.

The Quest (Jean Claude Van Damme, dir.). J.C.'s impressive debut behind camera and a large-scale scope make this a winner. Former 007 Roger Moore is on board for a highly involving tale about the ultimate kung fu competition, with a dozen experts appearing. For Van Damme fans, this is as good as it gets; for others, its as good as *he* gets.

Maximum Risk (Ringo Lam, dir.). Jean Claude's in double trouble again, this time realizing that he's a ringer for a man that both the criminals and cops are out to get. Lots of action, well staged by chop-socky expert Lam. Natasha Henstridge co-stars.

Jan-Michael Vincent

Born July 15, 1944, in Denver. The family moved to California, where J.M. devoted himself to surfing. His striking "California-dude" looks won the youth a Universal contract during the final days of the old Studio system. Introduced (along with James Caan, Michael Sarrazin, Harrison Ford) in *Journey to Shiloh*, a minor-league showcase for the new studio talent. Significant early roles included a wiseass kid in big budget items: *The Undefeated* with John Wayne, *Bite the Bullet* with Gene Hackman, and *Hooper* with Burt Reynolds. Won the lead in *Tribes* (1970), a high-quality TV movie about the generation gap in the military, *World's Greatest Athlete* (1973), a Disney live-action comedy. Universal tried to convince Spielberg he should play "Hooper" in *Jaws*; the director saw it otherwise. *Buster and Billie* (1974) and *Baby Blue Marine* (1976) flopped, so J.M.V. turned to TV, with the lead on an action series, *Airwolf*. After that, everything that could go wrong did. An August 1996 car crash left him with a broken neck. Arrested on July 20, 2000 for a "physical altercation" with wife Patricia Christ. The fast-fading star then violated his parole by instances of public drunkenness, three times in six-month period. A sixty-day jail term followed, after which J.M. entered a live-in substance-abuse treatment program.

ACTION FILMOGRAPHY

Bandits (1967); *Journey to Shiloh* (1967); *The Undefeated* (1969); *The Mechanic* (1972); *White Line Fever* (1975); *Bite the Bullet* (1975); *Shadow of the Hawk* (1976); *Vigilante Force* (1976); *Damnation Alley* (1977); *Hooper* (1978); *Big Wednesday* (1978); *Alien's Return* (1980); *Defiance* (1980); *The Last Plane Out* (1983); *Enemy Territory* (1987); *Hit List* (1988); *Alienator* (1989); *Raw Nerve* (1991); *Xtro II* (1991); *Hangfire* (1991); *Divine Enforcer* (aka *Deadly Avenger*, 1991); *Beyond the Call of Duty* (1992); *Deadly Heroes* (1994); *Codename: Silencer* (1995); *Russian Roulette* (1995); *The Last Kill* (1996); *The Thundering 8th* (2000); *Escape to Grizzly Mountain* (2000); *White Boy* (2002).

MUST-SEE

The Mechanic (Michael Winner, dir.). Moody actioner with Charles Bronson playing an aging hitman, Vincent his young protégée. Peckinpah might've made something special out of John Lewis Carlino's script; Winner merely gets the job done. But this does contain one of Jan-Michael's finest performances.

White Line Fever (Jonathan Kaplan, dir.). One of many trucker-as-modern-cowboy films, unaccountably popular during the mid-seventies, and easily the best of its type. Vincent (with Kay Lenz his female lead) excels as a rugged individualist taking on slimey corporate badguys via CB radios.

Bite the Bullet: See chapter 15.

Damnation Alley: See chapter 21.

Big Wednesday: See chapter 15.

21
BEST OF THE Bs

Before 1950, the term "B-movie" referred to sleazy quickies churned out by Poverty Row companies with names like Mascot and Monogram. Each ran under 90 minutes, available for rental to small theaters that didn't have access to upscale Hollywood products. Then, a new era dawned—television kept middle-aged people home except for weekends. Young producer-director Roger Corman sensed the presence of an emerging youth audience that craved its own films to augment the rock 'n' roll music they'd discovered. Shortly, he produced junk movies that, with the passage of time, have come to be thought of as an edgy alternative art form. Originally, they played at urban theaters and Drive-Ins, later showing up on home video and DVD. Here are some of the most impressive postwar examples.

Action Jackson (1988). Most ambitious of several projects designed to turn Carl Weathers, Stallone's sparring partner in *Rocky* films, into an action star. He plays a sophisticated Bondish hero, matched in martial arts combat against the obligatory megalomaniac villain (Craig T. Nelson), romancing beauties Sharon Stone and Vanity.

Arena, The (aka *Naked Warriors*, 1973). One of the best teamings for two 1970s Glamazons, black Pam Grier and blond Margaret Markov. The gladiator girls battle each other until they join forces, turning against the Roman patriarchy. Steve Carver deftly directed the action sequences for producer Roger Corman.

Army of Darkness (1993). The title entity is a fighting force of skeletons, out to destroy King Arthur's court until B-movie icon Bruce Campbell puts a violent end to their plot. Sam Raimi's follow-up to the incredibly popular *Evil Dead* movies goes more for hard-edged action than gross horror; A-list actress Bridget Fonda appears.

Assault on Precinct 13 (1976). Early low-budget item from John Carpenter makes clear why he was once considered an exciting director. A modern version of Howard Hawks's *Rio Bravo* (1959). The plot focuses on a small group of cops at an isolated police precinct, besieged by gang members. Brilliantly staged fights.

Avenging Force (1986). Two of the lesser lights of B-action stars, Michael

Dudikoff and black buddy Steve James, take on an evil secret society led by John P. Ryan, who makes his character almost believable. Features both martial arts and traditional shoot-outs, impressively staged by director Sam Firstenberg.

Battle Beyond the Stars (1980). Roger Corman's Concorde studio produced this outer space action epic (to capitalize on *Star Wars*), yet another variation on *The Magnificent Seven* theme, with Robert Vaughn reprising his old role. Sybil Danning memorable as a Valkyrie. Impressive F/X later endlessly recycled by Corman.

Beastmaster, The (1982). Low-budget *Conan* ripoff, engaging thanks largely to the hero (Marc Singer) being part Noah, collecting animals who help him in his one-man war against obligatory magalomaniac villain (Rip Torn). Tanya Roberts, as the requisite action babe, has a memorable nude bathing scene. And you gotta *love* those ferrets!

Black Belt Jones (1974). A solid director with impressive action/martial arts credentials, in this case Robert Clouse, makes all the difference. This is the best Jim Kelly vehicle from the black-exploitation era. He's a kung fu teacher in Watts, fighting the Mob for the brothers and sisters. Gloria Hendry is the gorgeous female lead.

Bloody Mama (1970). Umpteenth ripoff of *Bonnie and Clyde*, directed by Roger Corman. A demented family rides around the Depression-era south, terrorizing the populace. Good-natured attitude toward horrific action leads to darkly anarchistic comedy, Shelley Winters plays the bravura title role, with Robert De Niro as her most maniacal (and Oedipal) son.

Bold and the Brave, The (1956). The finest B-movie ever about World War II, with Wendell Corey an embittered soldier, Mickey Rooney (Oscar-nominated for Best Supporting Actor) the company wheeler-dealer, Don Taylor softspoken recruit. Lewis R. Foster's direction of one-man's war with a huge German tank is something to see!

Born Losers, The (1967). Tom Laughlin, dir. A karate-chopping, half-Indian Vietnam vet (Laughlin) takes on bikers (led by Jeremy Slate) to save a bikini-clad babe (Elizabeth James). Far better than later, more expensive (and pretentious) *Billy Jack* movies. Best moment: leather villain dying in slow motion against James Dean's iconographic image.

Breakout (1975). One of the best Charles Bronson vehicles. He's a cowboyish bush pilot hired by Jill Ireland to rescue her husband (Robert Duvall) from the high mountain fortress where villains hold the man prisoner. Intriguing moral crisis for the hero as he does so, despite falling in love with the lady. Elaborate, exciting acton, well staged by Tom Gries.

Pam Grier has another close call in the black exploitation flick, *Coffy*.

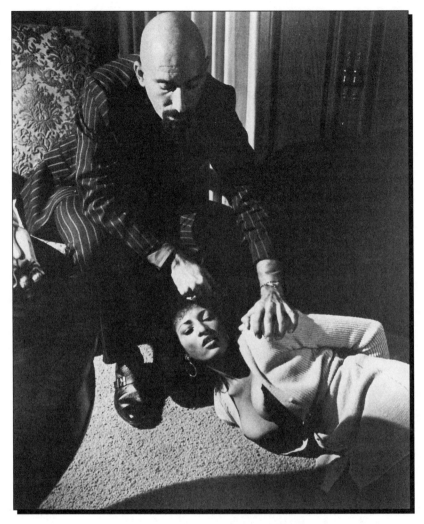

Coffy (1973). The best (and best remembered) of all female action-hero films to come out of the black exploitation craze features Pam Grier at her most seductively dangerous. Director Jack Hill spins a semi-surreal story of a beautiful nurse who moonlights as a lady killer and wipes out the drug dealers who caused her sister's death.

Damnation Alley (1977). George Peppard, Jan-Michael Vincent, and European glamour girl Dominique Sanda are the last people alive after nuclear war destroys Earth. They travel in a souped-up tank, fighting giant killer cockroaches that crawl up out of the earth. Undemanding fun, directed *without* tongue in cheek by Jack Smight.

Dark City (1998). Audiences are transported to a ruined Metropolis—the grimy future of our worst collective nightmares—this time with a witty script and convincing action. Thanks to director Alex Proyas, this Aussie entry emerges as the *Blade Runner* of B-pictures as Rufus Sewell and Jennifer Connelly search for futuristic Jack the Ripper.

Deadlier Than the Male (1967). This is the film that launched the hit-woman genre, with Elke Sommer and Sylva Koscina as a pair of magnificently endowed mercenaries, donning bikinis before they kill off unsuspecting targets on the beach, or seducing rich men in their penthouse apartments, then hurling them down to their death.

Death Race 2000 (1975). At top of the heap for low-budget futuristic films, as David Carradine and pre-*Rocky* Sylvester Stallone compete in bloodthirsty sports car competition, points scored for killing innocent bystanders. Think *Rollerball* by way of *The Gumball Rally.* Director Paul Bartel neatly combines action and satire.

Dirty Mary, Crazy Larry (1974). Of all the post–*Bonnie and Clyde* action flicks about an attractive outlaw duo, director John Hough's Drive-In favorite was the best. Peter Fonda is the bad-ass dude, Sue George (from *Straw Dogs*) his Lolita-like companion. They wildly tear across the rural South, shooting at cop Vic Morrow in between crashing cars.

Duel (1971). Steven Spielberg made his first big impact with this TV movie (from a Richard Matheson short story) about a traveling salesman who finds himself locked in a deadly conflict with a huge rig. So good that it was expanded, released to theaters, though the ultra-tight 74-min. TV print is superior.

El Mariachi (1992). One man, one movie, or so the auteur theory goes: Robert Rodriguez wrote, directed, edited, co-produced, and photographed (on a $7,000 budget, in two weeks) this absorbing actioner about musician Carlos Gallardo, mistaken for a dangerous criminal in a small town. Tarantino saw it and invited Rodriguez to collaborate.

Faster, Pussycat! Kill! Kill! (1962). Russ Meyer graduated from purveyor of softcore porn to junk-movie genius with this wild (for its time) sex-and-action extravaganza (shot on a miniscule budget). Tura Sultana loves and fights her way through an army of despicable men, setting pace for Lara Croft and other action babes to come.

Firecracker! (1981). Umpteenth variation on *TNT Jackson* (by the same director, Craig H. Santiago). A strong-willed woman seeks revenge for the murder of her sister in Asia. Jillian Kessner is the topless blond kickboxing beauty who ultimately kills her own lover (Darby Hinton, once the kid who followed Fess Parker around on TV's *Daniel Boone*).

Fistful of Dollars (1964). People forget this was such a minor item that Clint Eastwood, second-billed on TV's *Rawhide,* got the lead role only when twelve other actors turned it down. Created international sensation; finally released in America two years later, making Clint a star. Brilliant revision of western movie clichés by Sergio Leone.

Futureworld (1976). Belated sequel to surprise hit is superior piece of action moviemaking, thanks to director Richard T. Heffron, who makes the premise click perfectly. Peter Fonda and Blythe Danner are well cast as a journalist couple who visit futuristic theme park, then face off with Yul Brynner's killer cowboy-cyborg.

F/X (1986). Taut, terrific combination of thrills and action with Bryan Brown as a quiet special-effects artist who realizes a fake "hit" he created may have been a cover up for the real thing. Brian Dennehy is menacing as the big guy out to make sure the truth doesn't come out. Robert Mandel's surefire direction of action and chases helps.

Godzilla (1954). The modern Japanese monster/action movie was born with this Hiroshima-inspired nightmare-fantasy about a leapin' lizard reawakened by nuclear waste, terrorizing Tokyo. Ishiro Honda was the original director of the film, then called *Gojira*; Terry Morse shot new footage (with Raymond Burr) to make it marketable in the United States.

Hard Ticket to Hawaii (1987). Former *Playboy* centerfolds Donna Speir and Hope Marie Carlton are action babes who hang by the pool, caress each other in the hot tub, make it with hardbody guys, slip in and out of *Frederick's of Hollywood*–type lingerie and, when they're not otherwise engaged, shoot it out with vicious drug dealers. From Andy Sidaris.

Hidden, The (1987). Dynamite blend of sci-fi and street action. Michael Nouri and Kyle MacLachlan are the buddy-buddy cop team out to stop a violent serial killer. Their target turns out to be an evil alien with the ability to slip in and out of anyone's body. Then again, Kyle isn't what he appears to be. Smart direction by Jack Sholder.

Macon County Line (1974). Alan and Jesse Vint may be forgotten today, but the brothers were stars (at least in the cult sense) of inexpensive action flicks during the mid-seventies. Director Richard Compton skillfully spins the story of two wild-living, fun-loving boys on the road who run afoul of a big, mean Georgia sheriff (Max Baer Jr.).

Mad Max (1979). Impressive Aussie import about a future cop who finds himself at odds with crazies tearing back and forth across nearly

The monster formerly known as "Gojira" ransacks Tokyo in *Godzilla*.

deserted roads. Mel Gibson made his first notable appearance as the character he'd later play (for director George Miller) again in far more ambitious
items; this one has verve and panache.

Ravenous (1999). Apparently inspired by John Fremont's expeditions of
the 1840s, in which starving explorers ate their comrades, this postmodernist
western stars Guy Pearce (well cast) as frontier army officer happening on
blizzard-baraged outpost. What occurs next is shocking, exciting, disgusting,
fascinating, and a must-see for action fans.

Michael Madsen, Quentin Tarantino, Harvey Keitel, Chris Penn, Lawrence Tierney, Tim Roth, and Steve Buscemi in *Reservoir Dogs*.

Reservoir Dogs (1992). Film freak/video-store clerk Quentin Tarantino penned a script combining elements of film noirs (*The Asphalt Jungle, The Killing*), added the nihilistic violence of Asian actioners by John Woo, talked Harvey Keitel into headlining, raised a small budget, and turned out a movie that changed the course of modern filmmaking.

Seven (1979). Early effort from Andy Sidaris, still formulating his unique approach to softcore porn and 007 action, is a redux of *The Magnificent Seven*, with tough guy William Smith perfect as the group leader. *Playboy* models on view (and how!) include brunette Barbara Leigh and blond Susan Kiger. Spielberg lifted one great gag for *Raiders!*

Sky Riders (1976). Soldier of fortune James Coburn must rescue politician's wife Susannah York from a high mountain in Greece, employing hang gliding to get the job done. Sounds pat, but director Douglas Hickox makes something special out of what could've been routine action thriller by capturing the beauty and thrills of the sport.

Southern Comfort (1981). Group of soldiers is massacred, one man at a time, by unseen enemy. Tradition-laced formula (*The Lost Patrol, Badlands, Bataan*) never fails, neatly updated here by director Walter Hill. Keith Carradine, Powers Booth and Fred Ward are among National Guardsmen shooting it out in the swamps with angry Cajuns.

Superfly (1972). While most black exploitation flicks rate as engaging junk, this is the exception: a dazzling action film (wonderfully directed by Gordon Parks, Jr.) that transcends urban crime-drama elements to become a controversial though valid "serious" movie, Ron O'Neal is explosive as a drug dealer exploiting his own people.

Sword and the Sorcerer, The (1982). Of many low-budget epic-fantasy films made to cash in on the *Conan* craze, this is easily the best, Lee Horsley effective as the musclebound hero, Kathleen Beller the obligatory threatened princess (catch her encounter with a phallic snake). Above par F/X. Director Albert Pyun's best film.

Thunder Road (1958). Alone among A-list actors of the fifties, ever-iconoclastic Robert Mitchum dared write and star in this Drive-In exploitation flick about hillbilly moonshiners. He also wrote and recorded the title song, casting his son Jim as his younger brother when Elvis Presley turned down the part. A real wild ride on rural backroads.

Toy Soldiers (1991). Marvelous action fun as a group of terrorists take over a military academy, and the beloved school leader (Lou Gossett, Jr.) whips the kids (including Sean Astin and Wil Wheaton) into a first-rate fighting force. Every red-blooded boy's blood-fantasy of licking evil adults, effectively realized by director Daniel Petrie, Jr.

Tremors (1990). Giddily senseless throwback to B-budget sci-fi action films of the fifties, now with a large enough budget for fine special effects. Giant earthworms come tearing up out of the ground, menacing the riff-raff in an isolated part of the southwest. Kevin Bacon and Fred Ward star; kudos to director Ron Underwood.

Trespass (1992). Neat little combo of action and suspense as treasure hunters search a destitute ghetto neighborhood for hidden money, running afoul of drug dealers using the place as their hideout. Edge-of-your-seat suspense in time gives way to blazing shoot-outs between Bill Paxton, Ice T, William Sadler, and Ice Cube. Walter Hill directed.

Valley of Gwangi (1969). Did Steven Spielberg catch a rerun of this shortly before setting to work on *Jurassic Park 2*? Cowboys capture dinosaur, put him in big show; the thing escapes and destroys town. Terrific F/X by (you guessed it) Ray Harryhausen, from an old and previously unfilmed script by Willis S. O'Brien (*King Kong, Mighty Joe Young*).

Walking Tall (1973). Fifties action-expert Phil Karlson revived his career with what might be considered the hick version of *Dirty Harry:* Real-life rural sheriff Buford Pusser (Joe Don Baker) cleans up corruption in a small town by taking Teddy Roosevelt's advice ("Speak softly and carry a big stick!") literally.

Warriors, The (1979). A rash of gang films in the late seventies (*The Wanderers, Walk Proud,* etc.) made way for this mini-classic, based on the Greek legend of Xenophon. A group of "soldiers" find themselves cut off behind enemy lines and must fight their way back to home turf. Michael Beck and James Remar star in Walter Hill's breathless film.

When Dinosaurs Ruled the Earth (1970). Nowhere near as well known as *One Million Years, B.C.*, this is just as good. Victoria Vetri (aka "Angela Dorian") is a blond cave girl, mixing it up with violent men, assorted dinosaurs—one of them surprisingly motherly. Great F/X by Jim Danforth as well as inspired direction by Val Guest.

22
THE ARENA: CLASSIC FIGHT FILMS

One of the original action heroes, Wallace Beery, won a Best Actor Oscar playing a prizefighter in King Vidor's early talkie, *The Champ* (1931), a sentimental favorite that set the pace for this subgenre's future. Occasionally, the title character would be an arrogant snit in need of a take-down, the case with James Cagney in *Frisco Kid* (1935). More often than not, the hero was portrayed as entering the ring to achieve something idealistic on the outside, including Robert Taylor in *The Crowd Roars* (1938), William Holden in *Golden Boy* (1939), and James Cagney in *City of Conquest* (1940). Even the Bowery Boys got into the act with *Kid Dynamite* (1943). And there was the occasional biopic, such as *Gentleman Jim* (1942), with Errol Flynn as James Corbett, the man who brought class into the ring. The fight film allowed actors previously written off as pretty boys to transform into action heroes, true of both Holden and Kirk Douglas. Here are the most significant fight films made during and since the postwar era.

Ali (2001). Michael Mann, dir. Will Smith, Mario van Peebles, Jamie Foxx. Story of the man once known as Cassius Clay, from first fights to boxing greatness. Told earlier in cheesey biopic *The Greatest*. Here, the story is related by a world-class director, yet not a lot better than the first go-around, despite fine impersonation by Will Smith. ★★

Body and Soul (1947). Robert Rossen, dir. John Garfield, William Conrad, Canada Lee, Lilli Palmer. As a consolation prize for never having had the opportunity to play *Golden Boy* onstage or on film, Garfield received the lead in what may arguably be the best boxing film of all time. Unsparing, unforgettable expose of the fight game. ★★★★★

Boxer, The (1997). Jim Sheridan, Daniel Day-Lewis, Emily Watson, Ken Stott, Brian Cox. Ambitious, highly successful attempt to bring the boxing genre into our contemporary world of complex politics. Day-Lewis is a prizefighter with a troubled past as an IRA operative, now focusing his violence on ring bouts. ★★★★

Champ, The (1979). Franco Zeffirelli, dir. Jon Voight, Ricky Schroder, Faye Dunaway, Strother Martin, Jack Warden. Why, after winning Oscars for *Coming Home* and *Network*, did Voight and Dunaway choose to do this career killer? Schlocky rendering of the popular favorite about a fighter and his boy. Bad!   ★

Champion (1949). Mark Robson, dir. Kirk Douglas, Arthur Kennedy, Ruth Roman, Marilyn Maxwell. Previously typecast strictly as whiners and wussies, Douglas excelled (and won an Oscar nomination) in his first action role, as a heel-as-anti-hero boxer who spares no one (in or out of the ring) in his climb to fame.   ★★★★★

Diggstown (1992). Michael Ritchie, dir. Louis Gossett, Jr., James Woods, Bruce Dern, Heather Graham. Delightful throwback to old-fashioned studio yarns about a boxer (Gossett) and lovable con man (Woods), out to take tyrant (Dern) who runs an out-of-the-way town. Familiar material, appealingly updated.   ★★★★

Fat City (1972). John Huston, dir. Stacy Keach, Jeff Bridges, Susan Tyrell, Candy Clark. Young Bridges has the talent but needs know-how he can only learn from washed up Keach. Film contains some of the best boxing sequences of all time, thanks to Huston's unsparing approach. From a Leonard Gardner novel.   ★★★★★

Fight Club (1999). See "Brad Pitt" in chapter 3.   ★★★★

Gladiator (1992). Rowdy Herrington, Cuba Gooding, Jr., Brian Dennehy, Robert Loggia. Bottom-of-the-barrel film plays like a *Blazing Saddles/Airplane*! spoof of previous films in the fight genre, only this is (believe it or not) intended as serious stuff. Gooding is the decent kid manipulated by unscrupulous manager Dennehy.   ★

Greatest, The (1977). Tom Gries, dir. Muhammad Ali, James Earl Jones, Robert Duvall. Despite the obvious thrill of seeing Ali play himself in the company of a stellar cast, this mediocre program-picture disappoints on almost every level—from the human drama aspect to the uninspired boxing sequences.   ★★

Great White Hope, The (1970). Martin Ritt, dir. James Earl Jones, Jane Alexander, Lou Gilbert, Beah Richards, Chester Morris. Howard Sackler's searing, well-received play about black boxing great Jack Johnson and his other lifelong fight (against racism) makes an uneasy transition to the screen. Acceptable but surprisingly uninspired.   ★★★

Harder They Fall, The (1956). Mark Robson, dir. Humphrey Bogart, Rod Steiger, Jan Sterling, Max Baer, Mike Lane. Scathing indictment of the

Muhammad Ali (as himself) in *The Greatest*.

fight game and its crime-world connections. Inspired by the real-life case of
Primo Canera (Lane), a manufactured champ who didn't know that all his
fights had been fixed, until too late.   ★★★★★

Hard Times (1975). Walter Hill, dir. Charles Bronson, James Coburn,
Jill Ireland. Terrific teaming of stars who a decade earlier, as character actors,
shared scenes in *The Great Escape* and *The Dirty Dozen*. Downbeat Depression-era tale of boxer Bronson, manager Coburn, and bare-knuckle New
Orleans fights. Strong stuff.   ★★★★

Hurricane, The (1998). Norman Jewison, dir. Denzel Washington, Liev
Schreiber, Rod Steiger. The story of real-life boxer Rubin Carter, who was
imprisoned (some say unjustly) for a street crime, is simplified and fictionalized. That aside, it is a powerful tale, featuring great ring action.   ★★★★★

Jeff Chandler in Iron Man.

Iron Man (1951). Joseph Pevney, dir. Jeff Chandler, Stephen McNally, Joyce Holden, James Arness. Rare case of the remake being superior to the dated 1931 original. Chandler is most convincing as an itinerant coal miner who cautiously enters the ring, only to realize he possesses violent impulses that are released once he gets there. ★★★★

Kid Galahad (1962). Phil Karlson, dir. Elvis Presley, Charles Bronson, Lola Albright. Early attempt to balance the typical Presley musical with a strong story and solid cast, this star vehicle for the king effectively balances several musical performances with solid boxing sequences and a believable drama. Remake of a 1937 flick. ★★★

Let's Do It Again (1975). Sidney Poitier, dir. Sidney Poitier, Jimmie Walker, Bill Cosby. Talented black cast, most of whom had previously appeared in *Uptown Saturday Night*, breathe fresh life into clichéd story about a youth (Walker) who is hypnotized by Cosby and becomes a legend in the ring. Lots of undemanding fun. ★★★★

Power of One, The (1992). John G. Avildsen, dir. Stephen Dorff, John Gielgud, Morgan Freeman. *Rocky*-like tale, from same director, strives for uplifting sensibility, comes close to clicking. This time, there's a civil rights theme, Dorff is an Anglo in South Africa who enters the ring with black boxers. Starts strong, dissipates toward the end. ★★★

Raging Bull (1980). Martin Scorsese, dir. Robert De Niro, Joe Pesce, Cathy Moriarty. From Jake LaMotta's autobiography of the same title comes this searing drama about the least likable prizefighter of all time, unsparingly presented by a great star and director combo. De Niro won Oscar, but Marty should have, too. A great film. ★★★★★

**Robert De Niro in
*Raging Bull.***

Requiem for a Heavyweight (1962). Ralph Nelson, dir. Anthony Quinn, Julie Harris, Mickey Rooney, Jackie Gleason, Cassius Clay. Originally a "golden age" TV drama starring Jack Palance. Rod Serling's script makes a tragic figure of a washed-up boxer who takes a wrestling job to survive. Ali plays himself in the opening sequence.   ★★★★

Rocky (1976). See "Sylvester Stallone" in chapter 10.   ★★★★★

Rocky II (1979). Sylvester Stallone, dir. Sylvester Stallone, Talia Shire, Burt Young, Carl Weathers, Burgess Meredith. The whole gang is back again for the follow-up in which Stallone and Weathers go at it once again, only this time you-know-who wins. Not so electrifying as the first, but rated high because the final fight is fabulous.   ★★★★

Rocky III (1982). Sylvester Stallone, dir. Sylvester Stallone, Mr. T, Carl Weathers, Talia Shire, Burgess Meredith. A tough newcomer named Clubber Lang (Mr. T) beats Rocky while his guard is down, causing the hero to question his values, become friends with Apollo Creed (Weathers). So-so, with okay fight scenes.   ★★★

Rocky IV (1985). Sylvester Stallone, dir. Sylvester Stallone, Dolph Lundgren, Brigitte Nielsen. Several years before the Cold War came to a close, Stallone caught the belligerant attitude of Reagan-era America, as Sly (wrapped in the flag) takes on the (then) Evil Soviet Empire's champ (Dolph) after the man kills Apollo. Over-ripe.   ★★

Rocky V (1990). John Avildsen, dir. Sylvester Stallone, Tommy Morrison, Richard Grant, Sage Stallone, Burt Young. Rocky comes full circle (with a return to the original director) as the aging boxer muses about what it was all about. The fight scenes are tame, the drama turgid. End of the line for Rock . . . so far, at least.   ★

Set-Up, The (1949). Robert Wise, dir. Robert Ryan, James Edwards, Audrey Totter. Will Ryan take a fall in order to get the money he needs to quit for good? If the premise sounds overly familiar, you're in for a surprise, as this searing drama, told in real time, is one of the best boxing movies ever.   ★★★★★

Somebody Up There Likes Me (1956). Robert Wise, dir. Paul Newman, Pier Angeli, Sal Mineo, Steve McQueen. The *original* "Rocky" (Graziano) was to have been James Dean's next role before his untimely death; Newman performs ably, opposite Dean's former girlfriend Angeli. Top-notch ring sequences, superb drama.   ★★★★

Triumph of the Spirit (1989). Robert M. Young, dir. Willem Dafoe, Edward James Olmos. Can you imagine *Rocky* by way of *Schindler's List*? That's what you get in this one-of-a-kind film, based on fact, about a Jewish boxer sent to Auschwitz, where he encounters the most unique "ring" ever. Little-seen gem is worth your time!   ★★★★

When We Were Kings (1996). Leon Gast, dir. Muhammad Ali, George Foreman, Don King, James Brown, Spike Lee. Ali versus George, circa 1974, in Zaire is the subject for the best documentary film ever made about the fight game. You'll learn a lot more about the man once known as "Cassius Clay" here than from the biopic *Ali*.   ★★★★★

23

OUR FORGOTTEN WAR: THE KOREAN CONFLICT ON FILM

Movies made about the Korean Conflict during the early 1950s differ drastically in tone and theme from those turned out during World War II. In place of patriotic jingoism coupled with fervent optimism in spite of all odds, such films are darker and full of edgy commentary on the absurdity of war as an enterprise. The reason for such a departure is simple—they were written and produced at a time while we were involved in a very different kind of combat.

With the latest "war to end all wars" behind us, America found itself plunged into a so-called police action that was claiming the lives of young Americans. Yet our reason for being in Korea remained a mystery to most citizens, while the eventual outcome seemed ever less clear. Hollywood approached our "prelude to Nam" with caution—unwilling to fully embrace this patently unwinnable situation while attempting on some level to support the effort. Understandably, only a handful of films were made about Korea. The ratings that accompany each (one through five stars) are intended to indicate the degree to which they will appeal to today's action fans.

All the Young Men (1960). Hall Bartlett, dir. Alan Ladd, Sidney Poitier, James Darren. This attempt to do a *Walk in the Sun*–type of drama for Korea falls flat. Dull Ladd looks comatose, though Poitier is better than his material. Awkward tone veers between rah!rah! and condemnation of the conflict. ★★

Battle Taxi (1955). Herbert L. Strock, dir. Sterling Hayden, Arthur Franz, Marshall Thompson. Low-budget but convincing portrait of the helicopter pilots who risk their lives attempting to airlift wounded men out of combat zones. Hayden particularly forceful as a dedicated officer. ★★★

Bridges at Toko-Ri, The (1954). Mark Robson, dir. William Holden, Grace Kelly, Fredric March, Mickey Rooney. The single masterpiece to come out of the conflict. Director Robson vividly realizes James Michener's account of a family man who must fly a dangerous but necessary mission. ★★★★★

Cease Fire (1953). Owen Crump, dir. Crump joined the Seventh Division, observed their combat action, and hastily wrote a script about a fictional mission, based on the reality of what he observed. All the characters are played by real GIs. An amazing experiment and one-of-a-kind-film. ★★★★

Fixed Bayonets (1951). Samuel Fuller, dir. Gene Evans, Richard Basehart, James Dean. From the pen of an auteur who had served in World War II comes an offbeat yarn about a group of GIs find themselves surrounded. Rare glimpse of winter fighting. Yeah, *that* James Dean! ★★★★

Glory Brigade, The (1953). Robert D. Webb, dir. Victor Mature, Lee Marvin, Richard Egan. This intermittently involving film concerns the role Greece played in supporting America's commitment in Korea. Mature no better or worse than usual. A young Marvin reveals his already potent charisma. ★★★

Hell in Korea (1956). Julian Amyes, dir. Robert Shaw, Stanley Baker, Harry Andrews, Michael Caine. British-lensed actioner emphasizes that country's contribution to the UN force. A few strong action scenes. The production is burdened by ordinary script, uplifted by terrific cast of future stars. ★★★

Hook, The (1963). George Seaton, dir. Kirk Douglas, Nick Adams, Robert Walker, Jr. Highly impressive pacifist film. Three GIs, burdened with a Korean prisoner, are given the order to "dispose" of him. Each must wrestle with his personal moralities. Unforgettable ending. ★★★★

Inchon (1982). Terence Young, dir. Laurence Olivier, Ben Gazzara, Jacqueline Bisset, Toshiro Mifune. Top-flight cast in a famed cinematic debacle, produced by the Rev. Sung Myung Moon as an anti-commie diatribe about American action in title City. Olivier as General MacArthur is a hoot! ★

Manchurian Candidate, The (1962). John Frankenheimer, dir. Frank Sinatra, Laurence Harvey, Angela Lansbury. Granted, only the opening sequence takes place in Korea. Still, we can't help but recommend this landmark film about Cold War political paranoia. One of the great ones. ★★★★★

Men of the Fighting Lady (1954). Andrew Marton, dir. Van Johnson, Walter Pidgeon, Dewey Martin. Even the ever-bland Van can't hold back this excellent depiction of the navy's understated contribution to the Korean war. The characterizations are honest, Pidgeon a standout. ★★★★

General MacArthur's troops take a Korean harbor in *Inchon*.

One Minute to Zero (Tay Garnett, dir.). Robert Mitchum, Ann Blyth, Richard Egan. Too much emphasis on Bob's romance with gorgeous Blyth detracts from an otherwise strong war story. An officer wrestles with moral concerns about innocent people caught in the crossfire. ★★★

Pork Chop Hill (1959). Lewis Milestone, dir. Gregory Peck, George Peppard, Woody Strode. From one of Hollywood's finest directors of war movies comes this intense, impressive account of a costly combat mission and its role in "the big picture." The Korean war equivalent to *Paths of Glory*. ★★★★

Retreat, Hell! (1952). Joseph H. Lewis, dir. Frank Lovejoy, Russ Tamblyn, Richard Carlson. In fact, retreat is precisely what the marines must do, as they abandon the Changjin Reservoir under fierce fire. Effective focus on combat. ★★★

Richard Loo (front, kneeling) and Steve Brodie (far right) lead their squad into action in *The Steel Helmet.*

Steel Helmet, The (1951). Sam Fuller, dir. Gene Evans, Steve Brodie, James Edwards, Richard Loo. Low-budget but high-quality mini-epic, written by the cult director, focuses on the absurdity of war as a newly integrated outfit occupies deserted monastery with ironic results.   ★★★★

Take the High Ground (1953). Richard Brooks, dir. Richard Widmark, Karl Malden. First-rate film documents the training of GIs under a tough topkick at Fort Bliss. Fatalistic approach shows them surviving or dying in combat in the pre-title sequence, then studies each man's lonely road to his destiny.   ★★★★

Target Zero (1955). Harmon Jones, dir. Richard Conte, Charles Bronson, Chuck Connors, L. Q. Jones. One more account of an officer attempting to keep his men alive during a hazardous mission. Familiar stuff, though the solid cast helps.   ★★★

Time Limit (1957). Karl Malden, dir. Richard Widmark, Richard Basehart, Dolores Michaels. First-rate suspenser about an American who may or may not have collaborated with the enemy after being captured during a ferocious battle. Produced by Widmark, and actor Malden's only attempt at directing.   ★★★★

Torpedo Alley (1953). Lew Landers, dir. Mark Stevens, Bill Williams, Dorothy Malone. Terrific title, mediocre results. Two servicemen in love with the same lady must head into combat (this time, in a submarine) together. Sound familiar? Not enough action to redeem a tepid, tired story.   ★★

War Hunt (1962). Dennis Sanders, dir. John Saxon, Robert Redford, Sydney Pollack. Terrific, little-known anti-war diatribe. New replacement Redford realizes his squad's great "hero" (Saxon) is a psychopath hooked on killing. Redford's first film and Saxon's best performance.   ★★★★

24
ESSENTIALS: THE FIFTIES

During this decade, the emergent postwar world gradually found its own sensibility, more often than not expressed in a series of delicately balanced polarities between old and new: Eisenhower and (at the back end) Kennedy, Frank Sinatra and Elvis Presley, James Stewart and Marlon Brando, Main Street, U.S.A. and Madison Avenue, New York, conformist and beatnik, the man in the gray flannel suit and the rebel without a cause, *Life* and *Playboy*, McCarthyism and Civil Rights reform. The movies, of course, responded to social change with an altered approach. If Hollywood's output began with modest black-and-white features for small screens, theatrical entertainment soon transformed into color extravaganzas, with stereophonic sound and wide screens to lure an ever more apathetic citizenry away from their TVs.

The African Queen (1951)

CREDITS

Directed by John Huston; written by Huston, James Agee, and Peter Viertel (uncredited), adapted from the novel by C. S. Forester; producers, Sam Spiegel and (uncredited) John Woolf; original music, Allan Gray; cinematography, Jack Cardiff; running time, 105 min.

CAST

Humphrey Bogart (*Charlie Allnut*); Katharine Hepburn (*Rose Sayer*); Robert Morley (*Rev. Samuel Sayer*); Peter Bull (*Captain, "Louisa"*); Theodore Bikel (*First Officer*); Walter Gotell (*Second Officer*).

THE FILM

John Huston, already legendary for such pre- and postwar hard-edged classics as *The Maltese Falcon* (1941) and *The Treasure of Sierra Madre* (1948), both starring Bogart, reteamed with his star to create a prime example of the nouveau-action film. *Queen* was shot on actual Congo locations with a non-glamorous attitude taken toward the film's ostensibly "romantic" leads—

a world-weary, vulgar anti-hero who must be convinced to do "the right thing," and a liberated heroine who plays an equal role in defeating their enemies. Huston created exciting action sequences (including running the rapids), staged a huge final explosion, and added a tongue-in-cheek edge to what previously would have been played as a straightforward adventure. The film appears at times to be spoofing itself, yet without taking the edge off the intense action, an approach Lucas and Spielberg would perfect in their *Indiana Jones* trilogy. The setting is Africa during the early days of the first World War, Bogie (who finally won the Best Actor Oscar) plays a dishevelled, alcoholic captain of a small steamer. His irascible "Charlie Allnut" is transformed into a reluctant hero by "Rosie Sayer" (Hepburn), the surviving sister of a deceased minister who'd been overseeing friendly natives until the German arrival. In turn, she also arcs from uptight spinster to sensuous woman during their shared odyssey downriver to demolish an enemy battleship. Huston makes this "fairy tale for grown-ups" happy ending work, despite striking realism along the way, such as a horrifying incident when the shocked Rosie must burn black leaches off Charlie's body.

Ivanhoe (1952)

CREDITS

Director, Richard Thorpe; screenplay, Aeneas MacKenzie, Noel Langley, and Marguerite Roberts, from the novel by Sir Walter Scott; producer, Pandro S. Berman; original music, Miklós Rózsa; cinematography, F. A. "Freddie" Young; editor, Frank Clarke; running time, 106 min.

CAST

Robert Taylor (*Sir Wilfred of Ivanhoe*); Elizabeth Taylor (*Rebecca*); Joan Fontaine (*Rowena*); George Sanders (*Sir Brian De Bois-Guilbert*); Emlyn Williams (*Wamba the Squire*); Robert Douglas (*De Bracy*); Finlay Currie (*Cedric*); Felix Aylmer (*Isaac*); Norman Wooland (*Richard the Lionheart*); Harold Warrender (*Locksley*, aka *Robin Hood*) Sebastian Cabot (*Tuck*); Guy Rolfe (*Prince John*).

THE FILM

Ancient notions of the action hero, more often than not expressed in poetry and ballads, found their modern incarnations in novels. This began with Sir

Robert Taylor in
Ivanhoe.

Walter Scott's 1819 epic, a classic combination of adventure, romance, and—lest we forget—sharp social commentary, notably an attack on anti-Semitism. The good knight of the title, returning to England from the Crusades with hopes of funding the release of captive King Richard, must oppose evil Prince John. Ivanhoe's greatest ally is Isaac of York, an ancient Hebrew whose people put to shame, through their generosity, both Normans and Saxons. Even as the film was being readied for release, the Civil Rights movement was growing. Earlier, such films as Elia Kazan's Oscar-winning *Gentleman's Agreement* (1947) attacked prejudice against Jews. Now, movies were helping shape a consensus against racism. On one level, *Ivanhoe* can be "read" as a thinly diguised allegory for what was then taking place in the United States. First and foremost, it is a period piece, mounted with incredible accuracy as to every aspect of medieval life, thanks in large part to the on-location shooting in England and Scotland. As in the original novel, Ivanhoe (with some much-needed help from Robin Hood) must rescue two beautiful women, the highborn Rowena and the Jewess Rebecca, from the evil clutches of De Bracy. In Thorpe's film, the attack on an enemy castle, though far from the first such sequence to show up on screen, is notable for the length of the battle and graphic depiction of violence. However mild by today's standards, it proved as much a landmark, in terms of brutality for its era, as *The Wild Bunch* would some fifteen years later.

The Crimson Pirate (1952)

CREDITS

Director, Robert Siodmak; screenplay, Roland Kibbee; producers, Harold Hecht and Burt Lancaster (uncredited); original music, William Alwyn with Muir Matheson; cinematography, Otto Heller; running time, 104 min.

CAST

Burt Lancaster (*Captain Vallo*); Nick Cravat (*Ojo*); Eva Bartok (*Consuelo*); Torin Thatcher (*Humble Bellows*); James Hayter (*Prof. Prudence*); Leslie Bradley (*Baron Gruda*); Noel Purcell (*Pablo Murphy*); Dana Wynter (*La Signorita*); Christopher Lee (*Joseph*).

THE FILM

After escaping the studio system and forming an independent production company, Burt's partnership was with Harold Hecht, with whom he brought to fruition a number of ambitious projects. The audience was ready for something new, though not *too* new, and *Crimson Pirate* fit the bill. It was a pirate movie, a Hollywood staple, yet there had never been a pirate movie quite like this. In the opening, Lancaster as Vallo swings across the screen, in vivid color, to address the audience directly. "Remember, believe only what you see." Then, with a naughty wink and a toothy grin, he adds, "No, believe *half* of what you see!" Incredibly, he reverses his movements, though we grasp that the film has been reversed. We are in on the joke, a striking comparison to pirate movies Errol Flynn and Tyrone Power had starred in, mostly shot on studio backlots and played "straight." This was a pirate movie that *knew* it was a pirate movie, and knew that the audience knew. Lancaster's giddy athletic feats have more in common with a three-ring circus than an old-fashioned adventure movie. The plot may be old hat, but the treatment appears entertainingly fresh. And Burt slips in a political message of a liberal order. The hero, originally a rugged individualist interested only in himself, is won over (by a beautiful woman) to the revolutionaries who take on the corrupt Establishment. This theme aggrandizes the development of a community composed of common men who fight enemies of freedom.

War of the Worlds (1953)

CREDITS

Director, Byron Haskin; screenplay, Barre Lyndon, from the novel by H. G. Wells; producer, George Pal; original music, Leith Stevens; cinematography, George Barnes; running time, 85 min.

CAST

Cedrick Hardwicke (*Narrator/voice of H. G. Wells*); Gene Barry (*Dr. Clayton Forrester*); Ann Robinson (*Sylvia Van Buren*); Les Tremayne (*Major Gen. Mann*); Lewis Martin (*Pastor Collins*); Robert Cornthwaite (*Dr. Pryor*); Jack Kruschen (*Salvatore*).

THE FILM

During the early 1950s, most science-fiction and/or fantasy films were low-budget affairs, cheaply produced for a non-discriminating market. A few notable exceptions included *Them!* (1954), *Forbidden Planet* (1956), and this handsomely mounted adaptation of Wells's classic about an invasion from the Red Planet. The film was produced by George Pal, rightly famous for his fascinating *Puppetoon* shorts, which brought the charm of European marionette theater to the Hollywood cartoon during the 1940s. *War of the Worlds*'s screenplay updated Wells's story to the then-present time, shifting the action to California. Screenwriter Lyndon also added an obligatory romance between a brilliant doctor (Barry) and a typical 1950s' career woman (Robinson), precursor of the liberated ladies who would dominate future action films. Otherwise, the essence of Wells's vision remains intact. Earth is nearly devastated by gigantic slow-flying ships of destruction, shaped like manta rays, with extended antennae that fire devastating white-hot blasts. Only when humans turn away from their own weapons of destruction (including, in this version, an A-bomb), embracing both science and old-time religion, is the planet saved. Specks of bacteria kill the martians who, behind their formidable flying armor, are in fact weak and vulnereable—God and/or Nature saving the day.

20,000 Leagues Under the Sea (1954)

CREDITS

Directed by Richard Fleischer; written by Earl Felton, adapted from the novel by Jules Verne; producer, Walt Disney; original music, Norman Gimbel and Paul J. Smith; running time, 127 min.

CAST

Kirk Douglas (*Ned Land*); James Mason (*Captain Nemo*); Paul Lukas (*Professor Pierre Aronnax/narrator*); Peter Lorre (*Conseil*); Robert J. Wilke (*First Mate, the Nautilus*); Ted de Corsia (*Captain Farragut*).

THE FILM

This film rates as a key work for the Walt Disney Company at a major moment in their corporate history. Disneyland (the park) was nearing completion and *Disneyland* (the TV show) had debuted only two months before this movie's premiere. Though the company was financially strapped, "Uncle" Walt insisted no expense be spared on this film, shot on a then-extravagant $5 million budget. A box-office star (Kirk Douglas) and an esteemed actor (James Mason) were hired. This film is in most respects true to Verne's 1869 novel, one of the early classics of modern science fiction, with its once fanciful notion of an atomic-powered submarine. In command is an environmental extremist who torpedoes gunboats from all countries on the globe in hopes of ending militarism. Nemo is a radical who employs violence in hopes of bringing about world peace, simultaneously ending mankind's destruction of the natural world, particularly its oceans. A harpooner (Douglas), a noted scientist (Lucas), and his personal manservant (Lorre)—survivors of a downed vessel—are taken aboard the Nautilus, where Land sets about sabotaging Nemo's plans. High-tech F/X (dazzling for the time) are obvious in the construction of the ship itself, notably modern on the outside but with garish gothic interiors, and the giant squid with which the crew engages in fierce combat. This, and the final large-scale battle with society's armies, qualifies the film as a watershed work in the development of modern action, with its reliance on special effects. Mason's Nemo is a person of dignity who achieves full tragic dimension, a great man who does evil terrible things for an idealistic cause, while Douglas plays his role with great showmanship, perfectly complementing Mason's understated work.

Moby Dick (1956)

CREDITS

> Director, John Huston; screenplay, Huston, Ray Bradbury, and (uncredited) Norman Corwin, from the novel by Herman Melville; producers, Huston and Jack Clayton; original music, Philip Sainton; cinematography, Oswald Morris; running time, 116 min.

Gregory Peck in *Moby Dick*.

CAST

Gregory Peck (*Capt. Ahab*); Richard Basehart (*Ishmael/Narrator*); Leo Genn (*Starbuck*); Friedrich Ledebur (*Queequeg*); Orson Welles (*Father Mapple*); Royal Dano (*Elijah*); James Robertson Justice (*Capt. Boomer*); Harry Andrews (*Stubb*).

THE FILM

In many respects, *Moby Dick* is the original American "guy story." There are no significant female characters in Herman Melville's tale of redemption through violence. A wanderer, Ishmael, and his dark friend, Queequeg from the South Seas, sign on board *The Pequod*, a Nantucket whaler. What they don't know is that Captain Ahab is obsessed with tracking down and killing the great white whale that tore off one of his legs. What follows is a grand action adventure with allegorical underpinnings, a biblical vision full of Old Testament thunder-and-lightning histrionics (a tattered man who predicts the coming doom of all "save one" is named Elijah). This by way of Greek tragedy, both sources brilliantly brought into a uniquely mid-nineteenth American setting. If not "*the* great American novel," *Moby Dick* is certainly *one* of them, and it was the *first*. Essentially, though, it is the story of a community of rugged men, following a remarkable though flawed leader as he tries to strike, through the "purity" of the whale's whiteness, at Nature and/or God. Wisely, director John Huston (working with sci-fi writer Ray Bradbury) understated though did not eliminate the story's symbolic dimension. Huston plays his film as a rugged sea yarn, the "boy's toy" here being the harpoon. Various locations around the world add to the authentic recreation of the whaling industry, while a superb cast (mostly British) conveys the essence of iron men in wooden ships. Peck perfectly captures Melville's conception of a great man who has misdirected his genius, a fallen Puritan grappling with moral issues that finally cannot be resolved by any one person, this man's immense hubris leading inevitably to the story's moral resolution.

Around the World in 80 Days (1956)

CREDITS

Director, Michael Anderson and (uncredited) Sidney Smith; screenplay, John Farrow, S. J. Perelman, and James Poe, from the novel by Jules Verne; producers, Michael Todd and William Cameron Menzies; original music, Victor Young; cinematography, Lionel Lindon; running time, 178 min.

CAST

David Niven (*Phileas Fogg*); Cantinflas (*Passepartout*); Shirley MacLaine (*Princess Aouda*); Robert Newton (*Fix*); Finlay Currie, Robert Morley, Ronald Squire, & Basil Sydney (*Reform Club Members*); Noel Coward (*Hesketh-Baggott*); numerous guest stars, including John Gielgud, Marlene Dietrich, Fernandel, Charles Boyer, José Greco, Frank Sinatra, Red Skelton, Luis Miguel Domínguín, and Buster Keaton, among many others.

THE FILM

Whether or not one buys the "one man, one movie" concept of the auteur theory, there's little question that *Around the World in 80 Days* did *not* express the artistic personality of its nominal director, competent craftsman Michael Anderson. From day one, this was the work of flamboyant producer Mike Todd, who insisted that his conception reach the screen. What he imagined—and provided—stands as a milestone in the development of motion pictures, if not as an art, then as entertainment. During the fifties, films had become ever "bigger" in scope, though none nearly so huge as this. The movie was literally shot, as the title insists, around the world, employing film crews in every country Todd visited. The making of *Around the World* was every bit as audacious as the adventures that the Jules Verne's characters embark on: As in that 1872 classic, Phileas Fogg, English gentleman, bets members of his club that he and his manservant Passepartout can navigate the globe in eighty days, a feat considered impossible in the mid-1800s. They are accompanied by Fix, a seeming friend who undermines their every effort, and (after arriving in India), the beautiful Princess Aouda, whom they rescue from a death cult. Her presence allows for romance as well as adventure and action—a balloon ride over Paris, Indians chasing a train through the wild west until the cavalry arrives in the nick of time, storms at sea, and so forth. The performance of a flamenco dancer is provided by the great José Greco—Todd (then married to Liz Taylor) peppered his film with other celebrities as guest stars, creating the concept of a "cameo performance" that would be imitated by endless others. Taking bigness one giant step further, he developed his own huge projection system—70-mm Todd-AO—to further heighten the effects, bringing ordinary motion pictures one step closer to Cinerama. The movie was a "big con" that paid off—besides rating as a huge box-office blockbuster, *Around the World* won the Oscar for Best Film of the Year.

The Bridge on the River Kwai (1957)

CREDITS

Director, David Lean; screenplay, Carl Foreman and Michael Wilson (uncredited), and Pierre Boulle, from his novel; producer, Sam Spiegel; original music, Malcolm Arnold; cinematography, Jack Hildyard; running time, 161 min.

CAST

William Holden (*Major Shears*); Alec Guinness (*Colonel Nicholson*); Jack Hawkins (*Major Warden*); Sessue Hayakawa (*Colonel Saito*); James Donald (*Major Clipton*); Geoffrey Horne (*Lt. Joyce*).

Alec Guinness and Geoffrey Horne in *The Bridge on the River Kwai*.

THE FILM

The WWII movie, which remained popular after 1945, was redefined by this Oscar-winning Best Picture. *Bridge* is a strangely satisfying cross between action film and arthouse cinema, expressed in the wide-screen spectacle style, complete with all-star cast. Set in Southeast Asia (and, perhaps, pointing our way to Vietnam), the film focuses on an American, Mears (William Holden) who escapes from a prison camp, then is persuaded by a special forces officer (Jack Hawkins) to lead a patrol back into the jungle. They plan to bomb a recently completed bridge, thereby destroying the enemy's transportation lines. Ironically, the bridge couldn't have been completed without the expertise of a captured British officer (Alec Guinness). Colonel Nicholson initially refuses to cooperate with the Japanese commandant (Sessue Hayakawa), owing to that man's insistence that officers work alongside enlisted men. Once this is resolved, Nicholson becomes so obsessed with getting the job done properly that he loses all perspective about whom he is completing it for, and why, until an attack by the commando squad sets his mind to reeling. This allowed for, however paradoxically, an anti-war statement to be made within the context of a rah!rah! action movie. None of the characters come off as clichés, but are unique human beings, as vivid and three-dimensionally realized as in any "serious" drama. Yet there were limits to how far the filmmakers would go in terms of such integrity. In the original book, the futility of war is driven home by the fact that the bridge is *not* blown up at the end. Sensing that an audience, having watched for nearly three hours, would feel let down by the lack of a big explosion, the filmmakers altered the ending.

7th Voyage of Sinbad, The (1958)

CREDITS

Director, Nathan Juran; screenplay, Ken Kolb, adapted from ancient Persian legends; producers, Charles H. Schneer and Ray Harryhausen; original music, Bernard Herrmann; cinematography, Wilkie Cooper; running time, 87 min.

CAST

Kerwin Mathews (*Sinbad*); Kathryn Grant Crosby (*Princess Parisa*); Richard Eyer (*Baronni the Boy Genie*); Torin Thatcher (*Sokurah the Magician*); Alec Mango (*Caliph*).

Ray Harryhausen's Cyclops menaces the crew in *The 7th Voyage of Sinbad*.

THE FILM

Ray Harryhausen had been providing the special effects for various creature features throughout the 1950s, including the fanciful dinosaur in *The Beast From 20,000 Fathoms* (1953) and an immense octopus (his tentacles reduced to six for economy) in *The Creature From the Ocean Floor* (1956). Those were tight-budgeted items in which special effects were given full rein only in the concluding act. Harryhausen's dream was a return to big-budget F/X films on the order of *King Kong*, in which interaction between human characters and the fantastic elements were constant. He finally had the opportunity to create a renaissance for such stuff with this, the first film he personally supervised.

Sinbad must team with the evil villain Sokurah to retrieve a magic lamp from the horrible Cyclops and restore a shrunken princess to normal size. *Voyage* features handsome color photography, a wide array of dazzling table-top creations (Cyclops, monstrous bird, snake-woman dancer, battling skeleton, etc.), and a phenomenal orchestral score by the man who had done such honors for many of Hitchcock's movies. Harryhausen left little room for doubt that he was, like his contemporaries George Pal and Walt Disney, going against the then-current notion that F/X action movies were strictly for small children and non-discriminating adults. He helped prove that magical alternative worlds could and would be fully realized in films that would appeal to intelligent adults as well as children, inspiring young fans Spielberg and Lucas, setting the direction they would eventually travel across the landscape of the commercial motion picture.

Rio Bravo (1959)

CREDITS

Director, Howard Hawks; producer, Hawks; screenplay, Leigh Brackett and Jules Furthman; producer, Hawks; original music, Dimitri Tiomkin and Paul Webster; cinematographer, Russell Harlan; running time, 141 min.

CAST

John Wayne (*Sheriff John T. Chance*); Dean Martin (*Dude*); Ricky Nelson (*Colorado Ryan*); Angie Dickinson (*Feathers*); Walter Brennan (*Stumpy*); Ward Bond (*Pat Wheeler*); John Russell (*Nathan Burdette*); Estelita Rodriguez (*Consuelo*); Claude Akins (*Joe Burdett*); Bob Steele (*Matt Harris*); Bob Terhune (*Charlie the Bartender*); Pedro Gonzalez-Gonzalez (*Carlos Remonte*).

THE FILM

The film noir style, so prevalent at the decade's beginning, spilled over into the western. Henry King's *The Gunfighter* (1950) and Fred Zinnemann's *High Noon* (1952) set the pace for stark, grim, unpleasant "adult" oaters. They, and endless imitations, provided negative commentaries on the American Dream gone sour, in tune with the "lonely crowd" tone of the times. This did not sit well with either star John Wayne or director Howard Hawks, who had collaborated on the classic *Red River* (1948). They commissioned a script that would directly answer such negative westerns with a positive story. In *High Noon*, Gary Cooper's lawman (threatened by old enemies) begs the townspeople to help him, yet when they refuse, he turns down offers for aid from a cripple, a drunk, and a kid. In *Rio Bravo*, John Wayne's lawman (in similar straites) refuses to ask the locals for help, yet enlists three volunteers to get the job done—a cripple, a drunk, and a kid. The film also differed from *High Noon* in terms of style. The former was shot in black and white at a bleak location (Gene Autry's ironically named "Melody Ranch" in California). The latter was filmed, with the brightest color stock available, on the streets of

John Wayne, Dean Martin, and Ricky Nelson in *Rio Bravo*.

Old Tucson, a warm, inviting-looking recreation of a western town. *High Noon* was virtually humorless; *Rio Bravo* is played more as comedy than drama, though when the action does start, it is big-scale and brutal. In recent years, it has been pointed out that *High Noon*, featuring a hero who rejects his community, marching out to fight evil as a rugged individualist, actually offers a conservative statement, while *Rio Bravo*, in which John Wayne can't do the job alone and must rely on others, implies the importance of the group and is, therefore, liberal in implication. Yet *High Noon*'s Academy award–winning screenwriter, Carl Foreman, had been blacklisted during the mid-fifties for the radical, anti-American ideas he had supposedly slipped into that movie.

25
THE RACERS

There's something about the speed, danger, and emotional rush that makes the car-racing film irresistible to action moviemakers. Howard Hawks turned out the first impressive example—*The Crowd Roars* (1932) stars James Cagney at his wiseguyish best, playing the original example of the silver screen's anti-hero. Ever since, the form has been a Hollywood staple, running the gamut from big-budget extravaganza to Drive-In exploitation. Here are the most significant racing films shot since 1945, rated between one (low) and five (high).

Cannonball (1976). Paul Bartel, dir. Highly enjoyable B-budget race flick from the Roger Corman company. David Carradine enters a backwoods country competition, allowing for expected cornball comedy and engaging stunt work. The clichés work owing to a wink-at-the-audience approach. ★★★★

Cannonball Run, The. See "Burt Reynolds" in chapter 10. ★★★

Days of Thunder (1990). Tony Scott, dir. From Bruckheimer and Simpson, the "hot" producing team of the eighties, comes this by-the-numbers racing flick that plays like *Top Gun* relocated on the track. Tom Cruise plays pretty much the same character. Acceptable but way too predictable. ★★★

Driven (2001). Renny Harlin, dir. Arguably the worst racing movie ever made, despite the presence of Sylvester Stallone and Burt Reynolds as aging fanatics who can't give up the game. This dumb film seriously hurt the reputation of one-time up-and-coming action director Harlin. ★

Gone in 60 Seconds (1974). H. B. Halicki, dir. A striking example of the direct-to-Drive-In features, this one's worth catching. Halicki directed and stars (with Parnelli Jones) in a spirited caper flick, involving a bank robbery done by blackmailed world-class racers. Contains the longest (and one of the best) auto chase sequences ever filmed. ★★★★

Gone in Sixty Seconds (2000). Dominic Sena, dir. Huge budget, big Oscar-winning stars (Nicolas Cage and Angelina Jolie) don't help this embarrassing remake of the cult classic. Once again, top racer is blackmailed by criminals into pulling car theft. The original's scrappy sensibility is sorely missing this time around. Nothing works. ★

Grand Prix (1963). John Frankenheimer, dir. Not even the combination of a huge scale including employment of the Panavision 70 format and an all-star international cast (James Garner, Toshiro Mifune, Yves Montand) can compensate for a dull story and impersonal filmmaking. Exciting race sequences rate as too little, too late. ★★

Greased Lightning (1977). Michael Schultz, dir. Underrated film (from the director of *Car Wash*), with Richard Pryor enjoying his first dramatic role as Wendell Scott, the first African American to become a racing star. Fine stuntwork, intriguing performances by musician Richie Havens and politican Julian Bond! Pam Grier's the female lead. ★★★★

Gumball Rally, The. See chapter 8. ★★★★

Le Mans (1971). Lee H. Katzin, dir. Tailored specifically for the on-screen persona of real-life racing buff Steve McQueen. This rates as one of the best films ever made in this action subgenre. He's the American taking on European competition, a hackneyed situation endowed with new life owing to vivid, hair-raising stunt sequences. ★★★★★

Racers, The (1955). Henry Hathaway, dir. Routine racing flick, apparently put into production by Daryl F. Zanuck to give then-current inamorata, Bella Darvi, a shot at stardom. Kirk Douglas is the American daredevil taking on European drivers (Gilbert Roland, Cesar Romero). Routine. ★★★

Smash-up Alley (1972). Edward J. Lakso, dir. Run-of-the-mill direction keeps this from roaring, yet you won't want to miss seeing Richard Petty play himself. Darren McGavin plays Petty's father. Oddly, that actor's real-life wife, Kathie Browne, plays *Petty's* love interest! ★★★

Steve McQueen in *Le Mans*.

Speedway (1968). Norman Taurog, dir. The "King" himself takes a turn at the car-racing gambit. Elvis Presley is here cast as a stockcar champ who, on occasion, breaks into song (none of the tunes particularly memorable) in order to impress Nancy Sinatra. Richard Petty co-stars. So-so. ★★★

Stroker Ace (1983). Hal Needham, dir. The chemistry evident in the car comedy *Smokey and the Bandit* between star Burt Reynolds and stuntman-turned-director Needham fails to happen in this slightly more ambitious misfire about a rebellious racer. The kind of film that cut Burt's stardom short. ★

Winning (1969). James Goldstone, dir. Perhaps the best racing movie ever, thanks to an exceptionally intelligent script, solid performances, and fine track footage. Paul Newman is obsessed with winning, neglects his woman (Joanne Woodward), who takes up with Robert Wagner. Convincing and absorbing every inch of the way, with bang-up finale. ★★★★★

Paul Newman in *Winning*.

26

O PIONEERS!: PREDECESSORS TO THE MODERN ACTION STARS

As the modern action film was coming into being, numerous stars of the century's first half—John Wayne, Clark Gable, Henry Fonda, Humphrey Bogart, Errol Flynn, Gary Cooper, Tyrone Power—continued to make their mark in new films. By the end of the fifties, most had retired or passed away, replaced by younger stars who, beginning in 1946, hurried the transition from old-fashioned adventure to modern action-entertainment. Many maintained dual careers, doing other types of films as well. All are best remembered today, though, as the predecessors of our contemporary action stars. Here are the most significant ones.

Yul Brynner (Taidje Khan)

Born July 7, 1915, in Vladivostock, Russia. Often claimed his name was Taidje Khan, that he was half Swiss and half Japanese. In actuality, Yul was the son of an engineer, Boris Brynner, half European and half Mongolian, and his Russian wife. When father abandoned the family, mother Marousia moved to China, then Paris, where Yul attended Lycée Moncelle. He dropped out of school to become a vagabond, playing guitar with a gypsy band. Befriended filmmaker Jean Cocteau, then worked as a trapeze artist with Cirque d'Hiver before joining Michael Chekhov's theater troupe on a U.S. tour. Made his Broadway debut in *Lute Song* opposite Mary Martin, co-hosted an early TV talk show, *Mr. and Mrs.* with wife Virginia Gilmore. Directed television shows until Ms. Martin suggested him for the lead in *The King and I*. Film version (opposite Deborah Kerr) won him an Oscar (1956), though exotic image made Yul difficult to cast. Kicked off a long career as an action star opposite Charlton Heston in Cecil B. DeMille's final outing, *The Ten Commandments*. In later years, he toured in stage revivals of *The King and I*. Died on October 10, 1985, in New York City of complications due to lung cancer, caused by excessive smoking.

Yul Brynner in *Taras Bulba.*

ACTION FILMOGRAPHY

Port of New York (1949); *The Ten Commandments* (1956); *The Buccaneer* (1958); *Solomon and Sheba* (1959); *The Magnificent Seven* (1960); *Taras Bulba* (1962); *Escape From Zahrain* (1962); *Kings of the Sun* (1963); *Flight from Ashiya* (1964); *Invitation to a Gunfighter* (1964); *Morituri* (1965); *Return of the Magnificent Seven* (1966); *Cast a Giant Shadow* (1966); *Triple Cross* (1967); *The Long Duel* (1967); *Villa Rides* (1968); *Battle of Neretva* (1969); *Catlow* (1971); *Adiós, Sabata* (1971); *The Light at the Edge of the World* (1971); *Fuzz* (1972); *Westworld* (1973); *The Ultimate Warrior* (1975); *Death Rage* (1976); *Futureworld* (1976).

MUST-SEE

The Ten Commandments: See "Charlton Heston" in this chapter.

The Magnificent Seven: See chapter 18.

Solomon and Sheba (King Vidor, dir.). Yul stepped in for Tyrone Power, who passed away on location, for this lavish biblical epic, romancing Gina Lollobrigida, battling evil George Sanders. Terrific of its type.

Taras Bulba (J. Lee Thompson, dir.). Big-scale epic about Cossack chieftan, battling enemies on the Steppes, with Argentina sitting in for the Ukraine. Fabulously staged fight between sixteenth-century cavalry units and long siege of a fortress city. Only limitation—the dull subplot involving Bulba's son (Tony Curtis) with genteel princess (Christine Kaufmann).

Kings of the Sun (J. Lee Thompson, dir.). Underrated, impressive action spectacle involving members of Mayan culture, whose young leader (George Chakiris) brings surviving followers to New World by boats. Once there, they conflict with a local native leader (Brynner). Far better than its reputation, with sumptuously staged fight scenes.

Futureworld: See chapter 21.

Kirk Douglas (Issur Danielovitch Demsky)

Born December 9, 1916, in Amsterdam, New York. His father, Jacob, was an abusive ragman who had immigrated from Russia in 1912. Poverty in youth left Kirk determined to achieve the American Dream. He waited tables to put himself through St. Lawrence, where he wrestled as well as acted. Did WWII service in the navy, afterwards debuted on Broadway. Cast as a weakling in early film noir roles—*The Strange Love of Martha Ivers* (1946), *Out of the Past* (1947)—though boxing drama *Champion* (1949), for which he was Oscar nominated, convinced the public he could play tough guys. Kirk walked out on a studio contract in the mid-fifties to create his own film company (Bryna Productions, named after his mother), then hand-tailored own career. In time, he redefined the popular notion of a film's "hero," purposefully portraying ne'er-do-wells who are unaccountably appealing. Balanced "serious" dramatic projects (i.e., Van Gogh in *Lust for Life*, 1956), with hard-edged action epics. Returned to Broadway for role of McMurphy in Ken Kesey's *One Flew Over the Cuckoo's Nest* (1963). Frustrated at never winning an Oscar, it's worth noting that he turned down roles in *Stalag 17* (1953) and *Cat Ballou* (1964), which brought statuettes to Bill Holden and Lee Marvin. Partly disabled by stroke in 1995, Kirk still occasionally acts.

ACTION FILMOGRAPHY

Champion (1949); *Along the Great Divide* (1951); *The Big Sky* (1952); *The Big Trees* (1952); *20,000 Leagues Under the Sea* (1954); *Ulysses* (1954); *The Racers* (1955); *Man Without a Star* (1955); *The Indian Fighter* (1955); *Gunfight at the O.K. Corral* (1957); *Paths of Glory* (1957); *The Vikings* (1958); *The*

Devil's Disciple (1959); *Last Train From Gun Hill* (1959); *Spartacus* (1960); *The Last Sunset* (1961); *Lonely Are the Brave* (1962); *The Hook* (1963); *In Harm's Way* (1965); *The Heroes of Telemark* (1965); *Cast a Giant Shadow* (1966); *Is Paris Burning?* (1966); *The Way West* (1967); *The War Wagon* (1967); *The Brotherhood* (1968); *There Was a Crooked Man* (1970); *Light at the Edge of the World* (1971); *A Gunfight* (1971); *Scalawag* (1973); *Posse* (1975); *The Villain* (1979); *Saturn 3* (1980); *The Final Countdown* (1980); *The Man From Snowy River* (1982); *Tough Guys* (1986).

MUST-SEE

Champion: See chapter 22.

The Big Sky (Howard Hawks, dir.). Mountain men (Kirk and Dewey Martin) find their friendship tested upon meeting an Indian princess (Elizabeth Threatt) on a keelboat trip into the Rocky Mountains. Handsome, lavish historical episode, loosely based on book by A. B. Guthrie, Jr.

20,000 Leagues Under the Sea: See chapter 24.

Gunfight at the O.K. Corral: See "Burt Lancaster" in this chapter.

Paths of Glory (Stanley Kubrick, dir.). One-of-a-kind war movie, with Douglas as a WWI French commander who leads his company in impossible attack on enemy position, then must defend his defeated troops during a court-martial. Actionful first half, intelligent dramatic follow-up.

The Vikings (Richard Fleischer, dir.). Fabulous recreation of Norse life, shot on location, with Douglas as the brutal warrior who invades England by sea. This film revolutionized the action genre, as Douglas's "hero" is in fact the villain of the piece, in conflict with bland leading man Tony Curtis for the hand of Janet Leigh. The Viking attack on a British coastal castle is remarkable, with Kirk doing most of his own stunt work.

Spartacus: See chapter 18.

Tough Guys (Jeff Kanew, dir.). Irresistible reteaming of Douglas and Lancaster, playing old cons released into brave new world they can't comprehend. Eli Wallach is a show stealer as a crazed villain.

Charlton Heston (John Charles Carter)

Born October 4, 1924, in Evanston, Illinois. Attended Northwestern University, where Chuck mastered the traditional Shakespearean performance style. Following World War II, he appeared in several independent/educational films including an acclaimed low-budget version of *Julius Caesar* (1950) as

Charlton Heston in *El Cid*.

Mark Antony. Married Lydia Clarke in 1944, the two have been together ever since. Much stage work, in Broadway and stock, as well as golden-age TV drama preceded his Hollywood premiere in a non-descript film noir, *Dark City* (1950). Subsequent studio contract led to undistinguished program-mers, though they helped established Heston as a rugged action star. Big break came with casting in Cecil B. DeMille's *The Greatest Show on Earth* (1952) as the tough circus foreman. This led to star casting as Moses in DeMille's final film, though superstardom might have yet proven elusive had Burt Lancaster not walked off the *Ben-Hur* set. Chuck offered a portrait in stolid heroism, earning the nickname Old Granite Jaw. A Civil rights activist, he befriended Dr. Martin Luther King, Jr., joining that leader's marches into the South. In the seventies, Chuck maintained a viable career as other action pioneers searched for work by taking on offbeat sci-fi films and disaster epics. Switched parties to become a Republican conservative, eventually elected president of the National Rifle Association.

ACTION FILMOGRAPHY

The Savage (1952); *Pony Express* (1953); *Arrowhead* (1953); *The Naked Jungle* (1954); *Secret of the Incas* (1955); *The Far Horizons* (1955); *The Ten Com-mandments* (1956); *Three Violent People* (1956); *The Big Country* (1956); *The Buccaneer* (1958); *Ben-Hur* (1959); *El Cid* (1961); *55 Days at Peking* (1963); *Major Dundee* (1965); *The War Lord* (1965); *Khartoum* (1966); *Planet of the Apes* (1968); *Will Penny* (1968); *The Omega Man* (1971); *Call of the Wild* (1972); *Skyjacked* (1972); *The Three Musketeers* (1974); *Airport 1975* (1974); *Earthquake* (1974); *The Four Musketeers* (1975); *The Last Hard Men* (1976); *Midway* (1976); *Two Minute Warning* (1977); *Crossed Swords* (1978); *Gray Lady Down* (1978); *The Mountain Men* (1980); *Tombstone* (1993); *True Lies* (1994).

MUST-SEE

The Naked Jungle: See chapter 15.

   The Ten Commandments (Cecil B. DeMille, dir.). Apotheosis of old Hol-lywood epic style, Heston's Moses clashes with Brynner's Ramses, with Anne Bancroft (as Nefertiri) caught in the middle. The film attempts to be all things to all people—romance, spectacle, inspiration—and, in truth, rates as cardboard and corny by today's standards.

   Ben-Hur: See chapter 11.

El Cid (Anthony Mann, dir.). Perhaps the finest ancient-world spectacle of its era, with Chuck perfectly cast as Spain's guardian hero, opposite Sophia Loren his great love. Sharp attention to accuracy of historic detail and intimate moments beautifully balanced with large-scale action vistas.

Khartoum (Basil Dearden, dir.). Vivid, authentic, rousing version of 1885 siege of the title city. Heston surprisingly game as England's General Gordon, and Laurence Olivier nothing short of remarkable as his enemy, "The Mahdi." Shamefully overlooked and underpraised on initial release.

Planet of the Apes: See chapter 18.

William Holden (William Franklin Beedle, Jr.)

Born April 17, 1918, in O'Fallon, Illinois, into affluent family (Bill's father was a chemist and his teacher mother was descended from George Washington). Bill planned to follow in his father's footsteps and enrolled in Pasadena Junior College, where he was spotted by a Paramount scout and quickly signed to a studio contract. Shot to stardom opposite Barbara Stanwyck in boxing melodrama *Golden Boy* (1939), though all wrong for the John Garfieldish role. Served in the air force during World War II. Thereafter, found himself stuck in easygoing boy-next-door roles until Montgomery Clift turned down Billy Wilder's *Sunset Boulevard* (1950); Holden's performance, full of icy irony, revitalized his career. Director again tapped Bill for *Stalag 17,* and a Best Actor Oscar led to superstardom. Cast as tough guy with a romantic soul in *Picnic* (1955). Hemingway-esque in real life, Holden spent much time in Africa, always crusading for anti-poaching laws to protect wildlife. Often in the company of long-term mistress Stephanie Powers,

William Holden in *The Bridges at Toko-Ri.*

though married to Brenda Marshall, 1941–1971. Just when career seemed ready to ebb, won the lead in Peckinpah's monumental *Wild Bunch*, allowing Bill to continue into the 1970s with major movies like *Network* (1976). Heavy drinking took its toll—Holden passed away November 16, 1981, in Santa Monica, California, due to injuries sustained during a fall at home.

POSTWAR ACTION FILMOGRAPHY

Rachel and the Stranger (1948); *The Man From Colorado* (1948); *Streets of Laredo* (1949); *Force of Arms* (1951); *Submarine Command* (1951); *Stalag 17* (1953); *Escape From Fort Bravo* (1953); *The Bridges at Toko-Ri* (1954); *The Bridge on the River Kwai* (1957); *The Horse Soldiers* (1959); *The Seventh Dawn* (1964); *Alvarez Kelly* (1966); *The Devil's Brigade* (1968); *The Wild Bunch* (1969); *The Wild Rovers* (1971); *The Revengers* (1972); *Open Season* (1974); *The Towering Inferno* (1974); *Escape to Athena* (1979); *When Time Ran Out* (1980).

MUST-SEE

Stalag 17: See chapter 27.
    The Bridges at Toko-Ri: See chapter 23.
    The Bridge on the River Kwai: See chapter 24.
    The Horse Soldiers (John Ford, dir.). Striking Civil War action yarn. Holden plays the wiseguy company doctor, endlessly arguing with stolid commander John Wayne as their cavalry outfit invades the South. Brisk dialogue and memorably staged battle sequences. Heroic march of the little boy soldiers is one of the great moments in movie history.
    The Wild Bunch: See chapter 18.

Burt(on) (Stephen) Lancaster

Born on November 2, 1913, in New York City. Burt and four siblings were raised by their postman father. An informal education on NYC's mean streets led to early interest in athletics. Burt ran away from home, joined a circus, and found work as an acrobat. While serving in the army, he tried acting in USO shows. Postwar movie career began with excellent film noir, *The Killers* (1946). Burt excelled in action-hero roles, though also sought out (like buddy Kirk Douglas) more "serious" parts in heavily dramatic works, including a brooding Brando-esque lead in *The Rose Tattoo* (1955). Also like Douglas, Burt was one of the first postwar stars to break with the then all powerful studio system, incorporating himself with Harold Hecht and James Hill, tailoring his career to his own (not some movie mogul's) tastes. Produced some movies that he did not star in, including *Marty* (1955), an Oscar-winning "little" movie that hit big. Best actor Oscar winner for *Elmer Gantry* (1960), as a huckster with an irresistible toothy grin. Lifelong liberal, Burt always crusaded for civil rights and anti-war causes. When bubble burst for his era of stardom in early 1970s, he accepted leads in less prestigious action films as well as supporting roles in ambitious movies, even some TV-movie jobs. Thrice married, Burt passed away (heart attack) on October 20, 1994, in Century City, California.

ACTION FILMOGRAPHY

Brute Force (1947); *The Flame and the Arrow* (1950); *Vengeance Valley* (1951); *Jim Thorpe, All American* (1951); *Ten Tall Men* (1951); *The Crimson Pirate* (1952); *From Here to Eternity* (1953); *His Majesty O'Keefe* (1953); *Vera Cruz* (1954); *Apache* (1954); *The Kentuckian* (1955); *Gunfight at the O.K. Corral* (1957); *The Devil's Disciple* (1959); *The Unforgiven* (1959); *The Train* (1964); *The Hallelujah Trail* (1965); *The Professionals* (1966); *The Scalphunters* (1968); *Castle Keep* (1969); *The Gypsy Moths* (1969); *Airport* (1970); *Lawman* (1971); *Valdez Is Coming* (1971); *Ulzana's Raid* (1972); *The Cassandra Crossing* (1976); *Buffalo Bill and the Indians* (1977); *Go Tell the Spartans* (1978); *Zulu Dawn* (1979); *Cattle Annie and Little Britches* (1981); *The Osterman Weekend* (1983); *Tough Guys* (1986).

MUST-SEE

The Crimson Pirate: See chapter 24.

From Here to Eternity: See chapter 27.

Vera Cruz (Robert Aldrich, dir.). Animalistic outlaw Burt competes with civilized Gary Cooper for gold and girls in revolution-torn Mexico. This innovative oater set the pace for Sergio Leone westerns that followed.

Apache (Robert Aldrich, dir.). The last free Mescalero fights the Anglos after Geronimo surrenders. One-man army concept serves as prelude to many future films starring Stallone and Schwarzenegger.

Gunfight at the O.K. Corral (John Sturges, dir.). Best by far of all the Lancaster-Douglas teamings, as Wyatt Earp and Doc Holliday, respectively, versus Johnny Ringo (John Ireland) and the Clanton gang. Long and leisurely paced, bolstered by a wonderful chemistry between the stars. The final shoot-out serves as director Sturges's warm-up for his upcoming *The Magnificent Seven*.

The Unforgiven: See "Audie Murphy" in chapter 20.

The Train: See chapter 27.

The Professionals: See chapter 18.

Ulzana's Raid (Robert Aldrich, dir.). Burt's a grizzled scout leading an under-manned cavalry patrol after a bloodthirsty Apache band. Brutally honest depiction of Indian strife never degenerates into exploitive violence, though the action is rugged and non-stop.

Robert (Charles Durman) **Mitchum**

Born August 6, 1917, in Bridgeport, Connecticut. His dad (part Indian), who worked on the railroad, was killed in a train accident in 1919, leaving Bob and his siblings in difficult straits. Troublemaking in youth led him to run away during the Great Depression. Thrown on to a Georgia chain gang, Bob managed to escape. Oddest job was as a ghostwriter for Carroll Righter, a then-popular astrologist. During the war, Mitchum found work at Lockheed Aircraft and dabbled in amateur theatrics. Won bit parts in B-westerns, owing to sallow cheeks and cruel though lazy eyes. Led to several break-through roles in WWII action films, then superstardom when the postwar taste in leading men changed from conventional to offbeat. Always appeared to casually glide through films, without effort—that image, which he encouraged, actually disguised a deep dedication to the craft. Busted for marijuana in 1949 and served time in jail. Somehow, his career managed to survive. The bad boy of postwar stars, Mitchum remained a closeted art lover, composing an oratorio that Orson Welles produced at the Hollywood Bowl. Best performance ever was as a crazed preacher in Charles Laughton's *Night of the Hunter* (1955). Despite endless tough-guy roles, he was completely believable as a milktoast reverend in David Lean's *Ryan's Daughter* (1970). A big-time drinker and smoker, he passed away (from lung cancer) on July 1, 1997, in Santa Barbara, California.

POSTWAR ACTION FILMOGRAPHY

The Story of G.I. Joe (1945); *Pursued* (1947); *Rachel and the Stranger* (1948); *Blood on the Moon* (1948); *One Minute to Zero* (1952); *The Lusty Men* (1952); *White Witch Doctor* (1953); *Second Chance* (1953); *River of No Return* (1954); *Track of the Cat* (1954); *Man With the Gun* (1955); *Bandido* (1956); *Heaven Knows, Mr. Allison* (1957); *The Enemy Below* (1957); *Thunder Road* (1958); *The Wonderful Country* (1959); *A Terrible Beauty* (1960); *The Sun-*

downers (1960); *The Longest Day* (1962); *Rampage* (1963); *The Way West* (1967); *El Dorado* (1967); *Anzio* (1968); *Villa Rides* (1968); *The Good Guys and the Bad Guys* (1969); *Young Billy Young* (1969); *The Wrath of God* (1972); *Farewell My Lovely* (1975); *The Yakuza* (1975); *Midway* (1976); *Tombstone* (1993).

MUST-SEE

The Story of G.I. Joe: See chapter 27.

    The Lusty Men: See chapter 15.

    River of No Return (Otto Preminger, dir.). Solid Mitchum saddled with an over-acting Marilyn Monroe as they travel by raft through hostile Indian territory. Nice locations, but back-projection for the river-rapids action scenes hurts overall impact. Considered pretty sexy for its time period.

    Thunder Road: See chapter 21.

    The Longest Day: See chapter 27.

Gregory (Eldred) Peck

Born April 5, 1916, in La Jolla, California, to the wife of a druggist father. Parents divorced when Greg was 5, the boy thereafter raised by his grandmother. Escaped loneliness by spending time at the movies. Pre-med studies at Berkeley ended when Peck decided to head for New York and study drama at famed Neighborhood Playhouse. Broadway debut was in Emlyn Williams's *The Morning Star* (1942), followed by his Hollywood premiere in so-so WWII film *Days of Glory* (1944). Quickly slipped into a heroic mold, combining the bulk of John Wayne with the common decency of Henry Fonda. Became a regular in David O. Selznick productions, including Hitchcock's *Spellbound* (1945). Numerous Oscar nominations came his way before Peck finally won for his sentimental portrait of a southern lawyer in *To Kill a Mockingbird* (1962). Such "serious" work, as well as an occasional comedy and/or romance, alternated with action films, including westerns and WWII dramas. Ultra-liberal political orientation included civil rights activism in the early sixties and support for pacifist Berrigan brothers during the Vietnam War. In 1970, his career—like those of many contemporaries—floundered, though Greg did enjoy something of a comeback with an offbeat horror opus, *The Omen* (1976). Served as first chairman of the American Film Institute, which he helped to create.

Gregory Peck in *Duel in the Sun*.

ACTION FILMOGRAPHY

Days of Glory (1944); *Duel in the Sun* (1946); *Yellow Sky* (1948); *Twelve O'Clock High* (1949); *The Gunfighter* (1950); *Only the Valiant* (1951); *David and Bathsheba* (1951); *Captain Horatio Hornblower* (1951); *The Snows of Kilimanjaro* (1952); *The World in His Arms* (1952); *The Purple Plain* (1954); *Moby Dick* (1956); *The Bravados* (1958); *The Big Country* (1958); *Pork Chop Hill* (1959); *The Guns of Navarone* (1961); *How the West Was Won* (1962); *Behold a Pale Horse* (1964); *The Stalking Moon* (1969); *Mackenna's Gold* (1969); *Marooned* (1969); *Shootout* (1971); *Billy Two Hats* (1973); *MacArthur* (1977); *The Sea Wolves* (1980); *The Old Gringo* (1989).

MUST-SEE

Duel in the Sun (King Vidor, dir.). Halfway between the absurdity of *The Outlaw* (1943) and the grandeur of *Red River* (1948) in terms of style and subject as well as its release date. Overblown Freudian epic in the old west. All-star cast includes Peck in an uncharacteristic bad-boy role. Mighty sequence in which mounted cowboys descend upon a railroad crew is truly spectacular.

Twelve O'Clock High: See chapter 27.

Moby Dick: See chapter 24.

The Bravados (Henry King, dir.). Grim, "not for the squeamish" western about vengeance-driven Peck, tracking down men (Lee Van Cleef, Henry Silva) whom he holds responsible for raping and murdering his wife. Unforgettable twist-ending.

Pork Chop Hill: See chapter 23.

The Guns of Navarone: See chapter 18.

The Stalking Moon: See chapter 17.

Sidney Poitier (center) with Alan Ladd (left) and player in *All the Young Men*.

Sidney Poitier

Born on February 20, 1927, Sidney was raised on Cat Island in the Bahamas by a dirt farmer father, unable to raise his family above the poverty level. All but uneducated, Sidney was sent at age 15 to Miami in hopes of deterring rapid descent into juvenile delinquency. There he encountered racism, American style, for the first time, and became determined to do something about it. Headed for NYC, slept in a bus terminal, worked odd jobs in Harlem, then impulsively auditioned for the American Negro Theatre—only to be stonily rejected. Dedicated to succeeding, he studied hard and, on the second try was accepted. Appearance in Broadway revival of *Lysistrata* led to a Hollywood contract at 20th Century Fox, even as a civil rights cinema emerged. Film debut as a dedicated young doctor—radically changing the screen image of African Americans—in *No Way Out* (1950). Then, *Blackboard Jungle* (1956) and *The Defiant Ones* (1958). Won the Oscar (first black star to win Best Actor) for *Lilies of the Field* (1963). In the minds of some critics, such dignified casting eventually went too far, leading to an impossible ideal of perfection, as removed from everyday reality as were the previous negative screen clichés for blacks. Poitier often lent his image and persona to the action genre, emerging as the first black action superstar for a then-forming "new" interracial mainstream audience.

ACTION FILMOGRAPHY

Red Ball Express (1952); *Go, Man, Go!* (1954); *Blackboard Jungle* (1955); *Something of Value* (1957); *Mark of the Hawk* (1957); *The Defiant Ones* (1958); *All the Young Men* (1960); *The Long Ships* (1963); *The Bedford Incident* (1965); *Duel at Diablo* (1966); *In the Heat of the Night* (1967); *The Lost Man* (1969); *They Call Me MISTER Tibbs!* (1970); *Brother John* (1971); *The Organization* (1971); *Buck and the Preacher* (1972); *The Wilby Conspiracy* (1975); *Let's Do it Again* (1975); *Shoot to Kill* (1988); *Little Nikita* (1988); *Sneakers* (1992); *The Jackal* (1997).

MUST-SEE

Something of Value (Richard Brooks, dir.). Still-powerful drama of Mau Mau uprising in Kenya, based on a novel by Robert Ruark. Poitier plays the warrior vascillating between the extremes of violent action and pacifist ideals. Only liability is a dull Rock Hudson as his pal.

　　The Long Ships (Jack Cardiff, dir.). Bizarre big-scale film about Moor (Poitier) and Viking (Richard Widmark) fighting over a mythical lost bell and dazzling Rosanna Schiaffano. Written as a serious action epic, this was played as a goofy comedy instead, with intermittently entertaining results. Sidney and Widmark are both fabulous.

　　The Bedford Incident (James B. Harris, dir.). Taut conflict aboard a U.S. Naval vessel as cynical captain (Richard Widmark) battles idealistic mate (Poitier) over whether to fire atomic weapons at a Russian sub. Fascinating precursor to Denzel Washington and Gene Hackman in *Crimson Tide*. Marvelous acting all around.

　　In the Heat of the Night (Norman Jewison, dir.). More suspense than action, but a classic all the way, with Sidney as Virgil Tibbs, a sophisticated big city police detective who helps a redneck Southern sheriff (Rod Steiger) solve a murder case. Oscar-winning Best Picture.

　　Let's Do It Again: See chapter 22.

Anthony (Rudolfo Oaxaca) Quinn

Born April 21, 1915, in Chihuahua, Mexico, to an Irish father and Mexican mother. Raised in East L.A. barrio, Tony survived by shining shoes and selling newspapers. Other odd jobs included butcher, boxer, street-corner preacher, slaughterhouse worker, and prizefighter. A scholarship allowed him to study architecture with Frank Lloyd Wright. Picked to play an Indian warrior in Cecil B. DeMille's *The Plainsman* (1936), Tony married the director's (adopted) daughter, Katherine, leading to a twenty-five-year relationship. Won strong supporting roles through the late thirties and 1940s. With the birth of the civil rights movement, Quinn became an all-purpose ethnic in major movies. Won two Oscars (Best Supporting Actor) for *Viva Villa* (1952), and *Lust for Life* (1956), stealing scenes from Marlon Brando and Kirk Douglas. Achieved high marks for his paintings, which were influenced by Gauguin, whom Tony had portrayed in his second Academy-worthy role. During the 1960s, graduated to leads, notably *Zorba the Greek* (1964), for which he

Anthony Quinn in
Lawrence of Arabia.

was nominated for Best Actor Oscar. As the decade waned, he (like others) found work hard to come by, opting for top-billed parts in less ambitious/ prestigious movies, often tending to overact. Quinn passed away June 3, 2001, in Boston, of complications due to pneumonia and throat cancer.

POSTWAR ACTION FILMOGRAPHY

Back to Bataan (1945); *California* (1946); *Sinbad the Sailor* (1947); *The Brave Bulls* (1951); *Mask of the Avenger* (1951); *Viva Zapata!* (1952); *The World in His Arms* (1952); *The Brigand* (1952); *Against All Flags* (1952); *City Beneath the Sea* (1953); *Ride, Vaquero!* (1953); *East of Sumatra* (1953); *Seminole* (1953); *Blowing Wild* (1953); *Ulysses* (1954); *Attila the Hun* (1954); *Seven Cities of Gold* (1955); *The Magnificent Matador* (1955); *The Ride Back* (1957); *Warlock* (1959); *The Savage Innocents* (1959); *Last Train from Gun Hill* (1959); *The Guns of Navarone* (1961); *Lawrence of Arabia* (1962); *Requiem for a Heavyweight* (1962); *Barabbas* (1962); *Behold a Pale Horse* (1964); *A High Wind in Jamaica* (1965); *Marco the Magnificent* (1965); *Lost Command* (1966); *Guns for San Sebastian* (1968); *Deaf Smith and Johnny Ears* (1972); *Across 110th St.* (1972); *The Don is Dead* (1972); *The Destructors* (1973); *Long Shot* (1976); *Caravans* (1978); *The Passage* (1979); *Lion of the Desert* (1980); *High Risk* (1981); *Revenge* (1990); *Mobsters* (1991); *The Last Action Hero* (1993).

MUST-SEE

Back to Bataan: See chapter 27.

The Brave Bulls (Robert Rossen, dir.). First-rate film about bullfighting, cuts through all romantic hogwash, revealing the absolute horror of the moment of truth. Quinn and Mel Ferrer are competing matadors. Director's cut (114 min.) contains the really rough stuff!

Viva Zapata! (Elia Kazan, dir.). Brando and Quinn are common men who become political bandits when oppression in Mexico becomes too awful to bear. Intellectual if anti-revolutionary big-statement movie from former lefty Kazan. Terrific action scenes.

The Guns of Navarone: See chapter 18.

Lawrence of Arabia : See chapter 11.

Guns for San Sebastian (Henri Verneuil, dir.). Quinn is a faux priest who helps isolated villagers defend themsleves from Yaqui warriors led by Charles Bronson. Mucho action, all of it staged on an impressively large scale.

Richard Widmark

Born December 26, 1914, in Sunrise, Minnesota. Dick was raised in Princeton, Illinois, and began acting while a student at Lake Forest College. Later, he taught theater there, then became a radio performer in NYC. Made his Broadway premiere in *Kiss and Tell* (1943). 20th Century Fox introduced him in *Kiss of Death* (1947) as a wild-eyed killer who cackles while tossing wheelchair-bound lady down stairs. Later claimed the laugh was unintentional, at the silliness of the scene. Might have been typed as a villain, but the new postwar taste in leading men called for edgier types. Dick proved perfect for offbeat leads, mostly in rugged outdoor films and shadowy noirs. When his contract expired, he chose—like Douglas, Lancaster, and numerous others—to go indie, helping end the long-term studio contracts. Tried everything including comedy, opposite Doris Day in *Tunnel of Love* (1958), and serious dramas like *Judgment at Nuremberg* (1962). After starring in John Wayne's *The Alamo* (as Jim Bowie), Richard was unmistakably perceived as an early example of the new action hero, snarling and cynical. In the seventies, when his generation of stars lost their box-office appeal, he shifted to TV, starring as a tough detective in *Madigan*, a role he'd played in a film in which his character died at the end! Lived a quiet personal life, married to Jean Hazlewood from 1942 until her death in 1997, then Susan Blanchard since 1999.

ACTION FILMOGRAPHY

Kiss of Death (1947); *Yellow Sky* (1948); *Slattery's Hurricane* (1949); *Down to the Sea in Ships* (1949); *Halls of Montezuma* (1950); *The Frogmen* (1951); *Red Skies of Montana* (1952); *Destination Gobi* (1953); *Pickup on South Street* (1953); *Take the High Ground!* (1953); *Broken Lance* (1954); *Hell and High Water* (1954); *Garden of Evil* (1954); *A Prize of Gold* (1955); *Run for the Sun* (1956); *The Last Wagon* (1956); *Backlash* (1956); *Time Limit* (1957); *The Law and Jake Wade* (1958); *Warlock* (1959); *The Alamo* (1960); *Two Rode Together* (1961); *The Secret Ways* (1961); *How the West Was Won* (1962); *The Long Ships* (1963); *Flight From Ashiya* (1964); *Cheyenne Autumn* (1964); *The Bedford Incident* (1965); *The Way West* (1967); *Alvarez Kelly* (1967); *Madigan* (1968); *Death of a Gunfighter* (1969); *A Talent for Loving* (1969); *The Moonshine War* (1970); *When the Legends Die* (1972); *The Domino Principle* (1977); *Rollercoaster* (1977); *The Swarm* (1978); *The Final Option* (1982).

MUST-SEE

Take the High Ground!: See chapter 23.

The Last Wagon (Delmer Daves, dir.). Brutal western about a small band of survivors of an Indian attack, fighting their way to safety, and portrayed by a game cast. Surprisingly harsh battle scenes for the time.

The Alamo: See chapter 11.

Madigan (Donald Siegel, dir.). Terrific tough-cop film, setting the pace for *Dirty Harry* (same director) about a no-nonsense police detective, his battles with criminals but also with the "brass," particularly a hard-line commissioner (Henry Fonda). A winner all the way.

27

THE LAST GOOD WAR:
WORLD WAR II ON FILM

The modern action film was born during World War II. No sooner had the conflict begun than the Hollywood studios were turning their attention to churning out patriotic films. If the quality varied drastically, the tone remained constant. These were rah!rah! portraits of fine young Americans in action, taking on terrible odds and either winning grand victories or going down fighting. As the war drew to a close, several top-flight filmmakers were already attempting more intelligent and probing visions of combat. No sooner was the fighting over than WWII films took a decidedly different approach to the event, halfway between grim documentary and quaint nostalgia. By the mid-sixties, the WWII film became a source for big-scale spectacles, much like westerns and ancient-world action yarns. During the hippie era, the WWII film threatened to disappear, except for highly critical reconsiderations. Just when it seemed down and out, this subgenre of the action film was revived for the nouveaux patriotism of the new millennium. The WWII film may go away for a while but, like the western, is always waiting for the right moment to return. The following brief selection includes only those WWII movies that will most satisfy fans of action movies, rated between one and five stars.

Away All Boats (1956). Joseph Pevney, dir. Jeff Chandler, Lex Barker, Julie Adams, Richard Boone. A big-budget naval battle epic from Universal studios, at a time when they mainly churned out B-movies. In a noble attempt to turn Chandler into another Charlton Heston, he's cast as the intrepid commander of our young sailors. Impressively staged battles in the Pacific.   ★★★

Air Force (1943). Howard Hawks, dir. John Garfield, Gig Young, John Ridgley, Arthur Kennedy. The men of a fighting plane balance values of rugged individualism with the necessity for group activity, as only Hawks could express it. Garfield is particularly strong as a cynical loner. Devastatingly striking fight scenes, in the air and on the ground.   ★★★★★

Attack (1956). Robert Aldrich, dir. Jack Palance, Eddie Albert, Lee Marvin, Buddy Ebsen. A squad of misfits finds itself commanded by an incompetent coward (Albert, delivering his greatest performance) during the Battle of the Bulge. Spielberg's HBO-TV series *Band of Brothers* also included this true story. Palance's long duel with Panzer tank is a knockout!   ★★★★★

Back to Bataan (1945). Edward Dmytryk, dir. John Wayne, Anthony Quinn, Beulah Bondi. American officer Wayne and Phillipine-bred hero Quinn rescue soldiers captured on Corregidor and form a guerrilla outfit (with help from local natives) to fight Japanese. Admirable interracial slant to combat.   ★★★★

Bataan (1943). George Sidney, dir. Robert Taylor, Thomas Mitchell, Desi Arnaz, Lloyd Nolan. This terrific action drama about a single squad holding off invading Japanese army bears little resemblance to the historical title battle, though the film works well as a blood 'n' guts restaging of John Ford's *The Lost Patrol*. Final fadeout still strong.   ★★★★

Battle Cry (1955). Raoul Walsh, dir. Aldo Ray, Van Heflin, James Whitmore, Fess Parker, L. Q. Jones, Tab Hunter. Sprawling, spectacular tale of marines, their love lives, and combat situations, was lambasted by critics but beloved by audiences. Only sore spot is miscast Hunter in a role Paul Newman sorely wanted but was turned down for!   ★★★

Battleground (1949). William Wellman, dir. Ricardo Montalban, James Whitmore, Van Johnson, James Arness. Ultra-realistic study of an army squad, fighting to survive during the snow-swept Battle of the Bulge. Only liabilities are Van Johnson's sorry performance and some stereotype dialogue. Otherwise, grim, believable, and inspiring.   ★★★★

Battle of Britain (1969). Guy Hamilton, dir. Laurence Olivier, Michael Caine, Christopher Plummer, Trevor Howard, Susannah York. One more of the many post–*Longest Day* films, this one about the air war over England, fails to strike bulls-eye. Too much talk by too many stars, though the plane crashes, bombing scenes, and dogfights above London are standouts.   ★★★

Beach Red (1967). Cornel Wilde, dir. Cornel Wilde, Jean Wallace, Rip Torn. The U.S. Marines hit a well-fortified beachhead in the South Pacific. Controversial on initial release owing to a "new realism" in which blood and guts were vividly depicted, this film set the pace for everything from *The Wild Bunch* to *Saving Private Ryan*.   ★★★

Big Red One, The (1980). Samuel Fuller, dir. Lee Marvin, Mark Hamill, Robert Carradine. Carradine plays writer-director Fuller in this stunning account of his combat experiences with the famed fighting outfit during World War II. Only regret is that the director's longer cut has never been made available.   ★★★★★

Bold and the Brave, The (1956). See chapter 21.   ★★★★★

Bridge on the River Kwai, The (1957). See chapter 24.   ★★★★★

Das Boot (1981). Wolfgang Petersen, dir. Jurgen Prochnow, Klaus Wen-nermann. One of the rare WWII films made during the 1980s, this German production established Petersen as a top director of edge-of-your-seat sus-pense/action. A sympathetic but unsentimental portrait of Germans who manned a U-boat during the war's darkest hours.   ★★★★

Darby's Rangers (1958). William Wellman, dir. James Garner, Jack Warden, Stuart Whitman. Charlton Heston, originally set to play General Darby, jumped ship, at which point Wellman's second-to-last project was demoted from super-production to Warner Bros. programmer. Hokey, but at least the battle scenes are impressive.   ★★★

Desert Rats, The (1953). Robert Wise, dir. James Mason, Richard Burton, Robert Newton. Fine follow-up to Fox's biopic on Field Marshall Rommel, concentrates less on the original's psychology and more on action adventure. Burton is Brit commando who must stop "the Fox" in his tracks. Unofficially remade, with Burton, in 1971 as *Raid on Rommel*.   ★★★★

Destination Tokyo (1943). Delmer Daves, dir. John Garfield, Cary Grant, Dane Clark. Sturdy, imaginative portrait of personalities aboard submarine, with satisfying psychological portraits of all concerned, despite the overall aura of patriotic adventure. Action scenes hold up extremely well in com-parison to more recent films.   ★★★★

Devil's Brigade, The (1968). Andrew V. McLaglen, dir. William Holden, Cliff Robertson, Claude Akins. Obvious imitation of previous year's block-buster *Dirty Dozen* boasts none of that film's panache, as Andy is no Aldrich. Still, WWII action buffs won't want to miss the final assault sequence or Robertson's excellent performance.   ★★★

Dirty Dozen, The (1967). See chapter 18.   ★★★★★

Enemy Below, The (1957). Dick Powell, dir. Robert Mitchum, Curt Jur-gens, Theodore Bikel. Hunt-and-destroy action between Mitchum's vessel as he attempts to sink German sub commanded by Jurgens. Terrific suspense as well as action, devoid of the usual hero-versus-villain mentality, the two instead portrayed as equally sympathetic adversaries.   ★★★

Flying Tigers (1942). David Miller, dir. John Wayne, Jimmie Dodd, Anna Lee. Wayne as Major Claire Chennault, leader of the famed title organiza-tion, though given a fictional name here. Powerful depiction of the force's activities in China before and after Pearl Harbor raid, emphasizing the fight-ing major's maverick approach.   ★★★★

Frogmen, The (1951). Lloyd Bacon, dir. Richard Widmark, Jeffrey Hunter, Robert Wagner. One of a series of retrospectives on World War II lensed by 20th Century Fox in the early fifties, headlined by their top star. Unique for a vivid portrayal (the first ever on screen) of fighting tactics of frogmen; fabulous underwater photography.   ★★★★

Go For Broke! (1951). Robert Pirosh, dir. Van Johnson, Lane Nakano, Henry Nakamura. Even ever-dull Van can't take edge off this first-rate actioner. He plays southerner with racist biases who finds himself commanding a batallion composed entirely of Nisei (Japanese Americans) who have volunteered to fight the Nazis.   ★★★★

Great Escape, The (1963). See chapter 18. ★★★★★

Guadalcanal Diary (1943). Lewis Seiler, dir. Richard Conte, William Bendix, Anthony Quinn. Spectacular story of marines in the South Pacific during early days of the war will still knock your socks off. A fabulous cast in a completely convincing non-stop actioner, frank and brutal for its time, based on the book by Richard Tregaskis.   ★★★★★

Gung Ho! (1943). Ray Enright, dir. Randolph Scott, Robert Mitchum, Sam Levene. Of all the rah!rah! WWII films, this may be the most controversial today, as well as inspiration for *The Dirty Dozen*. Other films saluted all-American boys getting the job done, this is a paeon to the meanest men in the armed services!   ★★★

Guns of Navarone, The (1961).   See chapter 18. ★★★★★

Halls of Montezuma (1951). Lewis Milestone, dir. Richard Widmark, Jack Palance, Karl Malden, Jack Webb. From the director of 1930's Oscar winner *All Quiet on the Western Front*, a big-scale tribute (by way of Darryl Zanuck) to leathernecks. Widmark et al. in brutal jungle combat. Skip Homier's death scene will leave you speechless.   ★★★★

Heaven Knows, Mr. Allison (1957). John Huston, dir. Robert Mitchum, Deborah Kerr. A two-character chamber drama, though this "chamber" is a besieged island. Rugged marine finds himself burdened with a stranded nun, fights to protect her from encroaching Japanese forces while hopelessly falling in love. Terrific pairing of the stars.   ★★★★

Hell in the Pacific (1967). See "Toshiro Mifune" in chapter 10.   ★★★★

Hell Is for Heroes (1961). Don Siegel, dir. Steve McQueen, Fess Parker, Bobby Darin, Nick Adams, James Coburn. Memorable actioner about a WWII squad setting out on a difficult mission and the strange loner (McQueen) who finally gets the job done. In the tradition of *A Walk in the Sun*, with an unforgettable final battle.   ★★★★

Hell to Eternity (1960). Phil Karlson, dir. Jeffrey Hunter, David Janssen, Vic Damone. Searing presentation of the Guy Gabaldon story, about an orphaned Anglo-American raised by a Japanese family, facing a moral crisis when World War II breaks out. This is the film that established Karlson as a top director of tough action scenes. ★★★★

Home of the Brave (1949). Mark Robson, dir. James Edwards, Steve Brodie, Lloyd Bridges. Still timely tale of the belated integration of our armed forces toward the war's end, focusing on the plight of an African American soldier who fights not only the enemy but a deadly racist within the ranks. Precursor to the 1950s' civil rights movies. ★★★★

Kelly's Heroes (1970). Brian G. Hutton, dir. Clint Eastwood, Telly Savalas, Donald Sutherland, Carroll O'Connor, Don Rickles. Comic takeoff on both *The Dirty Dozen* (which introduced Sutherland) and Eastwood's own *The Good, the Bad, and the Ugly* (with treasure-hunting during a war). Grim irony, dark humor, large-scale action. ★★★★

Long and the Short and the Tall, The (1961). Leslie Newman, dir. Richard Todd, Laurence Harvey, Richard Harris, David McCallum. Thought-provoking study of the members of a small British patrol, setting out to knock off Japanese position, gradually coming to sense their own deep-seated conflicts are greater than those with the enemy. ★★★★

Longest Day, The (1962). Ken Annakin, Andrew Marton, Bernhard Wicki, dirs. John Wayne (commanding the airborne) and Robert Mitchum (in charge of the assault by sea) headline the all-star cast of Darryl F. Zanuck's final blockbuster, a triumphant account of D-Day, based on Cornelius Ryan's best-seller and hitting all the right notes. ★★★★★

Memphis Belle (1990). Michael Caton-Jones, dir. D. B. Sweeney, Sean Astin, Matthew Modine, Harry Connick, Jr. An appealing throwback to the rah!rah! WWII films (predating Spielberg's *Private Ryan*) with a lively young cast impersonating the crew of the legendary B-17 on its final mission. Expertly staged, non-stop aerial combat. ★★★★

Merrill's Marauders (1962). Samuel Fuller, dir. Jeff Chandler, Claude Akins, Ty Hardin. Near-great WWII actioner (thanks to top-notch co-writer and director Fuller) about special unit of commandos and their invasion of the Burmese jungle, with fierce hand-to-hand combat scenes. Chandler died during filming. ★★★★★

Midway (1976). Jack Smight, dir. Charlton Heston, Henry Fonda, Robert Mitchum, James Coburn, Toshiro Mifune. Awful melodramatics about fictionalized Heston (other stars play actual people) detracts from an otherwise engaging naval action epic, including new battle sequences, stock footage from old Hollywood films, and news clips. ★★★

Naked and the Dead, The (1958). Raoul Walsh, dir. Aldo Ray, Cliff Robertson, Raymond Massey. From the blistering best-seller by Norman

Mailer, based on his own combat memories, about an over-eager marine (Ray) and his idealistic counterpart (C.R.). Their conflict clearly inspired the moral tug-of-war in Oliver Stone's Nam-era *Platoon*. ★★★

None But the Brave (1965). Frank Sinatra, dir. Clint Walker, Tommy Sands, Brad Dexter, Tony Bill, Frank Sinatra. Only directorial effort by the "Chairman of the Board" is a didactic would-be allegory about an American squad locked in combat with the Japanese, gradually realizing that their enemies are also human. Uneven but worthwhile. ★★★

Objective Burma (1945). Raoul Walsh, dir. Errol Flynn, James (B.) Brown, Henry Hull. Vivid retelling of a near-impossible mission as Flynn and cohorts parachute into Burma, fight their way to a Japanese fortress, and engage the enemy. Another unrelentingly honest and brutal combat film from Walsh—but beware cut and/or colorized prints! ★★★★

Operation Crossbow (1965). See "George Peppard" in chapter 14. ★★★★

Patton (1970) Franklin J. Schaffner, dir. George C. Scott, Karl Malden, James Edwards. Oscar-winning tribute to iconoclastic general, a modern-day Custer wearing a pair of silver-plated pistols. A must-see, though not nearly as great as people remember. What would've happened had screenwriter Francis Coppola been allowed to direct? ★★★★

George C. Scott (as General George Patton) in *Patton*.

Pearl Harbor (2001). Michael Bay, dir. Ben Affleck, Josh Hartnett, Kate Beckinsale, Cuba Gooding, Jr., Alec Baldwin. Initial 84 min. relating a trite romantic traingle is unwatchable. That's why God created fast-forward on VHS and chapter choices on DVD. Title attack is even more incredibly staged here than in *Tora! Tora! Tora!* and there's a fine rendering of the later Doolittle Raid. ★★★

Play Dirty (1968). Andre de Toth, dir. Michael Caine, Nigel Greene, Harry Andrews. Yet another of the *Dirty Dozen* imitations that proliferated during the late 1960s, this is one of the best, thanks to grim sensibility created by Hollywood old-time reliable de Toth, as Caine leads assorted criminal soldiers on a suicide mission. ★★★★

Ben Affleck and Josh Hartnett head for their planes in *Pearl Harbor*.

Pride of the Marines (1945). Delmer Daves, dir. John Garfield, John Ridgley, Ann Todd. Fascinating transitional piece from the rah!rah! war movies turned out during combat to the more psychologically complex war films that followed. Garfield is first-rate as Al Schmid, a heroic leatherneck blinded during battle.   ★★★★★

Purple Plain, The (1954). Robert Parrish, dir. Gregory Peck, Bernard Lee, Win Min Than. Survival of fittest tale as an American soldier finds himself wounded and stranded in the wilds of Burma, hardening himself against the elements and surrounding enemy troops, becoming a one-man army, fighting his way home.   ★★★★

Sahara (1943). Zoltan Korda, dir. Humphrey Bogart, Rex Ingram, Lloyd Bridges, Dan Duryea. Yet another *Lost Patrol*–type film, though realized with such striking attention to accuracy for modern desert combat by its esteemed director that the clichés take on new life. Bogart and companions, surrounded by Nazis, make a heroic last stand.   ★★★★

Sands of Iwo Jima (1949). Allan Dwan, dir. John Wayne, Forrest Tucker, Adele Mara. The postwar psychological war film from Republic that forever solidified Wayne's image as the ultimate WWII screen hero, one of only six films ever made in which the Duke dies on screen. The three surviving flag raisers (including Ira Hayes) play themselves. Marred by over-obvious back-projection for the battle scenes.   ★★★★

Saving Private Ryan (1998). Steven Spielberg, dir. Tom Hanks, Matt Damon, Edward Burns, Vin Diesel. Hanks leads his own magificent seven inland, after the D-Day landing. They find the surviving son of a devastated family and return him to safety, with ironic results. This memorable film created a renaissance for WWII movies.   ★★★★★

Sink the Bismarck! (1960). Lewis Gilbert, dir. Kenneth More, Dana Wynter. Moment-by-moment depiction (with the British war room as the film's center of attention). Patriotic Englishman More, learning that the Germans have sunk the *Hood*, sends his entire fleet out to accomplish a do-or-die mission. Famed Johnny Horton song does not appear.   ★★★★

Secret Invasion, The (1964). Roger Corman, dir. Stewart Granger, Raf Vallone, Mickey Rooney, Henry Silva. Expensive-looking (at least for Corman) WWII adventure, released three years before *The Dirty Dozen* but with an identical theme. Extremely well-staged action scenes and big-scale explosions.   ★★★★

Stalag 17 (1953). Billy Wilder, dir. William Holden, Peter Graves, Otto Preminger, Robert Strauss. American soldiers in a German P.O.W. camp

The famed flag waving atop Mt. Siribachi, as restaged by Allan Dwan for *Sands of Iwo Jima*.

realize there's a traitor in their midst. Like the director's other films, a truly cinematic approach to what is essentially a one-room setting. Holden was never better than in his Oscar-winning performance.   ★★★★★

Story of G.I. Joe, The (1945). William Wellman, dir. Burgess Meredith, Robert Mitchum, Wally Cassell. Mitchum's awesome performance as a tough but fair lieutenant, whose exploits are seen through the eyes of legendary war correspondent Ernie Pyle (Meredith), won him instant (and deserved) superstardom. This is Wellman's sound-era masterpiece.   ★★★★★

They Were Expendable (1945). John Ford, dir. John Wayne, Ward Bond, Robert Montgomery, Donna Reed. American servicemen in the Philippines at the beginning of World War II gradually realize they cannot be reinforced in time. Rare for the war era—no clichéd characters, no phoney heroics, though lots of brilliantly staged battles.   ★★★★★

Thin Red Line, The (1998). Terrence Malick, dir. George Clooney, John Travolta, Nick Nolte, Sean Penn, John Cusack. The fascinating if overly clinical (and overly stylized) approach of filmmaker Malick robs a memorable James Jones story of any human dimension. Nonetheless, the battle scenes make it a must-see. Far superior to the abominable 1964 version.   ★★★

Thirty Seconds Over Tokyo (1944). Mervyn Le Roy, dir. Spencer Tracy, Robert Mitchum, Van Johnson. General Doolittle's near-suicidal attack on Japan, staged as an answer to Pearl Harbor, here presented in an effectively straightforward manner by a no-nonesense director. If only there were more of Tracy and Mitchum, less Van!   ★★★★

To Hell and Back (1955). Jesse Hibbs, dir. Audie Murphy, Susan Kohner, Jack Kelly. Murphy effectively underplays himself in this semi-factual account of his WWII exploits, putting the "professional" actors to shame. The finale, in which he takes on an entire German company, is incredible. Only liability— the GIs never look dirty!   ★★★★

Too Late the Hero (1970). See chapter 15.   ★★★★★

Tora! Tora! Tora! (1970). Richard Fleischer, dir. Martin Balsam, Toshio Masuda, Jason Robards, Kinji Fukasuka. Lavish attempt to do for Pearl Harbor what *The Longest Day* did for D-Day invasion comes pretty close to achieving its aim. Scorned in its time, this is a solid recreation from both U.S. and Asian points of view.   ★★★★

Train, The (1964). John Frankenheimer, dir. Burt Lancaster, Paul Scofield, Jeanne Moreau. Philosophic, highly moral (but never didactic) WWII action drama. Duel of wits between German officer (Scofield) stealing valuable paintings on his train while decimating the civilian population of

France, and resistance leader Lancaster interested only in saving human lives.   ★★★★★

Twelve O'Clock High (1949). Henry King, dir. Gregory Peck, Gary Merrill, Dean Jagger. On-target portrait of an air force commander (Peck) who, despite courage and strength, cracks under the strain of sending men to their imminent doom. The flying fight sequences are remarkably convincing. Don't miss!   ★★★★★

U-571 (2000). Jonathan Mostow, dir. Bill Paxton, Matthew McConaughey, Jon Bon Jovi, Harvey Keitel. Exceptionally well-wrought naval combat tale, as a heroic team aboard an Allied submarine pursues a German U-boat. All the expected clichés from 1940s' films are present, now done with state-of-the-art F/X for the big battle scenes.   ★★★★

Victors, The (1963). Carl Foreman, dir. George Peppard, George Hamilton, Eli Wallach. A financial disaster when originally released, this innovative and ironic anti-war film follows squad of GIs (Wallach's the sarge) through combat, focusing on their personal involvements in Europe. Stunning, but beware cut prints!   ★★★★★

Von Ryan's Express (1965). Mark Robson, dir. Frank Sinatra, Trevor Howard, Raffaella Cara. Often compared (unfairly) with the somewhat similar film *The Train,* this is a terrific if superficial action-chase movie with Sinatra and his company escaping the Nazis via locomotive chase across Europe. Cara's death scene is a pip!   ★★★★

Wake Island (1942). John Farrow, dir. Brian Donlevy, Robert Preston, William Bendix, Albert Dekker. One of the first rah!rah! films to appear was this tribute to heroes of Wake. Still stirring, to say the least, though film makes the battle appear to be an Alamo-like last stand, when in fact the marines ultimately surrendered.   ★★★★

Walk in the Sun, A (1945). Lewis Milestone, dir. Dana Andrews, Richard Conte, John Ireland, Lloyd Bridges. Oft-imitated (including Oliver Stone's *Platoon*), this fact-based story (from a book by Harry Brown) concerns a group of ordinary soldiers on a fateful mission in Italy to take a German-held farmhouse. Every character is an original, non-stereotyped gem.   ★★★★★

28

THE TALL MAN: A CAREER
TRIBUTE TO JOHN WAYNE

A man's gotta do what a man's gotta do.

—John Wayne, *The Alamo* (1960)

Duke Wayne is the last of the great traditionalists. When he passes from the scene, I do not think there will be another to replace him.

—John Tuska, *Views and Reviews* (1974)

The temptation is there to claim that the action film begins and ends with John Wayne, though the truth is something else entirely. There were action stars before Wayne arrived on-screen—his predecessors include Harry Carey, on whom the Duke consciously based his best-loved mannerisms. Even as Tuska made the claim that opens this chapter, six years before the Duke's death from lung cancer, Clint Eastwood and Charles Bronson had competed not with Wayne but each other for the status of the world's most popular action star.

Yet it's impossible to overstate the significance of this man's singular career. Wayne missed silent stardom by a few years, becoming an action headliner in the earliest days of sound. He would remain on top for the better part of five decades, long after others of his ilk and era—from Clark Gable to Gary Cooper—had slipped from the passing parade. Wayne was a survivor, off-screen and on—the man who gets the job done, then disappears into the desert. Perhaps that explains why the few films in which his character dies— including *Reap the Wild Wind* (1942) for Cecil B. DeMille, and his final (and fine) film, *The Shootist* (1976), directed by Don Siegel—fail to satisfy. Despite high-quality work, John Wayne "passing" at a film's end seems somehow as wrong as Montgomery Clift living at the end of one of his.

The distinction here is between traditional hero and contemporary anti-hero. Perhaps that explains why Howard Hawks's western *Red River* (1948) still holds such a grip on the public's imagination. The film marked Wayne's first time out as an older man and Clift's debut as a youthful star,

John Wayne in *Wake of the Red Witch*. The name of Wayne's later production company, Batjac, derives from the seafaring company he works for in this film.

and their pairing allowed us an on-screen choice between the two primary possibilities for postwar protagonists. Yet when Clift died prematurely, in 1966—the fate of so many rebels on-screen and off—the Duke was still walking tall, still surviving, still "getting the job done," whatever that job might be in any particular picture. His impressive body of work—152 films in all, counting the B-actioners and cliffhangers he labored in during his first decade—run the full gamut of action's subgenres. The western and the WWII tale remain the best remembered. Lest we forget, though, he also starred as a sea captain (*Wake of the Red Witch*, 1948); daredevil aerial ace (*Flying Tigers*, 1942); sports coach (*Trouble Along the Way*, 1953); boxer (*Conflict*, 1936); roadshow manager (*Circus World*, 1964); fireman (*Hellfighters*, 1968); soldier of fortune (*Seven Sinners*, 1940); railroader (*Hurricane Express*, 1928); fortune hunter (*Legend of the Lost*, 1957); foreign ambassador (*The Barbarian and the Geisha*, 1958); hockey player (*Idol of the Crowds*, 1937); big-game catcher (*Hatari*, 1962); freelance photographer (*I Cover the War*, 1937); airplane pilot (*The High and the Mighty*, 1954); government agent (*Big Jim McClain*, 1952); hillbilly farmer (*Shepherd of the Hills*, 1941); urban cop (*Brannigan*, 1975); a Mongol warrior (*The Conqueror*, 1956); and a Roman centurion (*The Greatest Story Ever Told*, 1965).

The latter two role entries are generally considered his least successful. Though equally at home in modern settings or period pieces, the essence of Big John was always *American*. One might wish that—had he been inclined to abandon the action genre even once—Wayne might have starred in a film version of Henry James's classic novel of that very title. Yet this would have involved acting, something the Duke flatly refused to do. "I'm a *reactor*," he chuckled when people inquired as to whether he thought himself any good as a thesbian.

Wayne did not, for example, "play" Davy Crockett in *The Alamo*. The Tennessee colonel instead became an extension of Wayne's ongoing personality—persona might better express it—as he reacted to the actors (Richard Widmark, Laurence Harvey) around him. Fine as they were, what we recall is Wayne. He could own a scene with the slant of his almost Oriental eyes, a sudden, subtle stooping of those broad shoulders, a pensive way of pulling himself inward when he heard something he didn't care for. "Never get caught acting" was the advice one legendary performer gave, ages ago, to an anonymous hopeful. If there was anyone in Hollywood history who lived by that precept, it was John Wayne.

For the record, he was born Marion Michael Morrison on May 26, 1907, in Winterset, Iowa. His pharmacist father moved to California five years later for health reasons, where the young Duke (the nickname came from a huge dog, always in the boy's company) had a chance to work on Mojave Desert cattle ranches. He graduated Glendale High School with high grades and football honors, later attending USC, where he again made a name on the gridiron. Cowboy star Tom Mix, a big football fan, learned the athlete's family was in financial trouble and found him a job as prop boy at Fox. Assigned to a movie called *Mother Machree* (1928), Duke fell into a friendship with its director. John Ford cast him in a bit part, then recommended the tall, rugged youth to colleague Raoul Walsh, who planned to use an unknown as the lead in the first epic sound western, *The Big Trail* (1930).

That film failed at the box office. In the thirties, adult audiences wanted their action films to be modern urban crime stories like *Little Caesar* and *The Public Enemy*. So Wayne slipped into kiddie westerns, becoming "Singing Sandy," with his musical numbers dubbed in by another performer, and a member of "The Three Mesquiteers." At decade's end, Ford—who sensed the western was poised for a comeback—picked Wayne for "Ringo" in *Stagecoach* (1939). From then on, it was the big leagues, often for Ford or Walsh, with their he-man sentimentality, or Hawks and Henry Hathaway, known for their rough-hewn sophistication. Wayne's instincts told him that an action film is only as good as its director. Always, he would seek out the best—John Huston, Nicholas Ray, Allan Dwan, William Wellman, Michael Curtiz, or Josef von Sternberg—helping to explain why so many of his films wear well today.

More than any other actor, Wayne's career spans the chasm from the adventure films of the Old Hollywood (1915–1945) to the action films of today (1946–present). Others who had excelled early on couldn't adjust to the drastic changes. Wayne casually kept on treading his own straight and narrow path, even when he mouthed the same ultra-patriotic views that had been widely popular while World War II raged during the unpopular Vietnam War. One did not have to agree with his politics to sense there was something majestic—and majestically American—in his every nod, wince, smile, and gesture.

His politics would, in the late sixties, be drastically exaggerated as extreme right-wing. True, Wayne believed in that oldest of American axions, "Don't tread on me." When it came to any combat his country might be involved in, The Duke was the ultra-hawk. Yet in *The Alamo* (1960), he insisted on portraying the roles that blacks, Hispanics, and women had played in the defense of that fort, never before featured in any such movie. In *The Green Berets*, he saw to it that the title outfit was populated by Asians and African Americans as well as Anglos.

On social issues, Wayne was a closet liberal, in favor of civil rights and dead set against censorship. Here, then, was the paradox of a tough guy who also happened to be the last gentleman. "The western hero," critic Robert Warshow wrote nearly fifty years ago, "is a figure of repose . . . his melancholy comes from the 'simple' recognition that life is unavoidably serious." No figure ever looked so melancholy, or quite so at repose, while riding tall in the saddle, as John Wayne. Legendary actress Louise Brooks had expected her cowboy co-star in *Overland Stage Riders* (1938) to be an insufferable rube. Instead, she fell under his spell, later claiming the quiet, unassuming man she met was Fenimore Cooper's "Hawkeye," alive and well and living in the twentieth century.

Such a shame, then, that Wayne never played the lead in a film version of *The Last of the Mohicans*. "Natty Bumppo" was, after all, the first all-American action hero in fiction, and ought at some point to have been incarnated by the greatest screen action hero ever. If Wayne served as an apotheosis of Carey, Mix, and every other he-man who preceded him, his image and vision of what a man ought to be set the pace for Arnold, Clint, Sly, and other action heroes to follow, in those films that—viewed from the present perspective to this point in the past—provide the essence of this volume.

INDEX

NOTE: *italic page numbers* indicate photographs; **bold page numbers** indicate Main Entries

ABOUT THE AUTHOR

Douglas Brode is the author of more than twenty previous books on the visual and performing arts, most often focusing on film. These include volumes on actors Denzel Washington and Robert De Niro, directors Steven Spielberg and Woody Allen, such significant eras as the 1950s and 1980s, and various genres including Shakespearean cinema and the crime film. The international publication of these and other works have earned him a considerable cult following, as well as frequent comparison with such legendary iconoclastic critics as Raymond Durgnat, Manny Farber, and Parker Tyler. An educator, Professor Brode teaches courses in film history at Syracuse University's prestigious Newhouse School of Public Communications. He also serves as the coordinator of Cinema Studies at Onondaga College. Professor Brode has lectured on cinema in places as diverse as the Hudson Valley Film Festival near Lake George, New York; the Buffalo Bill Museum in Cody, Wyoming; and the International Literary Festival in Aspen, Colorado. Leading newspapers including the *New York Times* and the *Washington Post* cite his opinions on the relationship of the media to society. His comments are

also included in varied installments of the Bravo TV channel's *Profiles* series and A&E's *Biography*. Popular magazines that have published his work include *Rolling Stone* and *TV Guide*. Brode's critical analyses have also appeared in more academic publications such as *Cineaste* and *Television Quarterly*. Two of his original plays, *Heartbraker* and *Somewhere in the Night*, have been produced in regional theater. His original screenplay, *Midnight Blue* (filmed by the Motion Picture Corporation of America and released on home video by Orion) was hailed by one reviewer as "the best of the low-budget erotic thrillers." Upcoming projects include two books on Walt Disney for the University of Texas Press, Austin, as well as a volume on westerns for that publisher. His most recent additon to the Citadel/Kensington library of film titles was *Sinema: Erotic Adventures in Film* (2002). His next will be *Edge of Your Seat* (2003).